FULL
DISCLOSURE

A MEMOIR

Published under licence by Brown Dog Books and
The Self-Publishing Partnership, 7 Green Park Station, Bath BA1 1JB

www.selfpublishingpartnership.co.uk

ISBN printed book: 978-1-83952-116-4
ISBN e-book: 978-1-83952-120-1

Cover design by Kevin Rylands
Internal design by Andrew Easton

Printed and bound in the UK

This book is printed on FSC certified paper

FULL DISCLOSURE

A MEMOIR

Vince Smith

BROWN
DOG
BOOKS

Disclaimer
Any resemblance to persons living or dead should be plainly apparent to them and those who know them. All events described actually happened, although on certain occasions I have taken liberties with the chronology.

FULL DISCLOSURE

On Monday, 21 January 1980, at 9 am, I was in the canteen at Kings Heath police station. The décor and the furnishings were bleak and easily matched the standard of the grub that was served. There were three small school dinner tables with an ashtray and a bottle of HP sauce on each. For those who wished to sprawl or nap, there was a well-worn sofa. For entertainment there was a television which was switched off, because *Play School*, the first programme, did not start until 11 am.

Because the school crossing lady had reported sick, I had been selected to ensure that the Wheelers Lane primary school children were not mown down on their way to school that morning. I queried this use of police resources with my shift Sergeant John Mason, suggesting that I had far more interesting and important things to do. He curtly told me that it was not a matter for debate. I had just arrived to start my refreshment break. As I ordered a bacon sandwich, Mason came into the canteen and spotted me.

"Ah, PC Smith, just the bloke. Have you ever remanded a prisoner in custody at the Magistrates' Court?" With only three weeks on the shift, it was unlikely that my answer could ever have been yes. I replied that I had not. "Excellent," Mason continued, "this will be a very good experience for you, then." I somehow doubted it. Through the serving hatch, the cook handed me my sandwich, three-day old bread and burnt bacon. Mason nodded towards it. "You can eat that on the way. We need to go now." A large dollop of HP sauce converted my sandwich into something I could actually eat.

I had never been to the Magistrates' Court before and was glad that I was with my sergeant. While he drove Mason briefed me. Gerry Donovan had stabbed his mate while they were both pissed in The Brighton pub, in Balsall Heath. Donovan was charged with wounding and remanded in custody. The CID wanted Donovan further remanded, so we were attending court to oppose any bail application.

"What will you say to the magistrates if he applies for bail, Sarge?" Mason smiled.

"I will say fuck all because I will not even be in the courtroom. I will be tucking into my breakfast in the canteen at Steelhouse Lane. You can come and get me when you're finished." Shit. I now had a million questions. Giving evidence in court was not something that I thought I was going to have to do for years. Mason handed me some case papers. I was desperate for help.

"Okay, Sarge, what should I say, then?"

"Didn't you cover this in your basic training? Just tell them he is a cunt. A cunt from a long line of cunts." Yep, that ought to do it, I thought. We pulled up outside the Magistrates' Court. "Right. Off you go. You know where I'll be. Oh, and by the way, Donovan's solicitor is John Morgan, and he's shit hot." Sergeant

Mason cheerfully drove off in the white supervision Allegro, the twat.

The Magistrates' Court building is a huge, daunting place steeped in tradition. The inside looked like a cathedral with stained glass windows, high ceilings and ornate wooden furnishing. The busy people inside, unlike me, all seemed to know exactly what they were doing. I remember the sound of metal tipped shoes click-clacking on the marble floor. I found the duty room and checked the court listings, Mr Donovan's hearing would take place in court 1. I entered the courtroom and shuddered.

In the centre of the court was the defendant's dock. Presiding over the court were three magistrates who sat in their raised wooden thrones so that they could assess the performances of the solicitors, witnesses and defendants, and whenever necessary reprimand the unruly occupants of the public gallery. The clerk of the court assisted the magistrates by ensuring that proceedings and rulings at least appeared lawful. The court was like something from the 18th century. I felt that everything had been designed just to intimidate me. The prosecuting solicitor told me that I would have to give evidence and explain the reason why the police objected to bail being granted, adding that he had no intention of being tackled by John bloody Morgan on a busy Monday morning. I told him that it was not my case and that I was only filling in for the officer in charge who was unavailable. I also told him that it was my first time at court. He wished me the best of luck. I felt like a lamb that was about to be slaughtered.

I had almost no police service, but I had heard of John Morgan. I saw him straight away. He was immaculately turned out and had a fop of impeccably groomed hair. He wore an expensive suit and a silk handkerchief dangled from his jacket's breast pocket. He looked like he owned the bloody place. Morgan was on the other side of the court, speaking to Donovan's family. He looked at me and sneered, and I could feel his contempt. John Morgan was reputed to eat probationary constables for breakfast. He did not see a uniformed police officer. What he saw was a full English fry-up, and he looked ravenous. Fraught with nerves, I left the court. I had a sudden and desperate urge to use the toilet. I click-clacked down the cold stone steps to the public lavatory. As I walked down, I saw a neatly written poem on the white enamelled tiled wall. It was just high enough for a cleaner not to be expected to erase it.

God Made Creatures Great and Small,
Some that Slither,
Some that Crawl,
The West Midlands police Employs Them All.

The police-recruiting message did not exactly fill me with confidence. I returned to court, and the usher announced that my case was next. I took a deep breath and re-entered the courtroom. I stood in the witness box. It is a lonely place. Mr Morgan smiled wolfishly and waited. The court usher handed me a Bible and a card with the oath written on it. My brain froze. I had forgotten how to read. The magistrates were waiting. I felt like the whole world was waiting. I was pretty sure that I was going to faint. Mr Morgan pierced my embarrassing silence:

"Surely to Christ you can get through the oath, Officer?" I was then led through the evidence of the case by the prosecuting solicitor, and I gave the reasons why the police objected to bail. I submitted to the court that Mr Donovan was an unpleasant individual who should not just go around stabbing people. Well, that was pretty pathetic. I was told to wait as Mr Morgan had some questions. I swallowed hard. Ding-ding, Mr Morgan came out slugging:

"Officer, was my client cautioned when he was arrested?"

"I think so, sir." Mr Morgan continued with jabs to my head and body.

"You think so, Officer. Nobody cares what you think. Was he... or was he not cautioned?"

"We always caution people we arrest, sir." I was trying to hide behind the mighty corporate shadow of the British police.

"Do you caution people that you arrest, Officer?"

"Yes, sir, always."

John Morgan looked around theatrically.

"Officer, please tell this court the wording of the formal caution. Which the police must give to a suspect at the time of their arrest."

Now that was a right hook I just never saw coming. Mr Morgan had just watched me struggle to read a card with the oath written on it. What were the chances of my being able to recite the caution? The lesson about the caution was so tedious that instead of learning it, I just counted the number of words

11

it contained: there were 24. I knew some of them, but I could not remember the exact order. I decided to give it a go, and soon wished I hadn't.

"You do not have to say everything... Sorry, let me start again. There is nothing you can say that will help. No, that's not right either... Hang on. It will harm your defence, so help me, God." Mr Morgan waited until everyone in the courtroom had stopped laughing. He winked at his client who responded with a fairly blatant thumbs-up. It was time to show off.

"Officer, I do recognise the tune and some of the words sound vaguely familiar, but that ridiculous jumble of nonsense is not the formal caution, is it?" After a brief and incredibly one-sided judicial skirmish, the magistrates bailed Mr Donovan. The court usher held the door open to let me out. He need not have bothered: I could have comfortably slithered under it. Feeling like a punch-drunk boxer, I staggered the short distance to Steelhouse Lane police station. In the canteen I watched my sergeant drain his cup of tea, and then push his spotlessly clean breakfast plate to one side. He took one look at the state of me.

"He got bail, didn't he?"

"Yes, Sarge," then sarcastically added, "thanks for all your help."

"I hate giving evidence at court," he said.

That made two of us.

CHAPTER 1
NO PLACE LIKE HOME

I was born in the City Hospital in Birmingham on 3 December 1956. My umbilical cord was so determined to prevent our separation that it wrapped itself around my neck and attempted to strangle me. It took an emergency C-section to save my life.

My dad, Tony, was short and stocky, balding with a - fooling absolutely no one - Bobby Charlton comb-over. He had a menacing Belfast accent and a hair-trigger temper. My mum Frances was slim and beautiful. Mum had a soft Northern Irish lilt and hailed from the picturesque seaside town of Newcastle, County Down. They were married just a few months before I was born. It was a hastily arranged ceremony, and the wedding photographs were taken from angles designed to hide Mum's embarrassing bump. My first home was number 1, back of 38 Alma Street, Aston, Birmingham. We had two small rooms and an outside toilet. It was not quite a slum, but it was close. I don't remember that much about my early years. I vaguely recall playing in the dirty street outside my house, with the other waifs and strays.

When I was just four, the five-year-old strumpet who lived

next door led me up an entry, a narrow passageway between terraced houses. She said I could have a look at her *tuppence*, but only if I showed her my *mickey* first. I declined. Sadly, I've probably left it too late to track her down and see if her offer still stands.

Dad was a factory worker at Henry Wiggin & Co, which produced nickel alloy. The company set up another production unit in Hereford and, in 1962, we moved to a terraced, three-bedroomed council house: 10 Powys Walk, Newton Farm, Hereford. Compared with our previous lodgings, it was a palace. We had a garden at the front and a slightly bigger one at the back. We even had an inside toilet. By the time I was eight years old, I had two sisters and a baby brother. Loads of kids roamed the estate, so I was never short of friends to play with.

In 1965, courtesy of Radio Rentals, a black and white television took up residence in the corner of our living room. It had to be fed sixpence coins to make it operate. When the sixpences ran out, the TV sulked, and four children stared at the blank screen but could only see their miserable reflection. The children's TV presenters of the 1960s and 1970s were not what they appeared to be. They included some notorious kiddy fiddlers: Jimmy Savile, Stuart Hall and that bloody Australian who, for some reason, kept trying to tie his kangaroo down, sport. I sensibly ignored the recruitment campaign of the pop sensation Gary Glitter, and his repeated requests of *Do You Wanna Be in My Gang?*

Behind our back garden, there was a row of garages and that area became Wembley, Lord's or Wimbledon, depending on the sporting season. It was floodlit; well, actually they were just streetlights, but to us they were floodlights. Matches paused for the duration of the popular kids' TV programmes - *Blue Peter*, *Fireball XL5* and *Thunderbirds*. As soon as they started, we would race into our houses, then as the closing credits began - *whoosh*, we would be back outside, and play would resume.

Cornfields, woods, orchards and farms were on the perimeter of our estate. Mum, Dad, four young children, a brand new house: it should have been perfect, and initially it was. Dad's local pub was the Belmont Inn, a brisk twenty-minute walk away. With a gallon of beer inside him, the return journey took considerably longer. My father never missed a Saturday night or a Sunday lunchtime drinking session. If he needed to justify himself, which he rarely ever did, then his attendance was required as a vital member of the pub's cribbage team. In the beginning, Mum did not drink as much as my dad, but that changed later.

Mum and Dad were both heavy smokers. Ashtrays were found on just about every flat surface in my house. I think that it was only the nicotine that held our net curtains together. During my childhood, I saw enough cigarettes being stubbed out into stinking overflowing ashtrays to last me a lifetime, and that is probably the reason I have never wanted to smoke.

The inside toilet we had, though an improvement, wasn't without issues. My father had a Sunday morning ritual: he sat on the throne and read the *News of the World*. He rolled his own cigarettes using *Old Holborn* tobacco and the smell, within the confines of our toilet, was unbearable. If I was desperate, and I mean desperate, then with one deep breath, I conducted whatever business was necessary and only breathed again when I was well clear.

There were quite a few Irish families who lived in my street but none from Belfast. I hoped that the speed at which my dad spat out his words meant that the neighbours did not always understand everything he said. Dad would stand at our back door and call us in for tea. If there was any delay in our response, then he raised the volume and hollered, "Get in the kitchen. You friggin wee *fuck pigs*!" Yes, in our house, a fuck pig was a term of endearment. His threats were unpleasantly graphic: "Vincent... stop kicking that frigging ball against the house, or I'll put my big toe up your hole, so I will!"

When I was nine years old, I learned two things that helped me through my childhood. Firstly, dock leaves reduce the pain of a nettle sting, and much more importantly, I noticed that just before my dad attacked whatever was annoying him, he curled his bottom lip over his teeth. Then he exploded and launched a flurry of punches, kicks and the occasional cricket bat at his target. Whenever I saw that lip curl and the evil grin that it produced, I just froze and took stock of what I was doing. When I was confident that I was not in his firing line, I watched with interest. I knew the touch paper had been lit, and the fireworks display was just about to start.

As for my theory, I witnessed incidents that confirmed that I was correct. They include a milkman who disturbed my father's pre-drink snooze. Dad was sleeping on our settee, wearing just a string vest and a loose-fitting pair of Y-fronts.

Rudely awakened by a loud and crisp, "Rat Tat a Tat Tat... Tat Tat", being played on our front door, probably with a coin, my dad produced a reflex lip curl and declared, "Cheeky fucking knock." He rushed to the door. There stood our milkman, who had not been paid for weeks. Nervously he asked my father for some money. Lip now fully curled and *thump*!

Our postman, who had not delivered Dad's expected benefit giro, was refusing to recheck his mailbag. Dad, furious that he may be denied access to government funds to buy beer, just because of this *jobsworth's* incompetence, called the postman, "a cunt of a whore's bastard". A lip curl followed, then *biff!* While I was upset by the violence: I thought my father had taken swearing onto a whole new level.

One incident even made the front page of the *Hereford Times* newspaper:

It was a sad afternoon for the residents of Powys Walk, Newton Farm when Mr Tony Smith called to see his neighbour, Mr Gordon Griffiths. Words were exchanged, and the two men began fighting. Mr Griffiths made the mistake of brandishing a cricket bat at Mr Smith who disarmed him and then struck Mr Griffiths several times with his bat. The police arrested and charged both men with assault. They have been bailed to appear before the Hereford Magistrates.

I had seen Dad's lip curl when Mr Griffiths picked up the cricket bat, so I had a pretty good idea what would happen next. Technically some of the strokes that my father struck the prone Gordon Griffiths with could have come from a cricketing manual.

Other blows he delivered had more of a baseball influence. Both parties were bound over to keep the Queen's peace and be of good behaviour for a year. My father was chuffed: Mr Griffiths had spent two days in the hospital, whereas Dad had a small sticking plaster applied to a tiny cut over his eye.

Mum took a part-time job at Wimbush's, a baker's shop in Hereford town centre. Extra income should have been good, but it wasn't: the extra money just meant they bought a lot more booze and cigarettes. As their drinking increased, so did the frequency of their fights. When Mum knew that Dad was about to kick off, she used alcohol as a pre-fight anaesthetic.

The only time that ever flew in our house was the mantelpiece clock: when hurled across the living room it was signal that hostilities were just about to commence. After their fights a few days of silence followed as they prepared for a rematch. I will never forget how sick I felt and how my stomach knotted and churned when my dad's anger was brewing. I knew that it was only a matter of time before Mum received another clattering, but I could do nothing. I just had to accept that this was how things were in my home.

I saw my mum's only victory. It happened the day after her usual Saturday night thumping. On that Sunday morning, my mum had a gap in her teeth that she had not had the day before. Still, in spite of the previous night's violence, she cooked a lovely Sunday roast chicken dinner. The food smelled good, it always did, but the meal that day had been seasoned with palpable domestic tension. Mum sternly called her children into the kitchen. When we were seated, she told us to tuck in then she screeched, "And here comes yours. You fucking bastard!" She threw a plate, full of food, which hit my dad on the head and sent him reeling. It was hilarious: the cabbage stuck to my father's bald head and he looked like he was wearing a mad green wig. Gravy and blood poured down his face. I wanted to cheer, so did my brother and sisters. We were so scared we didn't, and our silence was punctured by the abuse and threats that spewed out of my dad in the direction of Mum.

As a child, I peaked in my last year at junior school. I captained the school football team and passed the 11+. I was one of only two boys offered a place at the prestigious Hereford High School. The letter of acceptance was completed and put behind the broken clock on the mantelpiece: and that was as far as it went. The cost of the uniform was a bit cheaper at the Catholic secondary modern school, and that was the deciding factor.

From the age of twelve, I started wetting my bed. It was bad enough for me, but it was considerably worse for my little brother Anthony. He was eight years younger, and we slept top to tail in a single bed. I was taken to a doctor, and after a few tests, he established that my problem was not physical. I think what he really wanted to say to my father was: 'Mr Smith, perhaps if you were to stop punching the boy's mother, then he just might stop wetting his bed.'

When she couldn't take any more, Mum would flee, taking her four children with her. A taxi would arrive, and the five of us would jump in and travel to Birmingham. We would stay with one of my mum's sisters. Sometimes we would be there for weeks. Eventually, my very apologetic father would turn up and beg my mum to forgive him, and he would promise to change his ways. We would all return to Hereford - until the next time.

In the 1960s and early 1970s, a musical revolution took place. The Beatles, Elvis, The Rolling Stones and many others, with their energy and talent, were taking the world by storm. While the rest of the planet was rocking, the records my mum and dad played in our house were soul-crushingly depressing. The soundtrack for my childhood would definitely include such mawkish songs as *Old Shep* (dog dies), *Old Tige* (dog dies), *Nobody's Child* (blind, orphaned child wishes he were dead), *The Blizzard* (a man and his horse die in the snow, just a hundred yards from home). And let's not forget *The Green, Green Grass of Home* (a man reflects on his life, the night before his execution). Check them out but make sure you have a large box of tissues handy.

My dad had eight brothers, and mum nine sisters. If the families had been closer, by selecting seven from each litter, they could have arranged a group wedding. The event could have been filmed and shown at cinemas all over the country. The publicity poster would have read: "Now showing at a theatre near you, *Seven Brides for Seven Wife-Beaters*. Critics have acclaimed it as an absolute '*Noseburster of a movie*' a must see."

We lived in the fairly remote town of Hereford; sometimes one of my aunts or uncles would bring their families to visit. They only ever came once, having usually been turfed out of our house in the early hours of the morning by my drunken father who had taken umbrage about something real or that he had imagined. I served mass at my local church. I was a ten-year-old altar boy wearing a fetching outfit of a cassock and surplice. I knelt before a Catholic priest every week with my eyes closed and mouth wide open. Thankfully a Holy Communion wafer was the only thing that was ever placed on my tongue.

Academically my performance plummeted. At my secondary school, I was the only boy in my year who had passed the 11+. By my fourth year, I was average in a few subjects and pretty useless at the others. Tennis, rugby, football and athletics kept me fit. At weekends I followed Hereford United and watched their home matches with my school friends.

My school and church joined together and opened a social club. My mum and dad went whenever they could. When they were drunk it must have been highly entertaining for the other patrons, which included my teachers, priests and school friends' parents. I waited at home for my parents to return, while my stomach churned. My teachers never said anything to me, but I was old enough to feel embarrassed by the pity that I could see in their eyes. After school, I stayed out for as long as I could and played a lot of floodlit football. I kept hoping things at home would improve: they never did.

The last year that a child could leave school without having to stay on, until sixteen, was 1972. If I joined the British Army in that September, I could drop out of school and say farewell to my miserable home life. Some of my teachers were exceptional, but I was only trying to survive. Whatever I learned during the school week was erased by my dad's weekend outbursts. I also knew for sure that my fifth year GCE exam results would have been abysmal.

I popped into the Army Careers Office in Hereford. If it had been an option, I would have completed the necessary forms, then climbed into the back of a camouflaged three-ton truck, ready to be delivered to any country that Great Britain was either occupying or at war with. A recruiting sergeant showed me some glossy brochures, and following a discussion, I decided that the Junior Leaders looked to be my best option. I could be a soldier, see the world, and maybe, just maybe, one day drive a tank. The sergeant explained that as I was only fifteen, my parents would have to give their permission for me to apply. I knew their consent was not going to be a problem, and it wasn't.

In May 1972, with 80 other potential junior Army recruits, I arrived at St George's Barracks, Sutton Coldfield for a three-day physical and medical assessment followed by written maths and english tests. On the third day, I lined up with the other candidates. I was confident that I had performed well enough to become a Junior Leader. We lined up in alphabetical order. A sergeant eventually addressed me.

"Ah, Smith V. Is that correct?"

"Yes, Sergeant."

"You have applied to become a Junior Leader, is that also correct?"

"Yes, Sergeant."

"Well, Smith V. Following three days of extensive tests you will be disappointed to learn that the British Army has discovered that there is a brain inside that big, fat head of yours. You, *Professor*, will be joining the Royal Army Pay

Corps. You will attend their Apprentice College in Winchester. Good luck." I had never heard of the Royal Army Pay Corps, and there did not appear to be an appeal process. I was now on my way to a college where 'O' levels and possibly 'A' levels were going to feature. The selection panel assessed me as 'a pleasant, smart and sensible boy who was of an above-average educational standard'.

Swapping domestic violence to join the British Army and become part of an organisation which faced armed conflict held no fears for me. My weekly wage was going to be £2 - so what more could I want? I enjoyed five very happy years in Hereford. Unfortunately, I lived there for ten. With a school report that, in a nutshell, said that I was quite good at games, I joined the Army, and I never wet my bed again, ever. Maybe it was just a coincidence, but I doubt it.

CHAPTER 2
A PRIVATE'S PROGRESS

Basic training was a challenge. Boy soldiers remained at the college for almost three years. The recruits who found it the easiest to stand out were the ex-Army cadets amongst us. Bulling boots and sorting out their kit was second nature to them. I fell into the category of never having ironed clothes or polished my shoes before I joined. I was one of the many, at the very bottom of an incredibly steep learning curve. As recruits, we were shouted at a lot. We were all in the same boat, so the incompetents formed a bond and helped one another.

I took up residence in a new, cube-shaped accommodation block: there were three floors, and housed a total of 90 apprentices. The college was divided into three houses, and that separation created inter-house competitions, sporting and academic. I was in Bednall House on the top floor. The staff sergeant in charge of my house was 'Chopper' Cummings, he supervised the junior NCO's who ran the accommodation block. The upside of being in Bednall was the view of the surrounding fields and woods. The downside - bedding, uniform or equipment that did not pass inspection was thrown out of the nearest window. There were 30 apprentices on each floor, aged between fifteen and eighteen. We slept six to a room and believed that we had all mastered the art of silent wanking, we hadn't, we just chose not to ever talk about it.

The Army had working practices that had been in place for centuries, and they were not going to change them just for the benefit of the spotty *oiks* who had just joined. "Stand by your Beds", was shouted across the floors at 8 am. All apprentices, stood to attention next to their bed, with their lockers open, awaiting inspection. The Junior NCO's relished the parade and enjoyed logging every infraction. When someone was struggling with the standard of their kit, initially, the Army did not punish the individual, they penalised the group. That ensured that the *problem child* was encouraged, by his colleagues, to improve smartish. If an apprentice liked to have his hair just a little longer than Army regulations dictated, that soldier would be dispatched to the barbers three or four times that day. When the recruit had no hair left the problem had been addressed.

Kit preparation was a nightmare. I paid a lot of attention to those who seemed to know what they were doing. The sloppy use of the communal iron could result in a double crease that could take hours to correct. The Army issued every recruit with two new pairs of DMS boots. One pair was worn for routine duties, the other for parades. Once both pairs had been broken in, by a series of five-mile route marches around the woods and fields of Hampshire, the two pairs were separated. One pair was just kept clean and polished, the other pair required every spare minute to be spent cleaning and bulling them. Black shoe polish was delicately applied onto the boots using a finger tightly wrapped in a yellow duster. Adding spit, and hours of effort the toe caps would, eventually, shine like glass. For some reason smokers' spit produced better results, possibly because of the nicotine. The soldier, in the next bunk smoked, so I allowed him to unload into the lid of my Kiwi polish tin. It worked. Parade boots were hated, cherished, loved and protected.

In the beginning, everything I produced for inspection was, according to the junior NCOs, in shit order. I learned that the minimum acceptable standard was *tickety-boo*. The rank structure, of which I was at the very bottom, would continue throughout my time as a soldier.

After a month, the inspections became more individual. Any item that was not up to standard on the 8 am parade resulted in a requirement to attend 'a show parade', held by the duty corporal at 6 pm. The offenders reported for inspection, with whatever item of equipment that had failed the morning inspection. This was a nightmare: we finished classes at 4 pm, then paraded for tea. The rest of your mates would be changed and playing table tennis or snooker, while those attending the show parade prepared their kit. If the apprentice did not pass muster on the show parade, further parades would take place at two-hourly intervals until they did.

Meal attendance was a parade, which meant that you must attend, the only exception being Sunday morning breakfast which was optional. Physical Education was ramped up from anything most of us had ever done. The physical training instructors (PTIs) beasted us into shape. They were all muscular Adonises, squeezing their incredibly muscular legs into a pair of tight-fitting blue tracksuit bottoms, with white piping. Their perfectly buffed upper body covered only by the issued white, sleeveless T-shirt with red trim and crossed swords on the chest. They loved themselves, but as long as you didn't stand between them and a mirror, you would be fine.

The only thing I struggled with was the uniform. I have extremely sensitive skin: the issue shirt and trousers I wore were extremely uncomfortable. I felt like I was wrapped in barbed wire. They were produced for World War II and were built to last until at least World War III. I did not see anyone else who was suffering as much. In fact, some of the apprentices from the Scottish Highlands bloody loved the shirts and even wore them when they went on leave. They said it made them feel cosy and warm. I took my khaki flannel shirt back to the stores and swapped it for the oldest one I could find. Then I shaved my shirt and the inside of my battledress trousers.

As far as the Royal Army Pay Corps was concerned, the faster we shaped up as soldiers, the sooner they could get on with teaching us our trade as regimental pay clerks. The training's initial focus was on personal hygiene, fitness and turnout. All apprentice tradesmen were expected to take and pass a business group of GCE 'O' levels: Maths, English, Commerce, Economics and Accountancy. Over 95% of the apprentices achieved just that. Our teachers were very experienced and ensured that every apprentice's educational potential was realised. Plus we had no females in class which ensured there were no hormonal distractions. Believe me, running around a drill square carrying my rifle over my head for 30 minutes, on one occasion, ensured that I behaved, and my work was always submitted on time.

Our college was set apart from the main camp probably to, literally, separate the men from the boys, the only shared facilities being the gym and sports pitches. It did not matter how bad the Army was, I never considered leaving. I was a bit like Richard Gere, years later, in the film *An Officer and a Gentleman.* "I ain't got nothing, I ain't got no place else to go."

It was easy to train, work and study without the chaos I had at home. Our daily schedule was busy - reveille at 6 am, breakfast at 7 am, room inspections at 8 am. Lessons started at 9 am. Basic Army training dovetailed into our class timetable and included: physical education, marching, rifle drill, weapon handling, and on the range we were trained and tested to fire rifles, pistols and sub-machine guns. The assault course started with a twelve-foot wall and did not get any easier. All aspects of basic training were assessed and graded, and that grading had a direct impact on my weekly wage. Although being selected to represent the college in one of their sports teams was not difficult, the college staff and coaches expected the high standard of results that had always been achieved to continue. We took part in activities that had featured on the recruiting brochures, namely: canoeing, sailing, rock climbing and camping. Most apprentices collapsed onto their beds at about 10.30 pm, and it was lights out at 11 pm.

Every soldier indicated their religion when they joined; I was RC, Roman Catholic. Most recruits were C of E, Church of England. Church parades were held every Sunday at 10 am. The C of E apprentices attended the church on the camp. Initially, six RC apprentices were transported by minibus to Winchester to attend a Catholic church. After the service we were collected at 2.30 pm. This was brilliant. Winchester was an expensive taxi ride away, so a free return trip into town on Sunday with the pubs open from 12 am until 2 pm was a real bonus. After a month nine Catholics waited for the Sunday bus to Winchester. Our legs were a little wobbly when we returned. A less than impressed Company Sergeant Major issued an order that religious defections were to cease forthwith.

My first leave was in December 1972: I had just turned sixteen, and my dad met me at Hereford train station. I was in full uniform, looked smart and felt very fit. Three months of training and no bed-wetting meant that I was quite proud of myself. I sensed that there was something wrong. Dad was actually thinking about what he was going to say, and that was a first. We took a short walk to a café in the town centre: it had to be a café because the pubs hadn't opened. Dad had been drinking, and he looked like he had been on a bender for weeks: his eyes were bloodshot, and he stank of booze.

"She's gone son, your ma's gone." I was shocked.

29

"Dead? Mum's dead?" Dad just looked straight through me.

"Not dead, you fecking eejit, she has just moved in with someone else."

He was upset: Dad sipped his tea, then lit a cigarette. Hereford is a small place, and I had only been away for three months, so I asked:

"Do I know him?"

"Know who?" Dad winced and added a partial lip curl. Initially, I thought - Oh-Oh. But I was no longer the nine-year-old boy who shat himself when his lip curled. He didn't scare me anymore.

"The man that Mum's moved in with, do I know him?"

My father took the longest drag on a cigarette I had ever seen him take. He looked around, leant forward and quietly said:

"It's not a him, it's a fucking her. If it had been a him, he would be in his grave by now."

Over the Christmas break I watched my dad try to drink himself to death. I cut my leave short, and to be honest, I was glad to get back to normality. The Army was going to be my family for the foreseeable future. I could never work out why my dad was always so angry. He would never enter into a discussion, to resolve matters, until exploring every possible avenue of violence. My father had a job, a beautiful wife and four decent kids, but that was not enough. Growing up, I thought that my dad hated everyone. Looking back, I believe that the person that he despised the most was himself.

Five other apprentices shared my room. Until my first leave, I was the only one who had a mother and father living together.

I was now able to join their ranks of those apprentices from a broken home.

The Army allowed me to develop as a person, academically and as a sportsman, and that could never have happened if I had stayed in Hereford. I played in midfield for the college football team for the two seasons I was there. The first year we reached the final of the Junior Army Cup and lost 5-3 to Bassingbourn Junior Leaders. I felt sorry for our centre forward that day, Johnny Carroll, he scored a hat-trick and still finished on the losing side. The following year we played against the Scottish Infantry Depot (Bridge of Don) in the final and won 3-0. Our captain John Higgs lifted the trophy.

In July 1973 I reached the semi-final of the Army tennis championships, I lost to Bill Herlihy, who was also RAPC and in Bednall House. I didn't mind losing: Bill was a great guy, a little bit older and he looked out for me. The following year I reached the semi-finals again. I thought that I had a good chance of winning the tournament but lost the first set 6-0 and broken a racket string, on the last point of the set, my prospects were not looking good. I didn't have a spare racket. John Davies, my Bednall roommate, was watching my match, he ran onto the court and gave me his racket to finish my match. As he handed the racket over, he said:

"You do know that he doesn't have a backhand, don't you?" John was right. I changed my tactics and won the next two sets 6-2, 6-1. I went on to win the singles final in straight sets. I also won the doubles tournament, with Bob James. John Davies told me to keep his racket: I still have the big heavy wooden thing in my loft. Thank you, John.

In 1973 I was in the Royal Army Pay Corps team that took part in the Royal British Legion Army March and Shoot Competition.

- Each team consisted of eighteen junior soldiers, led by a commissioned officer and a sergeant. We wore full battledress and webbing.
- Junior soldiers carried self-loading Rifles - that weighed just over 9 lbs.
- The officer and sergeant carried Sterling submachine guns weighing 5 lbs.
- There was a full squad inspection, before and after a five-mile route march.
- Following the second inspection, squads were marched to the rifle range, and fired twenty rounds at a figure 11 target, from a distance of 100 yards.

All the elements of the competition were assessed and scored. The event was organised, marshalled and usually won by the Parachute Regiment. We had trained for weeks to avoid humiliation which, realistically, was the best we could do. Lieutenant Macleod, a fierce Scot, and Sergeant Mick Craig led our team. The pace that Sergeant Craig set resulted in a course record time. During the route march, whenever we slowed, Lt Macleod encouraged us:

"Run faster, you useless English bastards."

After the rifle range, all the teams waited for the result to be announced. To our delight, and the Parachute Regiment's chagrin, we had won. Our squad proudly lined up in front of the trophy table. We were soaked in sweat and generating a fog of *rugby scrum steam*. The major from the Parachute Regiment, in charge of the presentation, was not impressed. He chucked his cherished red beret to one side and said our result was a fluke, adding that he looked forward to presenting the following year's tankards to the Parachute Regiment.

The following year I was in the Pay Corps team again. The Parachute team lined up next to us. They looked determined. Their commanding officer fired them up with a speech that was probably more for our benefit than the Paras.

"Redemption... You cannot lose to the bloody Pay Corps again, get out there and do your job.' He went on for quite a bit. My teammate John Higgs had heard enough. He announced to anyone within earshot.

"Don't worry about them. If there is one regiment in the entire British Army that will find a way to fuck things up, it's the Paras." We achieved a competition score, not only higher than our Junior Shield challengers, but also better than the Senior Shield winners, the Depot Para and Airborne Forces. I now have two tankards that take pride of place in my dining room cabinet.

I passed the business group of GCE 'O' levels and added an RSA Stage 2 in Accounting that I passed with distinction. That would never have happened if I had stayed in school. I had the option to stay at the college and take GCE 'A' levels. I hadn't really wanted to take any exams in the first place: it was time to move on. I enjoyed my time at the college, and I was quite proud of my achievements. Historically the college's level of success academically, sportingly and in military competitions was so exceptional it was taken for granted. In 2011 I was going through some old photographs and realised that I did not have one of the 1974 March and Shoot winning team. I was given the telephone number of Dan Graham, as someone who may be able to assist: he had been my company sergeant major at the Apprentice College for the duration of my training. Now a retired lieutenant colonel. I gave him my college résumé. I waited, then he politely said, "I am sorry, Mister Smith, but you would have had to have done an awful lot more than that for me to remember you." He put the phone down. Well, that put my achievements at the college into perspective. I still do not have the photograph.

In December 1974, at 18 years of age, I graduated from the Apprentice College and joined my first regiment, the 16/5th Queen's Royal Lancers, based in Northampton Barracks, Wolfenbüttel, West Germany. It was 6 miles from the East German border and patrolling the border was a regular duty for the regiment. I worked alongside four RAPC clerks in the pay office. Within six months, I was promoted to full corporal and responsible for paying the 60 soldiers in 'A' squadron. They all expected to receive the correct number of beer tokens on their weekly pay parade.

Being a pay clerk sounds pretty cushy, and I had been well trained to do my job, but I had a further incentive. Every soldier in 'A' Squadron had access to firearms, and some fired 76mm rounds from their Scorpion tanks. I shared a barrack room with Al Griffiths (also Pay Corps) and Phil Reale, who was a lancer. I managed to force my way into the regimental football team and played in midfield, alongside Graham Moore who served with the Royal Electrical and Mechanical Engineers. Graham added the guile and craft to my sweat and graft in the engine room of the team.

Socially the NAAFI bar was always available, but most squaddies ventured out to local pubs, clubs and brothels to have some contact with the female of the species. British soldiers were not welcome at every establishment, and given how they often behaved, why would they be? Graham Moore and I played football for a local pub, and that ensured that we were made very welcome whenever we dropped in for a beer.

One Saturday afternoon there was nothing much happening, so with my room-mates Phil and Griff, I went to the public swimming pool and sauna. Swimming has never been an activity I was interested in, mostly because I can't swim. Wearing my snazzy blue Army issue swimming trunks, I led the way, walking straight past the pool towards the sauna area. Relaxing in a steam room, rather than flailing away in a swimming pool and possibly drowning, was a lot more appealing. I walked through the turnstile, and into the sauna area and was followed by Phil and Griff. Immediately a very pretty, slim, blonde lady challenged me. She was angrily pointing towards both me and some signs on the wall. My mates were delighted that I was having a problem. Griff, not really helping, said:

"Smudge, maybe you're just too fucking ugly to be allowed in." Cheers, mate. Exasperated, the young lady dropped to her knees, took hold of my swimming trunks and whipped them off. The effect this had on me almost resulted in her losing an eye. My penis had seen very little action and was determined to show that he was more than ready if called upon. The woman who I can still picture, because at the point she dropped to her knees and pulled my trunks down, I set my eyeballs to record. I had seen several adult films that started in a very similar fashion. I thought this might be an event that I could mentally replay well into my twilight years. The lady lobbed my trunks towards a bin and pointed me, and my penis, in the direction of an ice-cold plunge pool. I stopped recording. 30 minutes sat in icy-cold water did the trick. As we were leaving Griff said:

"Hey, Smudge, that woman who stopped us going into the sauna, she was pretty fit, don't you think?"

"Fit, Griff? She was bloody gorgeous."

A smiling Griff added, "I was thinking, when your dick sprang to attention, she had her chance... but she blew it." Phil sniggered, I said, "Oh if only she had, Griff, if only she had."

I served with the regiment in the Maze Prison, Northern Ireland and was awarded the General Service Medal. I was an ever-present in the regimental football team for the two years I was attached. Playing in the team that lost 3-2 in the final of Cavalry Cup in 1975 to the Queen's Royal Irish Hussars. The following year I played against the 15/19 King's Royal Hussars and we won the final 2-1. The Cavalry Cup had eluded the 16/5th for 43 years. That night our team attended the regimental association dinner at the Strand Hotel in London. We had a great time and as a reward the players enjoyed a free bar.

I got married to my German girlfriend in 1977. The only guests at the Bromsgrove register office were my Dad and brother. Nine months later I was posted to Krefeld, West Germany, and joined the 28 Signal Regiment. I lived in married quarters. My regiment were the reigning Army football champions. I was proud to be a part, if not always a regular, in their football team.

Throughout my time in the Army, I worried about my little brother Anthony. When my mum and dad went their separate ways, my youngest sister, Frances, lived with my mum, so I believed that she was going to be okay. I will never know why my mother never took my brother with her. My oldest sister Kathleen did whatever she liked and stayed wherever she wanted, and that did not end well. My little brother drew the shortest of short straws and lived with my father. The Army was looking after me, but who was looking after him? Whenever I went on leave, I stayed with my dad and brother, and had to pay the electricity arrears to get the power turned back on. I sent a weekly payment book to my father, and I increased the amount annually. I felt better, but I knew exactly where the money was going. I may as well have sent cheques directly to 'The Jolly Farmer' and the 'Sportsman's Arms'.

I wanted to spend Christmas 1977 in Germany, so I told my dad that I could not get my leave authorised. I felt a bit guilty, so in early December, I sent my dad a cheque for £136. I asked that a pair of spectacles I had ordered from Dollond & Aitchison were collected and the balance of £36 paid. The rest of the money was for my dad and my brother to enjoy Christmas. My glasses may still be at the opticians for all I know. My dad spent every penny in the pub. My thirteen-year-old brother went downstairs on Christmas morning and could not see any presents. He searched the loft, wardrobes and cupboards - nothing. He eventually realised that his presents were not well hidden; they simply did not exist. My dad lay drunk on the settee recovering from a night that he had hoped would never end. There was no food in the house, so Dad scrounged a Christmas dinner for himself and Anthony from a neighbour. The cheque that I sent would be worth £838 in 2019. My dad probably had his best Christmas ever; my brother had his worst.

I had to do something, so in January 1978 I made a decision. In Army jargon, *I purchased my discharge*. No, I did not turn up at a sperm bank and pay for the return of my previously donated sample. I applied to leave the Army and handed over the princely sum of £200 to facilitate my exit.

On my final night in West Germany, I popped into my local pub for what I thought would be my last ever stein of Pilsner and a Bratwurst. The guy who owned the bar, Helmut, was a mad keen Borussia Mönchengladbach fan. He took their defeat against Liverpool in the European Cup Final of 1977 very badly, and I thought he held me personally responsible. I bought enough beer and schnapps to get back into his good books. I told Helmut that I was leaving the Army, and this would be my last visit. Helmut stood to attention, clicked his heels together and said, in his pronounced German accent:

"So, for you Corporal Schmidt, the war is over. It is now time for you to return to Blighty."

I enjoyed my time in the Army, especially the Apprentice College and my attachment to the 16/5th Queen's Royal Lancers - a great regiment. I have stayed in touch with some of the guys I served alongside. I was always going to be a better person because of my time as a soldier. However, I did not feel the same about my next job.

CHAPTER 3
PASSING OUT PARADES

Terry Goodwin, who was serving with the 28 Signal Regiment, and who had quite enough of soldiering, was leaving at the same time as me. We hired a van, filled it with our belongings, then drove to the Hook of Holland and caught the ferry to Harwich. Terry deposited me and my wife at my dad's house in Redditch and then continued on his journey to Newcastle, County Durham.

I made my obligatory trip to the Midlands Electricity Board office to pay the arrears and have the electricity turned back on. Moving in with my dad was only ever going to be temporary. He was never going to change, and his entire life revolved around pub opening hours. Dad was a little bit miffed that the Army had cancelled my weekly payment book.

I had to sign on the dole to qualify for unemployment benefit, and the weekly amount I received meant that beans on toast became my staple diet. I applied for loads of jobs, and the swiftest response came from the Rates Rebate Department of Redditch District Council. I started working there in April 1978. I was 21 years old. My dad tried to show willing and even took the occasional job, but being paid cash on a Friday meant a weekend's drinking followed. He missed going into work on Monday, Tuesday and sometimes even Wednesday. Often he was sacked; other times he just never went back. Eventually, he stopped working altogether and, because of his failing eyesight, he became the worst shoplifter in Redditch.

Anthony had some degree of stability and the bonus of electricity. The colour TV I brought back from Germany meant that he was able to talk to his friends about the football matches that he actually watched, and not have to read the newspapers to contribute.

Anthony improved at school. He said that it was much easier to do his homework in the winter when he could turn on a light. That more than justified my decision to leave the Army, but Dad's behaviour deteriorated to the point that I had to do something. He was permanently drunk, and the house was rocked by what we called his *screaming heebie-jeebies*. At three in the morning, any morning, he would sit bolt upright and shout out a conversation that might have happened 25 years before. It was both scary and annoying. If Dad lost an argument in the pub, then with delayed frustration, he would wake up and start slamming his bedroom door in the middle of the night.

I applied for alternative accommodation, and the Council offered me a three-bedroomed terraced house on the new Churchill housing estate. We moved out and took my brother with me. As I was going to be responsible for Anthony, I asked Dad for the family allowance book: his lip curled. He never

41

handed it over, and the subject was never mentioned again.

After only three months at the council, I felt like a hamster on a treadmill. The job I did was mind-numbingly dull. I sat with six other people around a large desk, and for eight hours, I checked and then submitted rate rebate forms. My supervisor took great delight in finding my errors, regardless of how minuscule. She would saunter across the office and return my work with my mistakes circled in red ink. To make her feel even more important, I also received a lecture. The carpet between her desk and where I sat was becoming pretty well worn, and if I had stayed much longer it would have become a trench. I was so bored that it was only the threats from the public that made my job remotely interesting. The council sent out a standard letter to anyone who had not paid their rates demand. The wording started with:

Dear Ratepayer, to avoid the possibility of having your house taken from you, please pay (inserted amount) that you owe the Redditch District Council within 14 days.

The angry resident would phone our office and ask:

"Are you the cunt who is going to take my house off me... because I owe the fucking council £2.78?" They had a point.

Working for the council was not a job that I could do for much longer. I worked flexitime, and that meant I could arrive late or leave early, but my hours had to be made up before the end of the calendar month: if not, my paltry take-home pay would be reduced. Going in late and leaving early usually meant I had to work 22 hours straight on the last day of each month. I needed to find alternative employment. My colleagues were waiting for retirement or a visit from the 'Angel of Death', and they didn't seem too bothered which came first.

The works Christmas party was enjoyable, though. The ladies heavily outnumbered the men. The women were a little bit squiffy, and as soon as they became bored with dancing around their handbags, it was time to lasso any male in the pub that was under the age of 70. When the slow dances started, my supervisor dragged me onto the dance floor, gripped my arse and started grinding herself against my crotch. Things were looking up: maybe my time at the council could develop into a sort of *Confessions of a Redditch Council Employee* sex farce. No, that didn't happen. The following day my hatchet-faced supervisor returned one of my forms that needed an i dotting.

Following a promotion, my role became slightly more tolerable. The head of my department had a quick word with me before my advancement. He congratulated me on my progression and then explained that I would not get a pay rise because the council were a bit strapped for cash. I was in no position to argue. To torment me he dangled the possibility of a pay rise sometime in the future. I was not going to hold my breath waiting for the council to cough up.

In the spring of 1979, I read an article in the *Sunday Telegraph* magazine that followed a class of police recruits through their basic training at Hendon. Two reporters remained with an intake for the full twelve weeks. The training sergeants adopted an 'if they can't take it here, then they've got no chance on the streets' approach to the trainees. Women and anyone from an ethnic background got both barrels. It was noble cause abuse designed to build character and resilience for what the officers would face in the job. The comments would result in millions of pounds in compensation today, but back then, it was simply a part of the approved training programme. A lot of the lessons were scenario-based. Trainees dealt with mock situations and incidents, then they were assessed and debriefed by their instructors and fellow students.

The journalists were excluded from a lesson that contained sensitive information about the Official Secrets Act. That lesson took place at the end of the eleventh week. The students were told not to discuss the content with anyone. The following Monday the trainees returned for their final week at Hendon. The reporters sat at the back of the classroom just as they had done for the entire course. The students were in high spirits, as this was their last week of training. The instructors stormed in and were fuming. One of them yelled out the names of a male and a female trainee. He ordered them to take the contents of their desks and then collect their belongings from their rooms. They had been sacked. The ashen-faced male and female scurried out of the classroom.

There was a stunned silence, and then the students erupted, demanding the return and reinstatement of their colleagues. An instructor explained that, contrary to his direct order, both trainees had shared information about the Official Secrets Act lesson to the reporters, who nodded, confirming that it was true. The class exploded: students were screaming at one another, the journalists and their instructors. After ten minutes of carnage, a sergeant blew his police whistle and the class fell silent. The dismissed recruits returned and were grinning. They had not realised just how popular they were. A sergeant pulled a roller chalkboard down and displayed one word in block capitals.

- CONTROL -

The sergeants lectured the class about the importance of remaining calm and in control, no matter what the provocation. The whole incident was a scenario, and the students had bought into it hook, line and sinker. The reporters were impressed, and the instructors had made their point. I can still remember the article, almost verbatim, 40 years later. For the second time, I contacted the police about joining. My first enquiry had been in the summer of 1976 when I was a soldier on a tour of duty in Northern Ireland. However, the wages were so poor I decided to not even bother filling in an application form. I wanted a job where I could at least afford to eat.

In July of 1979, at the age of 22, I applied to join the police. Following Margaret Thatcher's landslide election victory, the Edmund-Davies Report was implemented and gave the police a decent wage - £4,300 per annum a £600 a year pay rise. Maggie had a load of trade unions lined up for a severe kicking, and she was going to need the support of the *Old Bill*. The floodgates opened, and everyone wanted to join. Hundreds were required to replace the officers who had left because of the poor wages.

I did the same amount of research that I did when I joined the British Army in 1972. I looked at some glossy colour brochures. I then applied to the West Midlands police. I asked a guy I worked with if he knew where the police headquarters was. He was from Birmingham, so he pointed me in the direction of Lloyd House in the centre of Birmingham. I submitted my application form and, thanks to the Army, I had the required educational qualifications and did not need to take the entrance exam. The policeman in the recruitment department was also pretty lenient when it came to my eyesight test. He confirmed my eyes were of the absolute minimum acceptable standard. I was pretty sure they were not. The vetting process included a home visit. A uniformed sergeant from Redditch came to my house. During our chat, he asked me why I had not applied to join my local force - West Mercia. What an idiot. I genuinely believed that I had. I babbled, "As I was born in Birmingham, I have always wanted to police the... the actual area of my birth." It sounds just as pathetic now as it did then.

Following an interview at Bournville Lane police station, I was offered a job and started in September 1979. I was part of the largest intake the West Midlands police ever had, over 40 trainees. I handed in my notice to the council. I had only worked there for sixteen months, but by God, it had seemed like an awful lot longer. Goodbye, Redditch Council. I was off to become a policeman. My dad had been pissed off when I joined the Army; my joining the police was even more painful for him.

The Birmingham Six may sound like a popular 1970s boy band, but they were actually a group of Irishmen convicted of committing the worst atrocity in mainland Britain. In

November 1974 they planted bombs in two busy Birmingham pubs which killed 21 people and injured hundreds more. Within hours of the bombings, six suspects were arrested. Following their trial in August 1975, they were each sentenced to a life imprisonment term, for each of the 21 victims they had murdered. It was reassuring to know that I was joining a robust police force that knew how to arrest and convict terrorists. Well, that was what I thought in 1979.

I had a two-week induction course at Bournville Lane, an ugly 1960s police station in the middle of the Quaker village of Bournville. I didn't drive so my journey to work required two buses, a train ride, and quite a long walk. On my first day, while other recruits were idly chatting between lessons, I had a more pressing matter. I needed to find someone who had a car, but more importantly, who lived in Redditch. I must have looked like a demented speed-dater. I flitted from group to group: once I ascertained that no one fitted my requirements, I moved on. During the afternoon coffee break, I hit pay dirt and met the man of my dreams. His name was Phil Wright, an ex-teacher, who lived in Redditch and who was the proud owner of an orange Ford Capri. Problem solved. I scrounged a lift to work from Phil. During my induction, dozens of pay, insurance and Federation forms required completion. Then the basics of the law, police powers and procedures were explained. At the end of the first week, I collected my police uniform and equipment. The little green issued torch could easily have been switched on during a Second World War blackout and not breached the government's civil defence instructions. The highlights, though, were the black leather gloves and the clip-on tie. The uniform fitted where it touched. I didn't realise the outstanding quality of the other police forces' uniform and equipment until I arrived at the Regional Training Centre at Ryton.

On Thursday of the second week, our class was told to attend in uniform. I met Phil at the Book and Candle pub in Churchill, Redditch - known locally as the Crook and Vandal. In the Army uniform was worn every day, so I dressed in my full police uniform to go to work. I can still see Phil sitting in his car, smoking and pissing himself laughing as I marched towards him. Ten days in the job and I was on independent foot patrol in another police force area. It turned out the police were just a little more covert than the Army. Attending the course in uniform meant wearing a civilian jacket over my tunic, and carrying my helmet in the issued bag. Phil told everyone. Fair play, I would have, too. I want to express my gratitude to Phil for my weekly lift to and from Ryton-on-Dunsmore. I'd meet Phil at 8 pm on Sunday, the course was residential Sunday through to Friday. Phil hated initial training. It was pretty tough for him as an experienced teacher; he thought his police instructors were a bit thick. He even talked about jacking it in. To avoid having to make alternative travel arrangements, I used to get Phil to stop at a pub en route, give him some moral support and buy him a couple of pints. Phil made it through training and completed a full 30 years' service retiring as an inspector.

At the police college, my trainers were Sergeants Bob Duxbury from Warwickshire and Paul Tomlin from

Staffordshire. Bob was a thoroughly decent man and an excellent tutor. Sergeant Tomlin reported sick in our second week, and we did not see him again. I remember Bob Duxbury told us if ever we were called 'Pigs' when we were patrolling the streets, then it should be treated as a compliment as it stood for Pride, Integrity and Guts. Really, Bob? Really. The aspirational police training buzzwords at the time were that we should be 'firm but fair'. My class consisted of eight females and sixteen males. I worked out there would be a 50% chance of carnal success. The good news for me was that only seven of my female classmates were looking for a dreamboat and not a shipwreck.

My class consisted mostly of West Midlands police officers but there were also students from Warwickshire, Leicestershire, Greater Manchester, Staffordshire, Hertfordshire and the City of London. While the other police forces looked smart in tailored uniforms, my force had used a one-size-will-fit-no-one-in-particular template to produce theirs. West Midlands trainees spent every night trying to iron creases into resistant trousers and floppy tunics, the other forces popped their clothes onto a coat hanger, and that was job done. It was with good reason that the West Midlands police were known nationally as *The Force of a Thousand Raincoats*.

As I had been a soldier, I was selected to be the class drill prefect. My role was to march our class to lessons, dinner and around the Training Centre. A graduate recruit challenged Sergeant Wood, the Training Centre's drill instructor:

"Sergeant Wood, why on earth, as police officers, do we

need to learn something as antiquated and pointless as how to march?" Woody had heard this before. He took a deep breath stared at the graduate, but addressed our entire class:

"Right, you lot. Listen in... Marching is the quickest and most efficient way of getting a group of individuals from point A to point B, at the same time and ready for action. Also, the commanding officer can see straight away if he has a man down or missing from the ranks. The Romans invented marching, and the British Army has just about perfected it. Now by the left, quick march!"

Basic training was reasonably strict, but nothing like the Army. I joined the Army and was not allowed to write home for a month. Conversely, if I had felt so inclined, I could have walked out of Ryton on the day I joined. In the police, I was allocated a bedroom with a toilet, shower, bed and lockable door, and set my bedside alarm for a 7.30 am start. In the Army at 6 am a demented lance corporal hit a metal bin with a stick and marched through our barrack room shouting:

"Hands Off Cocks... and On with Socks!" Basic training in the police was nothing like the Army.

Police training only skimmed the surface of what would be required. In first aid, the subject of childbirth was covered in about three minutes. We were told to make sure that the woman's tights were taken off as a priority. Otherwise, the baby might look like a bank robber as it was coming out. We were taught criminal law and police powers through the medium of an overhead projector. We had to learn legal definitions for all arrestable offences, and were tested, on the content of that week's lessons every Friday morning. Those who failed could retake the exam the following Monday, after a weekend's revision and hopefully a little bit of romance at the Training Centre.

One of the guys in my intake, Dave Yellowley, had a real expertise with brassieres. Any female on the course who walked past him was fair game. With a display of speed and dexterity, he would unclip their bra, and there would be a slight fall in the altitude of the now released breasts. Only a small drop, mind: the average age of the eight women in my class was twenty.

Basic training included scenarios just like I had read about in the *Sunday Telegraph*. As students, we pretended that we did not mind being selected, but deep down we did. WPC Maggie O'Hare from Warwickshire and PC Ada Nolan from the West Midlands were chosen to deal with a scenario, and it appeared rather sombre. They were allowed a few minutes to prepare. Ada looked nervous, whereas Maggie played it cool her 38DDs pointed impressively front and centre. Dave Yellowley had been eyeing up Maggie from a distance, just waiting for the opportunity to perform his party trick. I am pretty sure that Maggie would have murdered him if he had.

Meanwhile, back to the scenario, Maggie knocked on the door of another classroom. A female sergeant, playing the role of the occupant, answered. Bob Duxbury and the rest of our class were observing. Maggie introduced herself and confirmed that the lady was the right person to receive the message. Maggie also ascertained that she had a 25-year-old son: so far, so good.

"I am very sorry to have to inform you that your son has just died in a fatal road traffic accident." Right on cue, the role player went into a full *Coronation Street* audition. Well, that was what I thought, anyway.

"Oh, my God. My only son dead. Dead, oh my God, dead, dead, dead. He's dead." She threw herself about a bit. Ada seemed to forget that it was a scenario and appeared genuinely upset. Desperate to help in any way that he could, and following a complete rush of shit to the brain, he offered some wonderful reassurance:

"No, love. It's okay! He's not dead. It was only a fatal accident." It was hard for the class to objectively assess the student's performance through their tears of laughter.

Our classroom was a wooden hut with a blackboard at the front. We sat at a single desk in three rows of eight. Picture any 1970s public school. To speak, I put my hand up and, once acknowledged, I then stood to attention and spoke. I recall that there was only one lesson during the ten weeks where this rule was relaxed, and questions asked from a sitting position. It was the day we had a tutorial about pornography. Hardcore Danish porno books were handed out for our perusal. It was the first time some officers had feasted their eyes on such material.

It was not my first time. When I was eighteen, I played in a football tournament in Denmark. The Mayor took my regimental team to a porn supermarket as part of an official guided tour, which was very kind of him. Like all supermarkets, it was divided into sections. Our centre half, a seasoned squaddie, gave me the low-down. He pointed to each of the aisles in turn:

"Normal, lezzers, puffs, animals, and over there kids." Even from a distance, the children in the magazines looked incredibly young, so I queried this. My learned guide laughed and shook his head. "In some countries, they have two-year-olds who can't get enough sex. Honestly, they are just born nymphomaniacs." I did not believe him.

"What's that woman doing with that bloody Shetland pony?" I blurted out, pointing to another section. My colleague chuckled:

"You will not believe this but..." I did not accept his explanation for that either. It was aisles one and two for me.

Back to the class of 1979. The physical reaction to the pornography was immediate and awkward. Sergeant Duxbury knew that if some of the class had stood up, they would have sent their desks flying. So questions were asked from a sitting position. After the tutorial, the porn books were collected and counted. When it came to pornography, no one could be trusted. We had a short discussion, and ten minutes later, Sergeant Duxbury deemed it was safe for the male officers to stand up and go for lunch. Being firm had not been a problem, so now the policemen just had to work on being fair.

Ada Nolan was again the star when we learned how to give evidence in court. I think you probably appreciate that, with hindsight, I wish I had given that lesson my full attention. A mock court had been set up in a classroom. We could either swear an oath on the Bible or, if we did not believe in God, affirm that our evidence was true. In turn, we held the Bible in our right hand and read the oath from a card. When it was Ada's turn, he picked up the Bible but then he seemed to stand a little taller. Rounding on Sergeant Duxbury, he explained that he did not believe in God, adding that he was not going to swear an oath just because everyone else had. Sergeant Duxbury applauded Ada's stance and cited him to the class as an excellent example of having the courage of his convictions. Ada looked pleased. He reached down and picked up the affirmation card in his left hand and read from it. Unfortunately, that was while he still held up the Bible with his right hand.

There were, of course, some casualties amongst the trainees. Having allowed so many in at one time, some of the more deranged had to be sifted out. One weekend a student donned his uniform, jumped onto a bus and started checking the passenger's tickets. The real police were called, and the student only came back to Ryton to collect his belongings. Another guy wore his police uniform while he took part in a filmed gay orgy and he was asked to leave - the police force, that is, not the orgy.

In November 1979 the successful recruits from our intake had a passing out parade. It was a pretty drab affair. It rained, so we wore coats. Families and friends who were watching would probably have been trying to spot two West Midlands officers wearing matching raincoats. We clumsily marched onto the drill square and after a few minutes just as awkwardly shuffled off.

It was not my first passing out parade. In December 1974,

having completed two years' training at the Royal Army Pay Corps Apprentice College in Winchester, I was scheduled to pass out. The Army sent my father an invitation to attend my parade. Also included were directions to the barracks at Worthy Down plus a map of the camp. The parade location was marked with an 'X'. Separately I sent my dad some money to pay his coach fare. My father never acknowledged the invitation or confirmed that he received the money. Well, he came. He trousered the cash and in a typically Belfast way - he put a clean shirt, underpants, socks, toothbrush and his shaving tackle into a brown paper carrier bag (complete with string handles) which he tucked under his arm and set off. He allowed himself a full day to thumb a lift from Hereford to Winchester, a trip of 120 miles.

There was a national security crisis in Britain. The Birmingham pub bombings had taken place the week before, and the entire nation was on a terror alert. Bombs, bomb threats and hoax bomb calls were, unfortunately, a part of everyday life. The locals in Winchester were as vigilant as the rest of the country. The night before my parade, Dad arrived in Winchester at 7 pm. He phoned the college's communal payphone to update me. He was a regular caller, so his pronounced Belfast accent did not cause concern. Dad asked where I was and was told that the graduating soldiers would be on the piss, in one of the pubs in Winchester. The corporal also said that soldiers were not welcome in all the pubs, so to find me, he may have to have a good look around.

So it came to pass that at 8 pm my father walked into the

heaving Railway Inn carrying a brown parcel. In his sharp Belfast accent, he barked at the landlord:

"Do any soldiers use this here pub?" The landlord and three regular's rugby-tackled my father and restrained him. The police arrived and showed the locals exactly how, using unrestrained violence with just a smattering of Home Office-approved techniques, a terrorist should be beaten up. A policeman found the map of my Army barracks in Dad's jacket pocket and noticed the 'X' on the map. He assumed that was the location where the bomb was to be planted. Dad was handcuffed and taken to Winchester police station. Looking back, and given the mood of the country, I cannot believe that he did not get sentenced to at least 30 years' imprisonment based on the few facts that you have just read.

I was oblivious to my father's plight. I had been drinking in the Baker's Arms pub. Not long after I returned to barracks, two uniformed coppers woke me up and told me to get dressed, adding brusquely:

"You, sunshine, are coming with us." At Winchester police station a cell door was flung open. I could see a bloody mess huddled in the corner of the cell.

"Is that your bastard father?" a policeman with bruised knuckles asked me. I was very tempted to say no. Apparently, my father had resisted arrest and had got exactly what he fucking deserved. Dad roused himself and, slurring his words through bloodied lips, said:

"Six of them son, it took fucking six of the bastards." I rounded on the cop, who was massaging his knuckles.

"Why have you done this to my dad?"

"Beating up cunts like him is one of the few perks of this job, son, that's why." To be honest, I was a bit surprised that it had only taken six policemen: my dad must be getting old, I thought. I didn't get any sleep that night. Covered in cuts and bruises, my dad attended my passing out parade. He cadged fags off my instructors then stole and drank the bottle of sherry that had been put aside for the royal toast.

A few weeks before my police graduation, I thought long and hard and decided not to invite my father to my police passing out parade.

CHAPTER 4
A CONSTABLE'S TALE

During my last week of police training, all those who had completed the course received their postings. I was to be based at Kings Heath police station in Birmingham. In preparation, I visited Redditch bus station and collected a pocketful of timetables. On a cold December Monday in 1979, I set off for my first day as a uniformed constable. To avoid repeating my September faux pas, when I patrolled the streets of Redditch. I wore my Army combat jacket and carried a rucksack that contained my police helmet and equipment. I set off at 6.30 am and allowed a comfortable two and a half hours to catch the four connecting buses I needed to get to work for 9 am. The bus timetables were a complete waste of time. The only accurate detail they contained was the date. Standing at bus stops and alternately checking my watch and then the timetables only increased my level of frustration. All of my buses were late. I was going to have to find a more reliable way of commuting.

The last bus on my never-ending journey was the number 50. I stepped onto the platform and nervously tap-danced next to the driver. He could see enough of my uniform to ask if I was going to Kings Heath police station. I confirmed I was. It was 9.05 am, and the driver could see that I was agitated.

"Running late, mate?" My God, Birmingham bus drivers were astute.

"Yes, pretty late, and this is my very first day." I then muttered to myself, "And at this rate, it might well be my last." The driver did his best to get me to the station as quickly as he could, but the bus stopped every 50 yards. As he approached the police station, the driver opened the door and slowed down. This allowed me to jump off the bus and jog into the station yard. Jogging made it look like I was at least making an effort. It also put a bit of distance between the bus and me. I did not want to present my new colleagues with an open invitation to nickname me Stan, Blakey, or worse still, Olive from the television programme *On the Buses*. My first thought was horse shit. No, not because I was late. There were three stables for police horses adjacent to the station entrance, and they had just been mucked out. There was a steaming pile of horse shit outside the stables, and the smell was overpowering.

Kings Heath police station was referred to as the B-3 subdivision, and it was fully operational. The station telephonist pointed me towards a narrow flight of twisty stairs. She said that PC Tommy Burton, the sub-divisional clerk, was waiting for me in the office at the top of the stairs. I quickly changed, then rushed up the stairs.

Tommy Burton greeted me. He was ex-Army and recognised the Northern Ireland campaign ribbon on my tunic. Tommy gave me a big smile and a firm, possibly Masonic, handshake.

He called me into his office then partially closed the door. I glanced at a clock on the wall: it was 9.10 am. Tommy smiled.

"Don't worry about being a bit late, son. The boss doesn't know what day of the week it is, let alone what time it is." Tommy ushered me along the corridor to join two other recruits who were waiting outside the superintendent's office. We were there to see the person who Tommy allowed to think was in charge of the subdivision, Superintendent John Walters. Tommy knocked on his door, and I heard:

"Enter." We all walked in and Superintendent Walters added brusquely, "Right then Tommy, which of these clowns was late?" I feared the worst.

"Do you know sir, I actually think they all were." Tommy gave a withering look at the other two recruits, who deflected it in my direction.

"Thank you, Tommy, that will be all." Mr Walters looked up at the three of us.

"Officers, punctuality is imperative in today's police force. Do not be late again." I was the only one who nodded at that comment.

Mr Walters bore an uncanny resemblance to Clark Gable which he reinforced with a black and white Hollywood-style portrait of himself which hung on the wall behind his desk. Mr Walters was captured in a Clark Gable pose complete with a cheesy smile and moustache. My superintendent trotted out some old tripe about us being good apples, and that we should be careful that we didn't turn into bad apples. Incredibly it had taken me only fifteen minutes to get from horse shit to bullshit. I had the impression that, as far as new recruits were concerned, Mr Walters' attitude was: 'Frankly my dear, I couldn't give a damn.'

Mr Walters explained that the Kings Heath subdivision was divided into fourteen beat areas and that each beat had a permanent beat officer (PBO). As part of our development, we would be attached to three different beat officers for two weeks. Then we would be posted to one of the four shifts. The other two recruits were posted to Kings Heath police station. The next morning at 8 am I was to start work with a PBO at Billesley police station. I drew a blank. Billesley? He may as well have said Buenos Aires.

After the meeting, I went back to see Tommy Burton. I asked him where Billesley police station was. Tommy stabbed a sausage finger into a sub-divisional map, adding that it was on the Yardley Wood Road, opposite Billesley Park and that I couldn't miss it. He also told me that I would be attached to PC Pete Tetsall, who he said was a top bloke.

"Thanks for what you did earlier, it was appreciated," I softly said to Tommy. Nowhere near as quietly replied:

"No problem, mate, after all, we're both ex-squaddies." Tommy was only a couple of years away from retirement and was very much the man in charge. All overtime, expenses, courses and postings went through Tommy. If he liked you, then you were offered career development and overtime. If he didn't, then you might have to think about taking a second job. Beat allocation resolved. I had my first breakfast in a police canteen and was then allowed out in a panda car with PC

Steve Groome. We patrolled the streets of Kings Heath. Steve pulled alongside a car on the Bristol Road, as if he was going to overtake it. He told me to wind my window down and indicated to a startled driver that he should do the same. The other car was travelling at 42mph in a 40mph zone.

"Oi, fuck face, where's the fucking fire?" Steve shouted at the driver. That was actually one of his less offensive opening lines of customer contact that morning. We were then sent to my first job. Some horses were running loose in a field dangerously near a road in the Maypole area of Birmingham. Another panda car was already there with another recruit, my old chum from Ryton, Phil Wright, who used his handcuffs to secure a five-bar gate and save the day.

The following morning armed with Tommy Burton's directions I set off in search of Pete Tetsall and Billesley police station. I left my home at 6 am for an 8 am start. I decided that cycling had to be a lot less stressful than using the buses. I got as far as Billesley and cycled up and down the Yardley Wood Road, disappointingly there was no sign of a police station. The only person about was an elderly man. I asked him if he knew where Billesley police station was. He said that he had lived in Billesley all of his life and did not think Billesley had a police station. I cycled up and down the road again. Nothing. Was this a complete wind-up? I caught a glimpse of a uniformed police officer walking down a tree-lined path towards a huge house that was set 80 yards back from the road. In the absence of any other ideas, I just followed him. The officer walked straight into the house. It was the police station. There was no indication that it was even a police building. You can't miss it, my arse. Anyway there was no location that I couldn't miss.

Pete Tetsall was waiting for me and helpfully pointed me in the direction of the station kettle. He introduced me to the office man, PC John Hughes, as his "brand new pro-con, straight out of the box". Pete Tetsall was a proper old-fashioned Brummie, but he did not seem too enthusiastic about police work. This was explained on my second day with him: he told me that he had resigned and was joining his dad in the family painting and decorating business. We worked day shifts and, rather than fighting crime, we spent most of our time drinking - tea in the morning and lager in the afternoon. This caused me a bit of a problem, not any moral dilemma; it was just that I had to cycle ten miles to get home.

During my first week, I saw John Walters at Woodbridge Road police station. Mr Walters had forgotten his meet-and-greet speech to me a few days before. Superintendent Walters looked a little tired and troubled, being Clark Gable 24 hours a day seven days a week was taking its toll.

"Who are you, son?"

"PC Vince Smith, sir." I saluted. They don't do that anymore.

"Who is your tutor at the moment Smith?"

"PC Tetsall, sir."

"That is a shame, he will be missed. Who are you with next?"

"PC Jim Thomas, sir." The name seemed to cause Mr Walters to twitch. Eventually, he said, "Jim Thomas, Jim Thomas, watch that fucker, Smith. That's all I'm saying. Just keep your eyes peeled." I was a bit confused. Did Mr Walters mean that I could learn a lot from Jim? I later found out that the complaints department were watching Jim as he was suspected of living off the earnings of prostitutes. Regardless, I had an enjoyable two weeks with him. We patrolled the vice area of Moseley and Balsall Heath. For the record, I saw nothing untoward. Jim was a great guy good at his job and an excellent beat man. He completed his 30 years and left with his reputation intact.

The third of my tutors was PC John McAnneny, or Johnny Mac as he was known. John was highly respected and was a renowned thief-taker. That was the ultimate accolade for a police officer. John's area was Waldrons Moor in Kings Heath, Birmingham. John ruled his patch and was ruthless. He had a network of informants who produced results, and the local criminals despised him. If John had one weakness, it was his paperwork: the standard of his court files and general report writing was appalling.

On lates, John always drove into the darkest corners of car parks and shone his torch into the cars of what usually turned out to be courting couples. Initially, this was amusing. Still, after a while, I just found it embarrassing. Eventually, I challenged him.

"John, why the hell are we doing this?"

"Let's just say that I wish some nosey copper had shone his torch into the van that some dirty fucker pulled me into when I was a kid."

After a few days, John opened up and told me how things were at home when he was growing up. John's mum, Rose, was a part-time cleaner at Redditch police station. All the coppers loved her and enjoyed the never-ending supply of tea that she made for them. Rose was arrested one year just before Christmas. She had committed the heinous offence of using chopped halfpennies in her gas meter. The Redditch cops had a collection for the McAnneny family, who then had their best Christmas for years. Rose had a season ticket for the Accident and Emergency hospital, courtesy of her husband, John. Black eyes and bloodied noses were regular occurrences. The domestic violence that Johnny Mac had lived through was actually pretty similar to my childhood experience.

One school day at 5 pm, a nine-year-old Johnny Mac was at home with his parents. Following the previous night's hostilities, Johnny's mum had a black eye, and she had just returned home from work. There was a loud knock on the front door which young John answered. The caller was a burly uniformed policeman that, with a purposeful stride, walked straight into the house. The officer had been before, but this was different. He seemed friendly enough, but John could detect an edge.

"Hello, Rose. I was just passing and decided that it was time for one of your lovely cups of tea." Rose dutifully went into the kitchen to put the kettle on. John noticed his dad looked uncomfortable. The officer said nothing as he slowly unbuttoned his tunic, which he put on the back of a chair. Then he rolled up his shirtsleeves, took off his watch and after placing it carefully on the table, he turned to John's father.

"Right, then, John, let's go and have a look at your tomatoes, shall we? Let's see how they're getting on."

"No, er... you're all right, Officer. The tomatoes are doing just fine."

"Get in the fucking garden," hissed the copper. John senior and the policeman walked through the kitchen, and into the tiny back garden. After a few seconds, young John heard the all too familiar, sickening sound of fist on face, followed by a yelp of pain. Both men came back into the house. A cup of tea was on the table waiting for the policeman, who drained it and declared that it was well up to Rose's usual high standard. He rolled his shirtsleeves down and put his watch and tunic back on. As the policeman was leaving the house, he spoke to John's dad:

"Just so you know, I'll be checking on those tomatoes regularly. Understand?" Johnny's dad was holding his face.

"Fine, Officer, I will... I can assure you that there will be no more problems."

"There had better fucking well not be." The officer ruffled little Johnny's hair as he left. Johnny Mac said he was shocked, mostly because he did not know that his dad was growing tomatoes in their garden.

I had my first-ever arrest with Johnny Mac on Sunday 6 January 1980. When I was posted to Kings Heath, the recruits who knew the Birmingham area told me that because of the number of High Street shops, I would be dealing with shoplifters all day every day. Thanks to Johnny Mac's policing skills, my first prisoner was not a shoplifter. John saw a Jaguar motor car being driven by someone he knew had been disqualified from driving. We followed the vehicle to a house in Waldrons Moor, Kings Heath. I knocked on the front door, which just opened, so John and I walked in. The family had just sat down to their Sunday dinner. John pointed to the driver, who was trying to hide behind a roast chicken:

"Come here, son, we need to have a word." It was time to make the arrest. Tentatively, I began:

"Right. I am arresting you for driving a vehicle whilst disqualified. You are not obliged to say anything but... "

John interrupted. "Vince. That caution shit is only for training. We don't use it on the streets." He turned to my prisoner and snapped, "Phillip. You're nicked, get in the police car." John explained to the family that Phillip would only be with us for an hour or so. Thanks a lot, John. Honestly, when was I ever going to need to be able to recite the caution?

I proudly took my prisoner to the cell block, he was charged, and because John didn't like him, he was not granted bail. My fellow recruits were right, though: most of my days were spent dealing with shoplifters.

After my two-week attachment with John, I started work on B-Unit. During the time spent with my tutors, I learned some very subtle applications of the law. They included the Ways and Means Act, and the Birmingham Byelaws. Neither appeared in any format the public could check but were often used to remove a problem from the streets and place it securely into a police cell. Technically the 'detained' were just helping the police with their enquiries. The legal beagles in the station would get to work and create a charge, a summons, or draft a profound apology.

Most days I wore my Army issue camouflage jacket to work. Coincidentally in the winter of 1979, *Citizen Smith* starring Robert Lindsay was a popular programme on TV. My shift christened me Wolfie after the camouflage-clad eponymous hero, and that name has stayed with me for years. I didn't mind being called Wolfie: other pro-cons at Kings Heath were nicknamed Bonehead, Bog-brush and Sperm bank. Yeah, Wolfie was just fine.

I made discreet enquiries, and none of the B-Unit officers lived anywhere near Redditch. There was just no public transport that would get me to work on time for an early shift or get me home after nights. It was time for action: my bicycle needed some attention. I took it out of the shed, pumped up the tyres, sprayed WD-40 on the gears, and put some new batteries in the front and rear lights.

My first two years in the police would consist of foot patrol, training courses and assessments. A part of policing which was different to most other occupations was the requirement to carry a pocketbook, a small diary that was carried and completed during every tour of duty. My inspector and sergeant checked and signed my pocketbook on parade and during my tour of duty. My pocketbook was expected to include my refreshment times, arrests, interviews, property seized, evidence and, well, anything that I felt was noteworthy. It was also a discipline tool. If I messed up a job, then my sergeant or inspector would endorse my pocketbook with the appropriate advice.

Without any experience of policing, I discovered, any pocketbook separated from its owner was knobbed and returned. Knobbing was the act of drawing a penis, complete with bollocks and pubic hair, on several pages. Disgustingly, the penis was often ejaculating. Highly amusing unless of course you were scheduled to give evidence at court; as there was always a possibility that a defence solicitor could ask to inspect an officer's pocketbook.

Another lesson that I was to learn the hard way involved the retention of my issued fleece-lined, black leather gloves. If I was not wearing them, and they were out of my sight for a second, then they were gone. A colleague with just a little more service than I had would be presenting them to his mate before my shift had even finished. The station kleptomaniacs also targeted A-Z street map books. I had no idea where any street in Kings Heath was, and it was embarrassing having to ask for directions to every location to which I was sent. I realised that I had to do something when the controller piped up on the radio and announced.

"Wolfie, I know you are in the station somewhere... can you turn out to an immediate at the Hare & Hounds on the High Street? Just for your information if you walk out of the nick then turn right and keep walking until you reach the pub where chairs, tables and people are being thrown through the windows. Then you will have arrived at the right place." After that not so subtle prompt I purchased the latest copy of the Birmingham A-Z. I was given a security tip. I was told to use my collar number and circle the corresponding page numbers in the book. I did just that on pages 82 and 93. Within an hour, it had disappeared. I was not happy, and everyone at the police station was now a suspect.

At shift changeover times, I checked out the officers on the other shifts. I was looking for any new A-Zs, especially in the hands of some of the shiftier-looking fuckers. A week passed then I saw one in the hands of Mr Shifty himself, PC Hughie Friel, an officer who always seemed to have more than just one pair of issued gloves stuffed into his car coat pockets. I asked Hughie if I could have a look at the A-Z he was holding. The page numbers on pages 82 and 93 were circled. I demanded an apology. Hughie refused. I told him exactly how I could prove that it was mine. Hughie invited me to look at all the pages: every bloody page number had been circled. Hughie snatched it back and claimed that when he bought it, a sergeant told him that was how to make it identifiable. The lying bastard.

PC Ray Siddall was the senior PC on my shift he ran the tea fund and was a spokesman for the troops. He asked me why I didn't smoke. He was a chain-smoker himself and explained that smoking was an absolute must for two reasons. Firstly, it allowed critical thinking time, and secondly, it had been clinically proven that nicotine helped the decision-making process. While we were both at an incident, just to demonstrate his point, Ray took a long draw on his fag. Silence. He was deep in thought. He exhaled slowly, and by pointing at each of them in turn, addressed the people at the scene:

"Right, you, sunshine, are nicked. You are going to have to go to the hospital to get that wound stitched. While all that is going on you two fuckers will be making witness statements. Wolfie, did you see what I did there?" I have to admit he looked cool.

On a Sunday afternoon in my first month, a concerned neighbour reported to the police that a drunken man was threatening his wife and children. The caller added that this happened most Sunday afternoons. I arrived at the address at the same time as Ray Siddall, who was climbing out of his panda and finishing his cigarette, which he expertly flicked down a street drain. He saw me and said:

"Watch and learn Wolfie, just watch and learn." The front door was open, so we just walked into the house. I could hear shouting. Noticing our presence, the intoxicated male started barking threats in our general direction. No one had been hurt. His wife and kids had suffered years of listening to the twat, returning from his Sunday lunchtime drinking session then berating them. Ray Siddall looked straight at the slob, then slowly raised his police radio to his face with his left hand. He then overtly wrapped his truncheon strap around his right fist. Ray spoke clearly into his police radio.

"Bravo 3 Control from Bravo Mike 20, I am at the address with Wolfie Smith. An aggressive drunken male has sustained absolutely horrific head injuries... while resisting arrest. Please send an ambulance. Immediately!" Ray had not pushed the transmit button. The mouthy male sobered up fast and looked around the room, realising that he was just about to get bludgeoned. In a panic he said:

"Officers... would you like a cup of tea? I was just going to make the missus one. Kids, I think I can hear the ice cream van: here's some money, go and get some ice creams." I thought, wow, that was impressive. Everything was sorted, and nobody got hurt. It was even possible that the mouthy twat might just behave himself for a few months. Did the nicotine chemically assist Ray or was it all down to his experience? I hoped it was the latter, as I still had no intention of smoking.

People think police officers are opinionated and they are right. At every incident they attend, in their 30 years' service, they will form an opinion and make their decisions based on it. They will often have to justify those decisions to a court or to a senior police officer. In my first two years as a pro-con, I was considered to be available for everything. Although posted to an area on foot patrol, I would be collected by a colleague and dropped off at whatever location required the physical presence of a uniformed police officer. Tasks to which I would be airlifted included guarding crime scenes and directing traffic. This was where I first learned how to tell lies to the public. "Ladies and gents, can you all please move along. There really is nothing to see here." If the police are there, then there is plenty to see: murder scenes, fatal car crashes, suicides , they are the very incidents that the public has waited their whole life to see.

When the school crossing patrol person failed to show up, then, as a priority, a uniformed officer would be dispatched to carry out those duties. As I said earlier, I was given this task with only a few weeks on the shift. I queried this particular use of police resources with Sergeant John Mason. I suggested I had far more interesting and much more important things to do:

"Wolfie, your primary role in this job is the protection of life and property. There are four hundred children who attend that school, so just go and do the crossing patrol. Oh, and try not to let any of the kids get fucking killed while they are crossing the road. You gobby twat." A point well made, albeit the level of tact and diplomacy could have been tweaked. John Mason added, "I will see you in the canteen after you have finished: I may just have a little job for you to do." That was when he abandoned me at the Birmingham Magistrates' so I could make a complete dog's dinner of opposing the bail application of Gerry Donovan.

As a part of their continued development, and because no one else really wanted the job, probationers were tasked to deliver death messages. This is one of the toughest jobs that the police have. When knocking on someone's door at 3 am, it was rarely going to be to deliver good news. Felix O'Neill was a burly Irish police sergeant who was usually the radio controller. Felix had a deep, gruff voice and a pretty dark sense of humour. Here was one of his classics: it took place at 11 am on Christmas Day.

"Bravo 3 Control calling Bravo Mike 19... Can you attend 124 Sandford Road, Moseley and tell the lady of the house that her husband has just passed away in hospital." There was a pause: we were all tuned in, we knew Felix would add his own inappropriate comment that he would find hilarious. He cleared his throat and said, "Well. That is one man who will definitely not be getting any sixpences in his Christmas pudding this year. A Hur Hur Hur."

CHAPTER 5
'8293, ARE YOU RECEIVING?'

I felt safe patrolling the streets with a tutor but dealing with the local nutter's latest episode of batshit craziness in his house. On my own, I felt more than a little vulnerable. While I was doing my very best to be firm but fair, the nutter had his own buzzwords - violent and menacing. I just knew that we were going to have a fight. My problem was that I wore spectacles, so in anticipation, I took off my glasses. On reflection, it was a pretty clear statement of intent. I may as well have just rolled up my sleeves and spat on my hands. The nutter read the signs. He stopped shouting, then calmly asked me to put my glasses back on, which I did. No blows were exchanged, and the matter was peacefully resolved. I realised that I was giving the public far too much notice of my intention. So the next day, I went to an optician and was measured up for a pair of contact lenses.

When the controller shouted out your collar number (which should actually be called a shoulder number because that is where police numbers are) Then whatever the next job was, it was coming your way. At 7 am on a bright Sunday winter's morning, it was not long till breakfast, and I was feeling peckish. My radio, which had been quiet, piped up.

"8293 from Control, are you receiving?" I confirmed that I was.

"Good. Can you attend 43 Addison Road? We have just had a report from a neighbour that a Marjorie Davies, who is in her eighties, has not been seen for a few days. The neighbour is a bit concerned."

My response of "En route, Sergeant," sounded a lot more confident than I felt. I was close, and it only took me a few minutes to get there.

Outside 43 Addison Road was the neighbour who had called the police. There were four bottles of pasteurised milk on the doorstep. Not a promising start. I told the neighbour that she could leave things with me and asked if she wouldn't mind popping her kettle on as I was a bit parched. Intending to shout through the letter box, I first had to push some letters and newspapers through it. To my right was a net curtain which initially, I thought, was moving. Then I saw that it was covered in hundreds of flies. I dropped to my haunches and pushed open the letter box flap: the stench nearly knocked me out. I was reasonably sure that Marjorie was no longer with us.

I went around to the back of the house and found the kitchen door open. I put my leather gloves on and went inside. I put my hand over my face and reduced my breathing to a minimum. There was no sign that the house had been searched, or that a struggle had taken place. In the lounge lying on a sofa was

Marjorie Davies. The newspaper on the carpet next to her was five days old. The following four days newspapers were on a mat in her hallway. The central heating had accelerated the decomposing process. The image of her bloated, the seepage, the flies and maggots stayed with me for some time. However, the smell is something that I will never forget. I needed some fresh air and to regain my composure.

I retraced my steps to the front of the house. This was the first time I had seen a dead body. The concerned neighbour was waiting for me with a cup of tea. I broke the news to her that Marjorie had passed away in her sleep. She asked me if I would like some toast, which I declined: it was going to be days before my appetite returned. The neighbour said that it had been a couple of years since Marjorie's family had visited. I radioed the controller and updated the police log; I requested the attendance of a doctor to certify the death and a Scenes of Crime Officer. I did this in my best matter-of-fact voice. Had the controller detected any emotional wobble. Then just for his own amusement, he would have sent me to every sudden death report for the next two years. I went to my fair share of unexpected deaths, but I never forgot my first.

Not long after I dealt with my first sudden death, I was sent to 53 Kingswood Road, Moseley, where I was the first officer at the scene of a murder. Percy Black was 55 years old, had taken early retirement and probably for the first time in his life had a wallet full of £10 notes. Percy had brought a young woman home for an afternoon of sex. She tied Percy up, then let a couple of her criminal associates into Percy's flat to help her rob him. Percy started shouting for help: to silence him, a rag was stuffed into Percy's mouth. He choked and died. His attackers ran off.

Percy's daughter lived nearby, and after she was given the bad news, she attended the scene and identified her dad to me. For continuity reasons, before an autopsy could be conducted, I had to identify the deceased to the pathologist. PC Dave McClughen, affectionately known as 'Clug', volunteered to attend the mortuary. Clug wanted to see how the continuity procedure worked. I identified Percy Black to the pathologist Doctor Peter Acland, stepped back and stood next to Clug.

Detective Inspector Jim Kelly, who had brought his team of hard-nosed detectives with him, asked me if I wanted to stay and watch the autopsy. I was not looking forward to watching Percy being medically dismantled, but I knew it was a trick question. Had I opted to leave, then Jim Kelly and his team would have ripped the piss out of me for years. Also, in all likelihood, I would be dragged to every autopsy just to see if I would faint or be sick. I opted to stay, and so did Clug. The stench from the mortuary was awful. I took my contact lenses out and dropped them into my shirt pocket. I told Clug what I had done, and I was quite happy that the room was now a sterile blur. Clug quietly gave me a commentary:

"Fuck me, Wolfie, they have taken the top of his head off." I sagely nodded. "Now they have scooped his brain out and stuck it into a jar." I was glad that I couldn't see what he could. The smell was horrific. I just kept nodding and tried to look blasé throughout the procedure. Then events became a little bit weird. The detective inspector barked at Dr Acland:

"Did he get to have a shag before he died Peter?"

Clug quietly continued. "Wolfie, he is peeling back Percy's foreskin, he is bending over Percy's cock. Oh, fuck, Wolfie, Acland's mouth is about three inches from Percy's cock. If he starts to suck it, I fucking swear I am going to scream and just leg it." I anxiously waited for his next update. "Wolfie, it's okay... Acland has only taken a swab from Percy's bell-end." Phew. Following the autopsy, Jim Kelly asked me if I was okay.

"Sir, I was in the British Army for almost six years and have seen a lot worse," I lied. The smell of death has a permanency that does not wash out. I went home and threw every item of uniform that I had been wearing in the bin. I was grateful to Dave McClughen. The three offenders were traced, charged with manslaughter and each received a twelve-year prison sentence.

Throughout my service, I only attended a handful of autopsies. Because for some strange reason, there were always plenty of police officers who wanted to see them, and I was more than happy to step aside and let them.

Reporting sick was frowned upon, but plodding the beat and cycling the twenty-mile round trip to work, in all weathers, could really take its toll. One morning I woke at 4.30 am with the prospect of a 5.45 am start. I had the flu and didn't feel well. For the first time in my service, I phoned in sick. I spoke to the night's inspector and asked him to let my inspector know that I was reporting unfit for duty. I went back to bed and fell asleep. A thunderous knocking on my front door woke me. It was 6.15 am. I looked out of my bedroom window and saw my Inspector Colin Young and a sergeant. Mr Young was a straight-talking no-nonsense gaffer. My first thought was: 'bollocks, my message hasn't been passed'. I grabbed a towel and rushed downstairs; opened my front door and sniffled.

"Gents, I reported sick this morning, didn't you get the message?"

"I got the message, son," my inspector replied, leaning towards me to a point where our noses were almost touching. It wasn't menacing, but it made me feel uncomfortable: maybe that was because I was only wearing a towel. "By the way, you don't look very sick to me. We're a bit short-staffed, so get your uniform on smartish. You can do a shift at Billesley: John Hughes has just reported sick." I mulled this over while getting dressed. I climbed into the back of the panda car. My inspector ignored my sniffles, so after ten minutes, I spoke up:

"Sir. What's the difference between John Hughes reporting sick, and probably being at home in bed, and me reporting sick and getting dragged into work?"

"Because John Hughes has 28 years' police service, and you, my little pro-con, have about 28 minutes in the job. Let's hear no more about this."

I found myself at Billesley police station, feeling like death warmed up. No bike to get home and no money for the bus. The world seemed like a terribly cruel place. Surely nothing else could go wrong. About halfway through my shift, I managed to borrow £1 from Ray Siddall, so at least I wouldn't have to walk home. I asked Ray about something that had been bothering me:

"When gaffer Young came to my house this morning, he did a strange thing."

"What was that?"

"Well, when I was talking to him, he was so close I wasn't sure whether he was going to kiss or head-butt me. Any ideas?"

Ray smiled and took a drag on his ever-present cigarette. "Wolfie, he was giving you a breathalyser. You know, smelling your breath to see if you'd been drinking. Had you?"

"No, mate, not a drop." Ray took another drag and a sip of tea. "Just as well. As a pro-con, you don't want your personnel file-stamped, 'pisshead that struggles to get into work', mate." I had an awful lot to learn about this police malarkey.

The office handover time for a second watch was 1.30 pm. The office staff looked after each other and were always on time. At 1.45 pm, my relief had not arrived. I waited until just after 2 pm and phoned the B3 controller. He was on second watch, not my shift, and he couldn't have cared less about my predicament. He checked the postings and said:

"Oh dear, your relief is Hughie Friel. He's never early, but he usually turns up. Best of luck." I was fuming. Hughie still had my A-Z, and now he had not even bothered to relieve me. I waited and waited. At 2.30 pm, the entrance door opened. Right - I was going to give Hughie Friel a piece of my mind. Unfortunately, the man who came in was not PC Friel, it was just a local bloke clutching a fist full of driving documents.

"I'm sorry, sir," I spluttered at him, "but, technically, I am off duty and only waiting for my relief to arrive. You will just have to wait to produce your documents." Pathetic: I had turfed all of my toys out of my pram. The member of the public stood nervously in the lobby and tried his best to ignore me, while I ignored him. My rage built until, at 2.40 pm, a dishevelled man walked in. He looked like he had been living in the mountains for years: scruffy, unshaven and dressed like a tramp.

"All right, mate," Hughie Friel said, "I bet you thought I wasn't coming." He beamed. Was that an apology?

"Right," I snapped, "that guy wants to produce his driving documents. I'll leave it with you." I stropped off to use the toilet before my long walk to my bus stop, my long wait for a bus, and my long bus ride home. As I was leaving, I walked past the man producing his documents. On the other side of the counter, I saw Hughie Friel stripped to the waist. Hughie had a face full of shaving foam, a fag in his left hand and a BIC disposable razor in his right.

"I am reporting you for..." Hughie paused then shaved a portion of his face and knocked the razor's foam and stubble into the office bin. Hughie took a significant drag on his cigarette before puffing out. "... Driving without any insurance, mate."

All male officers below the rank of Inspector wore blue shirts. You could tell how much service an officer had by how faded his blue shirt was. Inspectors looked much smarter in their tailored uniforms, white shirts and brown leather gloves. They strutted around their areas: they were in charge, this was their shift, and this was their patch. Inspectors bullied their sergeants who, in turn, bullied the rest of us. They were the shift supervision, and in modern parlance, they probably would not be found amongst your friends on Facebook. They were paid to tell me what to do, and constables were paid to do what they were told. The inspector was referred to as sir, boss or gaffer. A sergeant, if you knew them well, Sarge. The shift inspector and their sergeants drank copious amounts of tea which was always made by the newest pro-con on the shift. The tea had better be up to standard. Otherwise you would spend all day making it until it was.

Here was my introduction to the shift bonding process. Having washed twenty dirty cups and made tea to the individual requirements of each shift member, complying, as best I could, with instructions about how strong and how many sugars. I was carrying a tray of freshly made tea into the parade room, and a policeman stood directly in front of me. He saw his mug: it had a Birmingham City FC motif emblazoned on it. He took a silver teaspoon from the sugar bowl and slowly stirred his tea, he removed the spoon, which by now was scalding hot and placed it on the back of my hand. I was in agony. I yelled, but I was not going to drop the tray: too much time and effort had gone into making the tea. When the spoon had dispersed its heat into my hand, the PC picked up his cup and smiled.

"It's Wolfie Smith, isn't it? Welcome to B-Unit." I made a mental note of the twat and, more importantly, his cup. The next time I made the tea, I ripped out as many arse hairs as I could stand to lose in one grab and dropped them into his cup. It was painful. Yes, there were tears, but it was worth it. For six weeks, I had a smug sense of satisfaction every time I made the tea. Still the price I paid was having an arsehole so sore that it would have forced a gay porn star to report unfit for duty.

A brand new pro-con, Dave Shaw, turned up on my shift and took over the tea-making duties. It was fairly evident that one of us was going to finish up as a chief constable. It was even more apparent, to anyone that knew us, that it was highly unlikely to be me.

Policewomen wore white shirts, their uniform was not tailored, so they looked as badly turned out as their male counterparts. Policewomen were paid a monthly stocking allowance. Some days when I was tired, bored and slowly losing the will to live, I would notice the tell-tale signs, two bumps upper-centre thigh on a policewoman's skirt. I knew what that indicated, and somehow those little bumps lifted my spirits. Policewomen were, unkindly, referred to as peewees, plonks or split arses. As if these names were not offensive enough, they were usually preceded by the word fucking and often the word useless, but mostly with both. As in, "Where has that fucking useless split arse gone?"

The parade room was also the report writing room. Ashtrays were everywhere, and a sea of partially completed forms swamped the tables. The forms had usually been abandoned because Yankee Mike, the force Control room which fielded 999 calls, had broadcast a job which required the immediate attendance of the police. Yankee Mike usurped the authority of the area controller. This was the emergency part of being an emergency service and was why most people had joined. We did not have a pole to slide down, like the fire brigade, but no one would have complained if we had. The shift was a place that existed before I arrived and would continue long after I had left. A pecking order was established, and length of service played a significant part. Four sergeants supervised my first shift, B-Unit, one of them would chauffeur Inspector Colin Young around the patch.

As a pro-con, there were hundreds of forms that I had to learn how to complete. Every one of them had to be submitted for checking. The paperwork sergeant was surrounded by crime files and reports, busily referring to the latest Archibald's Law Manual and Force Standing Orders. Submitted work had to be correct before the sergeant signed it and passed it along the chain of command. Sergeants meticulously hunted for mistakes, and they took great delight in the rejection and return of work for correction: it justified their existence. I sometimes felt like I was actually having more paperwork returned than I had submitted. Paperwork was a scary beast and one that could get you sacked: I needed to learn how to deal with it.

Respect was earned by what the shift saw, and previous achievements were ignored. Any bad reputations were heeded, though. The advantage of being a recruit, I was starting with a clean slate. My first lesson, which saved a load of time and effort, was to work out each sergeant's requirement regarding paperwork. They all did it differently, so a peep into their office before any submission was an absolute necessity. Senior police constables would often suggest advice, and this formed my second lesson, could I trust them?

Colleagues on B-Unit advised recruits to endear themselves to Sergeant Mason by talking about their athletic achievements at school, college or university. This would result in their being screamed at by Mason, "My son is a fucking paraplegic... you insensitive twat!" Actually, his son wasn't.

The sergeant who performed the role of the radio controller used practical psychology. Aligned to an intimate knowledge of all their officers' skills, abilities, shortcomings and developmental needs, to ensure they selected the right officer for the right job. Of course, if anyone had overstepped the mark by taking the piss out of the controller, then whatever the incident, and no matter how dangerous, that particular cheeky bastard was being sent.

A recently promoted, female, sergeant was working overtime as the controller on my shift. She was extremely nervous. I saw a couple of PCs whispering before they left the station. An hour into her shift, the new sergeant was coping quite well, until an officer shouted up on the radio. It sounded desperately urgent.

"Bravo 3... Mumble Mumble... six inches, Mumble Mumble... six inches, Mumble Mumble... six inches." Silence followed. The controller frantically responded:

"To the officer sending the urgent message! Please be aware that I am only receiving six inches! I repeat. I am only receiving six inch... you bastards."

On parade, officers were given their shift postings. We had two double-manned area cars: these were fast response vehicles with call signs Bravo Zulu 7 and Bravo Zulu 8. The Zulu cars had blues and twos - blue flashing lights and two-tone warning sirens. Our Zulu cars were Morris Marinas, and could only be driven by a grade one or grade two police drivers. Experienced drivers put a bag of sand in the boot to assist stability when cornering.

We usually had five panda cars, call-signed Bravo Mike and numbered 19 through to 23. The vehicle of choice for the West Midlands police panda car was the mighty Austin Allegro. These vehicles had blue flashing lights and not much else. Pandas would only be double-manned on nights. The Zulu drivers were the most crucial PCs on the shift, closely followed by the panda car drivers. Panda drivers aspired to one day become Zulu drivers. Neither role particularly appealed to me.

Those not posted to vehicles would be sent out to walk designated beat areas. The foot patrol area that nobody wanted was *flying the flag*, walking up and down the High Street. From leaving the station to being sent to deal with a shoplifter might only take five minutes. We were allocated refreshment times, first break or second break and that dictated which card school, snooker or table tennis match I would be involved in. The refreshment break entitlement is best explained by a conversation I overheard between Sergeant Mason and a probationer.

"Sarge, I didn't get a grub break yesterday. Everyone else seemed to get one, but not me." John Mason gave him a 'what sort of cretin are you?' look then said for the benefit of all those listening:

"Sonny, for your information, police regulations clearly state that your daily refreshment entitlement is 45 minutes, per man, per day, perhaps."

The shift was a tight-knit unit, and petty squabbles had to be quickly resolved. Officers relied on each other for support. With the police radio switched to talk-through officers could hear colleagues speaking to the controller. If an officer's voice so much as wavered, then other shift members would head towards their location, just in case. Officers only used the 'Urgent Assistance' or the coded call for help of 'Ten-Nine,' when absolutely necessary. Steve Groome was on a mobile patrol with Dawn Sheffield, a young pro-con. It was the middle of the afternoon. The radio shouted up:

"Burglary in progress. Man disturbed, by the occupant, the offender is possibly armed. He's now in the back garden of 140 Oxford Road, Moseley." Steve was already in Oxford Road and near the address. He pulled over, then athletically vaulted into the nearest back garden. Dawn Sheffield, hindered by her skirt, eased herself over a garden fence to join her colleague. When she did, she saw Steve and then she saw a wild-eyed, crazy-looking 'Jolly Mean Giant', who was wielding one half of a pair of garden shears. The man was running towards Steve and screamed:

"Fucking come on, then, I'll have you!" The three were in an enclosed garden. Dawn realised that she and Steve were in a life-threatening situation. She fumbled while trying to get her police radio out of her handbag. Two minutes later she yelled at her radio,

"Urgent Assistance Required. I am in the garden at the rear of 140 Oxford Road. Get here quick, I think he's going to kill him." In the background, a male voice could just about be heard: "Don't you ever, ever and I mean fucking ever..."

Just before Dawn's distress call, this was what happened. As the burglar charged at him, Steve adopted a karate fighting stance with his hands raised. His attacker attempted a machete strike; Steve used a textbook block that caused the weapon to drop to the floor. With lightning speed, Steve delivered a roundhouse kick to his would-be assailant's head. Steve straddled the now prone offender and punched him in the face while explaining that the man's behaviour was unacceptable. That was when Dawn shouted for backup: it wasn't Steve that needed urgent help, it was the burglar. If anyone pulled a weapon on Steve Groome, then in their own best interests, it had better be one that fired bullets. To be fair, that wasn't how most police assistance calls were played out.

A posting that I was not too keen on was covering the office; I had not left the Redditch Rates Department to do that. Some officers, who were about to retire, did not want to be on the streets. They were happy to see out their service in an office. John Hughes only had a couple of years left: he hated everyone, but especially senior police officers, policewomen and cheeky pro-cons. John was happy to be posted to Billesley police station: prisoners, evidence, pocketbooks and court appearances were all a thing of the past for John.

The shift pattern meant we worked seven nights in a row - Monday through to Sunday, working 10 pm-6 am. John was never going to let his job prevent him from enjoying a nightly tipple. John was always sober when he arrived for work. At the start of his shift, Inspector Young occasionally searched him for alcohol: none was ever found. Most mornings at 3 am, John would be sitting at his desk, drunk and grinning. His secret: he injected vodka into the large Jaffa oranges he brought in for his refreshments.

John left the job under a cloud: he had almost completed his 30 years, but he did not get to cross the finish line. He was not corrupt, just lazy, and could not be bothered reporting someone for some driving document offences. Following a brief internal investigation, John was sacked. I never saw John in the best of health, and without a job to at least reduce the amount he drank and provide some interaction with people, John died alone in his flat. Because he had been sacked, police officers were told not to attend John's funeral. I liked John and ignored the instruction. There were not many at his funeral. Most of John's family had lost touch or moved away. The priest said:

"John Hughes was a man who enjoyed his own company and did not suffer fools gladly." If the priest had listed all the people that John did not suffer gladly, we would still be there today. John had requested that no hymns were sung at his funeral. The priest announced: "This was John's favourite song." A guy sitting next to me opened a small case then put together a clarinet and played the most amazing rendition of the Acker Bilk song, *Stranger on the Shore*. Rest in Peace, John.

Sunday 25 May 1980 was my last shift on another long week of nights. I had plodded around an unusually quiet Balsall Heath for the full week. I was shattered. My wife was heavily pregnant with our first child and due to give birth any minute. I finished my shift on Monday at 6 am and was stood down. It was a Bank Holiday, and I was messing about on the snooker table, putting off for as long as I could my tedious bike ride home. At 6.30 am the station tannoy sparked into life. "Wolfie, your missus is about to have the pup. Get yourself to Solihull Hospital... Pronto!"

The early turn shift inspector gave me a lift and used my predicament to put his foot down. In the delivery suite, I sat next to my wife's bed and promptly passed out. I woke up just after 1 pm, and there was a lot of activity. I tuned in straight away. The doctor could not trace a foetal heartbeat and could not find what looked like a post office stamp, that worked. These devices were designed to discharge an electric shock and restart a baby's heart. A consultant paediatrician was summoned and assessed the situation: he looked fairly agitated. I didn't have time for fairly, so I skipped straight to extremely. I looked terrible, unshaven, knackered and still wearing the uniform I had started the previous night's tour of duty in. I was angry. I decided to get a grip on the situation. I took a firm hold of the paediatrician's throat, "Either you find one of those charging things that work, or you my friend, are on the next chartered flight through that window." The maternity ward was on the third floor. Before he could say anything, I heard, "Wah-Wah-Wah". Which, from a medical perspective, indicated that there was nothing wrong with my son's heart, lungs or vocal cords. I released my grip on the doctor and awkwardly turned it into an unreciprocated hug. My son, Peter, was born it was the best day of my life. I bought the doctor a bottle of Scotch as a peace offering.

23 years later, I was to have an equally proud day when Tommy was born. My collar number was 8293, Tommy was born August (8) 29th (29) 2003 (3). Yes, a personalised police collar number, date of birth. There were problems with both my sons' deliveries: Peter was induced with forceps, and Tommy was a Caesarean section. There are not many ways that a newborn baby can express their displeasure at being unwillingly brought into this world, but Tommy was able to. When the doctor held him up for a cursory inspection, Tommy piddled all over him.

If I make a child every 23 years, then the next one will be a real challenge, I will be 70 years old.

CHAPTER 6
50 SHADES OF PLEB

In July 1980 I was working again, albeit briefly, with Johnny Mac. Whenever there was a spate of burglaries or car crime in our area, the superintendent would set up a mini-crime squad to try to nip it in the bud. John and I were on a burglary team working in plain clothes. During a break, we walked up the High Street to get a sandwich. I saw my first prisoner. He was on the other side of the road. I wasn't sure if he had seen us or would even recognise us out of uniform. I was wrong on both counts.

"McAnneny, you bastard! You... you said I would only be in for an hour. Home for my Sunday dinner, you said. I have been in Winson Green prison for six fucking months. I only got out last week." Initially, I could not work out why he was so much braver than he had been when we last dealt with him, and then I saw that he was with his mum. They crossed the road to continue abusing John. Mum chipped in:

"You're an absolute fucker, McAnneny. I put his dinner in the bastard oven for him as well." John fielded as much abuse as he was prepared to take, then he pointed at Mum.

"Well firstly, I suggest you go home and take his dinner out of the oven. Secondly... I strongly advise you both to fuck off, before I arrest the pair of you for breaching the Queen's peace, and bastard swearing in public."

During my probation, I had to attend several training courses: these were held at Bournville Lane. The training was usually a two-hour input stretched out into a seven-hour working day. We were given an hour's break for lunch. I was eating a sandwich in the snooker room when a large, uniformed man asked me if I fancied a game. We were sizing each other up to see if there was any chance of making a profit. I declined the challenge.

"Not a bother," said PC Hughie McGowan, a mountain of a man, square-jawed, jet-black hair, a monobrow and a barrel chest. I was to discover that nothing ever bothered him. He could not have looked any more Irish, but even with my heritage, I couldn't quite place his accent. When I knew him better, he explained that he was actually born in a small place just off the east coast of Ireland, called England. Hughie and I were to spend a lot of time together over the next 30 years.

Another policeman who became a really good friend was Mark Blackburn. He was on D-Unit, which was the opposite shift to mine. While I cycled along the High Street to get to work for a 5.45 am start, Mark, purely for his own entertainment, would drive his panda car at me. The fucker.

Johnny Mac, as an ex-Royal Navy diver, was a member of the Nautical Club in Birmingham. John would proudly accompany his wife to the club's annual dinner and dance. With the next one coming up soon, John had put her best dress in for dry-cleaning and was due to collect it on Wednesday morning.

Crucially Wednesday was half-day closing, and the function was that night. At 1 pm most shops in Birmingham, including Sketchleys in Northfield, closed for the rest of the day.

John and I were in plain clothes and dealing with a burglar. John had lost all track of time, and at 2.30 pm he shrieked that he had forgotten to collect the dress, adding that the dry cleaners were now closed. He declared that his life was now over. We jumped into the squad car, and John drove like a maniac to Sketchleys. With an impressive turn of speed, we arrived only two hours after the shop had closed. I don't know what I or for that matter, anyone else would have done. But this was what John did. He walked up to Sketchleys and booted the front door quite hard. The glass didn't break, but John knew that the alarm had been triggered. He sauntered back to our car.

There was a short delay before the audible alarm sounded: that delay was to allow the police time to attend and arrest burglars. Two uniformed policemen arrived and summoned the keyholder. One of the policemen examined the footprint on the door. Still we waited. The keyholder turned up and was talking to the officers outside the shop. We approached. John identified himself and explained that we were on a local burglary squad. John added that he had a pretty good idea who was responsible for the attempted break-in. I suppose technically this was correct. John politely addressed the keyholder: "Excuse me, my colleague and I were just passing, you won't believe this, but I was actually going to collect my wife's dress tomorrow. Is there any chance I could get it while I am here?" I can confirm that Mrs McAnneny did go to the ball.

Interviews with prisoners were very different from what they later became. They were notes of conversations recorded in a pocketbook. They were written by the police officer, and often unsigned by the suspect. These notes included closing phrases such as "I am not signing anything, Officer, I never do", or "I do not need to sign it, I have seen you write it". One I remember seeing was, "I will not sign, I have committed the crime, I will now have to do the time". It read as if the defendant had sung it. The arresting officer could influence guilt or innocence by what they wrote in their pocketbook. The police decided whether a suspect was charged and whether bail was granted following that charge. Solicitors were imaginary people, rarely seen in police stations; they appeared at Court by which time the damage to their clients had already been done. Officers in the canteen crowed about how the magistrates would nod while the police gave their evidence and shake their heads if a defendant cast a slur on their integrity, I stayed quiet, as my own experience had been entirely different.

Remember the guy in my class, Ada Nolan, who delivered the worst death message in police training history. Well, he scraped through Ryton and was posted to Digbeth police station. He was a real hero when it came to the action stuff on the streets. While he was off duty, he arrested a bank robber armed with a loaded handgun. He also rescued a family from an overturned car that was on fire. His shift inspector would not let the fire crew or anyone else intervene as he thought the vehicle was just about to explode. Ada ran past his inspector and wrenched a door off the car, saving the family. Heroic stuff. However, for Ada, it was the suspects' statements that he never really mastered. In any written statement of admission, there were only two crucial areas that had to be covered, the *actus reus*, what the offender did, and the *mens rea,* what the offender was thinking. For a simple criminal damage admission, the defendant's statement could read, 'I threw the brick through the window', the actus reus, 'and I knew it was wrong to do what I did', the mens rea. Simple enough, but Ada always forgot to include the mens rea, and his sergeants were not happy with him.

One of Ada's defendants was charged with theft and bailed to appear before Birmingham Magistrates. No one was paying a lot of attention during the court proceedings it was, after all, a guilty plea. The prosecuting solicitor read out the defendant's statement of admission. The last line read: "And I knew it was wrong to do what I did". The defence solicitor casually glanced at his copy of the statement. He flagged up an issue. His statement did not include the last line, it must have been added by someone.

The Crown Court judge at Ada's subsequent trial blew away any chance Ada had of being acquitted. When he was summing up the case at the end of the trial: "Ladies and gentlemen of the jury, you have heard the evidence of the prosecution's handwriting expert. The possibility that the last line of the defendant's statement was added by anyone other than PC Nolan is so remote that you should dismiss it from your minds entirely." Ada was convicted of attempting to pervert the course of justice. He was sentenced to three months' imprisonment and sacked. I never saw him again.

The loss of a loved one will happen to all of us at some time in our lives. Hughie McGowan suffered such a loss. Hughie felt in many ways that he was responsible for Freddy's death. Freddy was Hughie's pet ferret. When the ferret escaped from its cage, Hughie reported to the police that his ferret was missing. I don't know anyone else who would have even done that. Incredibly Freddy was found and handed over to a less than impressed office man at Billesley police station. The local press picked up on the story. The *Birmingham Evening Mail* reported:

"It was a sad day for PC Hughie McGowan when his pet ferret, Freddy, escaped. They were inseparable. Freddy joined Hughie on his hunting trips and was his regular drinking partner at Hughie's local the Robin Hood pub in Hall Green. While Hughie quaffed pints of Mickey Mouse - half of bitter and a half of mild - Freddy would drink water from an ashtray. Freddy, while on a lead, ran around Hughie's body to his little heart's content. We are delighted to report that they have been reunited."

The article was accompanied by a photograph of PC McGowan with Freddy sitting snugly in Hughie's police helmet. A few weeks later Hughie was in the Robin Hood pub and had just sat down to enjoy a pint, that was going to be the first of many. Freddy was on his lead and happily running around Hughie. Without really thinking, Hughie picked a spot on his ear and it bled. Freddy, who was perched on Hughie's shoulder, noticed the blood and launched a frenzied attack on Hughie's bleeding ear. Ferrets have interlocking front teeth, and Freddy used them to good effect. Hughie screamed in pain, dropped the lead, leapt up and shook his head vigorously to shake off the ferret. Hughie looked like he was wearing one of Bet Lynch's earrings. Unable to shake the ferret off, he ripped it from his ear, and in his anger and distress just threw the ferret which tragically crash-landed into a large stone fireplace. Splat. Freddy the ferret, died instantly. Rest in Peace, Freddy.

Some weeks later, I was on nights and on mobile patrol with Steve Jordan, my new shift sergeant. He was a bit posh and was also an officer in the Territorial Army. Just after midnight, we were in Moseley village. It was a warm night, our car windows were open, and the police radio was quiet. The Queen's peace was shattered by the sound of an almighty crash. Looking up St Mary's Row, I could see a man reaching through the smashed window of a shop called Pottery and Pieces. Steve drove to the shop, and the offender ran off. I gave chase and caught the man near the junction with Oxford Road. He was in his early twenties and extremely drunk. The suspect had stolen a small novelty doorstop, and as I chased him, he was frantically ripping the traditional Welsh ladies' costume off it. I seized the doorstop and arrested the man for burglary. I considered an alternative charge of attempting to rape a doorstop but shrewdly decided that burglary was going to be easier to prove in court. We restrained the burglar, who was particularly unpleasant. He shouted abuse at us for the duration of the short trip to Kings Heath. We lodged our prisoner in the custody suite. My sergeant instructed:

"Smadge - a sort of posh Army Smudge - you deal with him.

I will write up the arrest in my pocketbook, and you can sign it. That will reduce your workload." I still had quite a lot to do, but at least I did not have to write up the arrest. After dealing with my prisoner, which took me a couple of hours, I went into the sergeant's office. Steve Jordan had left his pocketbook in his workbasket, I read his entry, sighed, then took my pocketbook out and started writing out the details of the arrest. Twenty minutes later, Steve Jordan joined me in the sergeant's office. "Smadge, I have already made a pocketbook entry, you don't need to repeat it."

"Sarge, I have read your entry, but I can't refer to your pocketbook in court."

"Is my entry incorrect? Have I missed something out, Smadge?" I flicked through his pocketbook and found his entry. "Here it is, 'En route to the police station, the prisoner was loquacious in his verbosity'. Sarge, I can't say that in court. I don't even know what it means."

"What have you written in your pocketbook, Smadge?" I read him my entry.

"En route to the police station, the prisoner repeatedly called me a cunt."

"Right, Smadge, understood. Carry on."

CHAPTER 7
THE SQUADRON LEADER
AND THE FLYING FISH

A specialist who was posted with the shift, but who only turned up when their skills were required, was the dog handler. This was someone I definitely wanted on my side. They responded to all persons-on-premises calls, foot chases and public order incidents: the transformation from an aggressive, threatening member of the public.

"Come on, I'll kill the fucking lot of you!" Into, "Good evening officer, I'm just going home. I hope you have a quiet night." Once the big, furry beast with the sharp, pointy teeth arrived was a joy to behold.

Mick Entecott was our dog handler. He was 6' 2", had a full beard and looked almost as fearsome as 'Shane', his huge Alsatian. Whatever incident they were at, I just loved the way Shane sat waiting for a command from Mick. I think Shane weighed up the situation deciding which part of the mouthy gobshite to chew on first, assessing developments just as Arnold Schwarzenegger did in *The Terminator*. Shane based his decisions on his previous experience. Biting a fleeing burglar on the face or neck, while effective, brought little praise, no treats, and was usually accompanied by repeated screams from Mick, "Shane! Shane! For fuck's sake, stop!"

Conversely, taking a massive chunk out of an escaping suspect's arse invariably brought reward and praise in equal measure. Mick seemed to take a shine to me. He pulled me to one side on the first night of the long week of nights.

"Wolfie, watch out for Shane, especially when I let him go for a person's-on-premises, make sure you stand absolutely still. Otherwise, he'll rip you to shreds." I thanked him. From a childhood experience, I knew just how painful a dog bite could be.

Later that week, my entire shift attended an intruder alarm at a factory in Balsall Heath. Mick hollered that he had released Shane. As instructed, I immediately froze. I heard a noise behind me, but I knew better than to move. I could hear something: it was close and getting closer, a wet, panting sound. Then it suddenly stopped, there was a moment of silence. I felt what I knew for certain was Shane biting my arse. I screamed and nearly jumped over the factory. Before I could reach behind to assess the damage, I heard Mick Entecott along with the rest of my shift roar with laughter. Mick had crept up behind me and gripped my arse hard with his hand. Shane was sitting about twenty feet away his head cocked quizzically.

The attitude of the senior police constables on the shift was unusual, though a lot more worldly-wise than us pro-cons: they didn't always feel inclined to assist, and they could still just be taking the piss. They spent their tours of duty sitting in the crew room, smoking and trying to look busy.

I was working nights, and there was a report of a disturbance on the 20th floor of Century Tower, Edgbaston. A blues party had been in full flow all weekend, and the noise could be heard for miles. The party involved over 150 people, mostly Rastafarians, enjoying music, alcohol and other substances that may not have been entirely legal. Our inspector rounded up fifteen officers, just in case. We used the stairs to make our way to the 20th floor. Unfortunately, tower block lifts were often used as toilets, and the stench could be overpowering.

On arrival, an older man approached us and very calmly explained that there had been dozens of people on the communal landing and a lad, in his twenties, had been leaning against a lift door which had suddenly opened. The young man fell down the lift shaft and was dead. The lift door was still open. I looked down the shaft and could see a motionless body on top of the lift. The atmosphere was sombre but not hostile. The fire brigade and ambulance recovered the body. The night detective was called out to deal with the incident.

In the crew room a couple of days later there was a gathering of old sweats, they were asking about the incident at Century Tower. One of them piped up.

"Wolfie, you were there. What happened?" I explained that there had been a party on the 20th floor with well over a hundred Rastafarians in attendance. A young man had been leaning against a lift door when it suddenly opened, and he had fallen to his death. The old sweats fell silent. As I walked out of

103

the crew room, I heard:

"The most disappointing thing about the whole incident for me, anyway, is that the twat hadn't been leading the fucking conga." Sadly this kind of snide racist remark was not uncommon in police stations back then.

Century Tower was becoming something of a free fall hotspot. A few weeks later, I returned to a report that a domestic dispute was getting out of hand. A man was having a swearing competition with his wife. When he couldn't take any more, he calmly said, "That's it. I've had enough. I'm off." His wife said later that she thought he was just going to storm out of the flat, slam the front door and go to the pub, which was what he usually did. Instead, he casually vaulted over the balcony of their 18th-floor flat and landed on the pavement with an almighty splat. He died instantly. His wife joined him, via the lift. In the circumstances, I don't think she would even have noticed the smell. I was one of the first officers at the scene. I took off my tunic and placed it over the splattered remains of the deceased. A senior PC shook his head at my naïvety and whispered in my ear:

"You do know that Tommy Burton will not give you a cleaning token for your tunic." I told the locals who came out to see what all the fuss was about:

"Ladies and gents... will you all please go back to your homes? There really is nothing to see here." By Christ, there was. I took the details and went back to the station to write up the sudden death report.

In the crew room were a couple of old sweats, and they were vaguely interested in the job I had just left. They were smoking, and then one of them asked:

"Hey, Wolfie... what was the name of that guy who just jumped off his balcony?" I checked my pocketbook. "It was James, James Patrick FISH."

"I wish I had been there, I really do." I needed to know what particular pearl of wisdom he could offer.

"Why, was there anything that you could have done?"

He took a drag on his cigarette, winked at his colleague and sneered:

"No, not really, but I have read about them flying fish... It would have been great just to actually see one."

As I had no aspirations to drive a police vehicle: my long-term goal might just be to become an old sweat, sit in the station trying to look busy and take the piss. It might be just perfect for me.

Just a word or two about smoking. The 1970s and early 1980s was the era when the smoker ruled. It was even referred to as a social habit. Smokers always knew, in their hearts, that one day their world would cave in and now it has. Currently, they have to stand outside buildings in the snow, 50 yards from shelter, so that their non-smoking colleagues can enjoy their discomfort from their thermostatically heated offices.

In 1981, I was in the canteen at Kings Heath, having breakfast and talking to a fellow pro-con from another shift. He had benefited from a university education. Two older PCs sat at our table. I assessed them, as I had benefited from time spent in the Army, as individuals who were not to be trifled with. Both were smoking and muttering about taking retribution on some poor bastard, just as soon as they had eaten. We were new recruits, light years away from being acknowledged by these battle-hardened veterans. My educated colleague spoke up:

"Gents, please. I'm trying to enjoy my breakfast here; would you mind extinguishing your cigarettes?"

In unison, they stubbed their fags out on the graduate's fried egg. "Happy now, cunt?" taunted one of them.

Over another Kings Heath canteen breakfast, I met PC John Dowling. He sat at my table with another guy from his shift. The other lad noticed the medal ribbon on my tunic and asked me what outfit I had served with. I told him I had been in the Army. He asked me if I knew John, who had served in the RAF. I pointed out that they were large and entirely separate organisations, so it was highly unlikely. John was tucking into his breakfast. He had a cartoon quiff of blond hair and looked like someone who could have smirked for England. I asked John what he had done in the RAF. His mate encouraged him.

"Go on, John, tell him." John moaned:

"Do I have to?" This appeared to be something that John had regularly been forced into repeating. "I was a jet fighter pilot, mate."

I did not know either of these guys and assumed this was a wind-up. John carried on with his breakfast. I must have looked slightly puzzled because John's mate challenged me.

"Don't you believe him?"

"Well, doesn't it take about four years to train as a fighter pilot? You can only be about, I dunno, twenty years old."

My challenge was expected. "Tell him how it worked for you John." Dowling put his knife and fork down and explained:

"Well, mate, it's Wolfie, isn't it? Normally, yes, you would be right, but my father was a fighter pilot, and that means that I was born with a fighter pilot's genes. So I didn't require four years of training. I joined the RAF at seventeen, and within a year, I was a fully qualified jet fighter pilot."

"Gosh, that's incredible," I said, what I actually thought was, what a complete crock of shit.

John was not on my shift, but I was keen to find out more about him. I thought he might be a train wreck waiting to happen and I wanted to know about all the stations he visited before his dénouement. What surprised me the most was that his colleague believed every word he said. John was on C-Unit, I was B-Unit, but news travelled fast around the station, and John Dowling was definitely going to be news.

Shift officers paraded fifteen minutes before the official start time. We were inspected and produced our appointments: handcuffs, truncheon and pocketbook. Policewomen presented their eight-inch batons and tried to ignore the lewd comments made by their unenlightened male colleagues. On parade, items of interest would be read out: we were told to keep a lookout for stolen cars and active criminals. Internal issues were dealt with, then a few rollickings and well dones dished out. We would then be turned loose on an unsuspecting public.

I remember our inspector telling us, on parade, about a female who would be joining our shift, adding that she'd been having a few personal problems. He was aware that some may have heard rumours, so on this occasion, he decided to share what he knew. I am not sure it went as well as he had hoped.

"Right, listen in, you lot. Diane is a competent policewoman with twelve years' service. She had an affair with her shift sergeant, who told Diane that he was going to leave his wife for her."

"Of course he was," muttered the policemen sarcastically.

"Anyway, Diane decided it was about time that she knew exactly where she stood, so she went around to the sergeant's house, to sort things out."

"Good on her," muttered the policewomen supportively.

"Please," said our inspector, trying to complete a task that he probably wished he had not started. He paused, in case Yankee Mike wanted to interrupt proceedings, and when they didn't, he took a deep breath and continued. "Diane invited herself in and sat on the settee in their lounge. Diane let the wife know that she had been having an affair with her husband for the past five years... and that she was only there to ask which of them he wanted to live with. The sergeant told Diane that their affair was over and that he would be staying with his wife and kids, then he asked her to leave. Diane produced a razor blade, slashed her wrists and nearly bled to death. Diane has been off work for just over a year." The parade room went quiet. Ray

Siddall punctured the silence with a question.

"So, boss, when exactly does Slasher start on our shift?" There was muffled laughter in the parade room at the outrageous insensitivity of Ray's comment. Unperturbed, Ray continued. "Well... I heard she refused to pay a fucking penny towards the cleaning of the carpet."

CHAPTER 8
SHIFT WORK AND SCOTCH EGGS

Whenever an inspector entered a room, the required code of behaviour was that all officers would stand up and the senior police constable would address the inspector with the words, "All correct, sir." At 3 am Ray Siddall, the office man at Woodbridge Road, discovered a dead prisoner in one of the cells. Inspector Young took me with him as he thought that it might be a good experience for a probationer. We arrived at Woodbridge Road. Ray Siddall stood to attention and snapped, "All correct, sir." I choked back a giggle: we were standing feet away from a cell that contained a 30-year-old man who had hanged himself. Just how correct could this actually be?

Not being a driver, I was posted to walk the beat areas of Kings Heath or, even worse, be stuck in an office. What I enjoyed most, though, was being in the Zulu car as the observer. It sounds impressive, but it only meant that I was the front-seat passenger. I worked with Tony Ayres. He was six feet tall, slim, had a full beard, drove a white MGB GT, and read

The Guardian newspaper.

In the Balsall Heath area, there was a sizeable Rastafarian community. Some of their practices were fascinating, and their outlook on life was totally relaxed. By the nature of my job, some that I encountered were criminals but no more so than in other communities. Tony decided that to broaden our horizons we should go to the cinema to see a film that had just been released. It was called *Babylon*.

"At night David is a 'Mic' controller at a local dance hall. The film centres around the racial divide of London in the early 80s, and the lack of opportunities available to black people. David loses his job, gets beaten up and charged by the police, forcing him to go on the run. Then breaking up with his girlfriend, all his frustrations culminate in the stabbing of a racist neighbour". Written by John Mulholland.

The film portrayed the police in a pretty poor light, but I did not feel any sense of outrage. In fact, some of it seemed disappointingly accurate. We did get some strange looks from the hundreds of Rastafarians in the audience. The film's title made reference to the fact that young criminal Rastafarians would suck their teeth and refer to the police as Babylon. In response, young, aggressive police officers would hit them on the head with their truncheons because they disrespected the cops. It was classic Betari's Box: their behaviour affected our behaviour, which affected their behaviour, and that continued in a loop. Add a sprinkling of hot weather, and almost any incident had the potential to result in a riot. Not many cops went to see the film. Perhaps if they had, then Brixton might not have exploded a few months later.

There was a Rasta shop on the Ladypool Road in Balsall Heath, on our patch, and it was open all day and night. The people who worked in the shop were not that talkative, but now that I had seen the film, I felt just a little more connected. One night I had just walked into the shop when Tony shouted for me to get a move on as we had been sent to a job. I bought a Mars bar and ran back to the police car. The call turned out to be a false alarm, and that was when I realised that I had left my police radio back at the shop. Deploying blues and twos, we returned. My desperate pleas for the return of my radio fell on deaf ears. I went back to the station and told Inspector Young that I had lost my Burndept police radio. He had no intention of authorising a search of the Rasta shop. That night a police radio on the Bravo 3 sub-division, my sub-division, could be heard broadcasting.

"Yo Babylon. Y'all Bloodclaatts, ya Bastaads," followed by sniggering. It could have been the guy from the Rasta shop, or it could easily have been any of my colleagues taking the piss. Luckily this did not last for more than the night, as the batteries only lasted an eight-hour tour of duty, thank God. The following Monday Mr Young called me into his office and told me that I would have to pay £200 to replace the radio. He allowed me to pay in instalments, £50 being paid directly to him on payday. Even being allowed to pay monthly caused me some severe financial hardship.

Four months later, Mr Young called me into his office to make my final payment. I wished him well, as he was leaving the shift to take up a post at the Central Lock-Up. I handed him £50. He opened a drawer and took out a brown envelope which had 'Wolfie' written on it; he placed my £50 into the envelope. A smile broke out on his face. "Wolfie, I can't keep this up any longer, here's your £200 back. We were only winding you up, mate."

Tony Ayres's serious approach to policing masked his dry sense of humour. Tony had three years in the job, and to me, that was a lifetime. When it was quiet, Tony and I played a silly little game. It worked like this - as soon as the radio shouted out "Bravo 3 Control to Bravo Zulu 7", then whoever's turn it was gave the other a name by which they had to address the first person they spoke to at the job. Early examples were easy: Mate, Mucker, Amigo, Pilgrim, Gringo and even Me Old China. I claimed game, set and match when Tony spoke to an 87-year-old Irish lady, who had witnessed a car accident and asked, "Right, then, Kimosabe, what exactly has occurred?"

I only ever saw Tony lose his temper once. We had to assist two social workers taking a couple of young children into care. I was talking to one of the social workers while Tony was going through the case papers. Just before we set off, I put my hand out, expecting the case papers to be handed over to me so that I could be briefed. Tony said quite curtly:

"Wolfie let's go, I've read the papers, so you don't have to." We set off to the Druids Heath estate; the social workers followed in their car. Tony was quiet and looked annoyed: this was unusual. We arrived at a block of flats, Tony rang the doorbell and a squat male, wearing only his string vest and underpants, opened the door. Two children aged about four and seven were standing in the sparsely furnished living room wearing just their underwear. The children looked thin and frail. Tony marched in, I followed, and the social workers waited near the front door. Tony formally explained to the man that the social workers had written authority to take his children into care. The squat male stood in front of Tony:

"No fucking social workers are taking my kids. You can all just fuck off." The man aggressively walked towards Tony, who put his hands under the guy's armpits, lifted him off the ground and threw him against a wall. Both children immediately ran into the arms of the social workers. We left while the guy was lying on the floor winded and muttering threats. On the way back to the station, I asked Tony why he hadn't let me read the case papers. "Wolfie, I think if you had read what he had been doing to his kids, you would probably have smashed his face in." That explained why the children had sprinted to safety. It was typically selfless of Tony, which was why I enjoyed working with him.

At 9.30 pm on a Saturday night, we were dispatched to the Masonic Hall, Kings Heath: a man had collapsed and was not breathing. We set off at speed and unfortunately arrived before the ambulance. Tony asked me if I was a Freemason. I confirmed that I wasn't and, if anyone is interested, I still am not. A lot of people think that those police officers, who are Freemasons, get special treatment in the police: a lot of people are right. Tony briefed me:

"Wolfie, it's ladies' night at the Lodge, and there will be hundreds of people in there and loads of senior police officers. They will be doing fuck all but watching us. Let's make sure we do things right. Put your flat hat on and straighten your tunic. Let's go." Not exactly John Travolta and Samuel L. Jackson, but we got into character. Lying on the floor near to the reception was a 60-year-old man, a smartly dressed, portly chap. Although he looked like he was fast asleep, no pulse or any other sign of life meant that he was probably dead. No sign of the ambulance and hundreds of people just watching. The men were in tuxedos, and the women were all in evening dresses. They were as much use as a platoon of Ken and Barbie dolls. A function that had been in full flow had paused. Silence. Everyone watched to see what we would do. I went straight to the man's chest to perform compressions. Tony knelt and put his mouth over the man's lips. My first compression pumped the contents of the man's stomach: a five-course meal, red wine, port and brandy into Tony's mouth. Tony vomited over the deceased. How could he not? One of the ladies watching fainted and I, unfortunately, started to snigger. The ambulance crew arrived and were at a complete loss as to who to deal with first.

35 years later, I bumped into Tony, who was out walking his dogs. I asked if he had it with him? Tony put his hand into his back pocket and produced a plastic Resusci-aid - a device the size of a handkerchief that assists mouth-to-mouth resuscitation. It prevents any blowback from the patient into the mouth of the first-aider. Tony told me that since the day of that incident, he had never left his house without it. He added

that just by seeing me, he remembered the foul taste of the dead man's vomit.

There were not many methods of escape from the strict, and exhausting, shift pattern of earlies, lates and especially nights. There were two quick changeover shifts a month, where I finished work at 10 pm and had to be back at 5.30 am. By the time I got home, it was almost time to return. Add a nursery run, an uncomfortable contact lens regime, and trying to drink with Hughie and Mark, as often as I could, I was absolutely shattered. It was not just the shifts. I was at the beck and call of a police radio that was mostly non-stop. It was particularly busy on earlies and lates. Nights could be quiet, but we worked seven in a row, and at the end of that week, I was exhausted.

My three long-term career prospects were: the Operational Support Unit - OSU. A force resource containing twelve serials of police officers. Each serial had a sergeant and ten constables, who were riot-trained and kitted out with decent public order equipment. They were call-signed phonetically, the Alphas, Bravos etc. I could become a beat officer - PBO working a designated area permanently. Finally, a detective on the CID - but their recruitment policy was based on invitation at that time.

The CID had two primary functions: to reduce the number of recorded crimes in their area and to detect recorded crimes. The first thing the CID established was: did the offence take place on their patch? If the offence could be shifted onto another subdivision, then it was not their problem. Where canals or roads were the sub-divisional boundary lines, legend has it, the first officers at the scene nudged dead bodies onto their neighbouring area. When officers were at a scene, once the exact location of the offence was established, the officer who did not cover that area would smile and say, "I will leave it with you."

Before anything was accepted as a crime, it had to be discussed with a detective. There was a level of artistic creativity which to be fully appreciated really had to be seen. When a dead body was discovered, several fanciful scenarios were put forward. Could the deceased have accidentally stabbed themselves to death? Could the victim have repeatedly fallen down the stairs until they had sustained sufficient injuries to die? There was one female detective at each station. They mostly dealt with rape victims and children. Often the treatment they dished out to some of the rape victims was worse than their assailant had put them through. "I heard she got shagged for a couple of hours by three blokes. That sounds like a good night to me," declared one of our more caring female investigators as she made her way to the rape suite to meet a victim.

Sexual offences have always been difficult to successfully prosecute at court, so if a stern approach was taken with the victim, they might just retract their allegation, and the crime would not be recorded. It has all changed now, but this was how it was back then. If an incident could be written up as an accident, then it was not a crime. I read a report that dealt with an allegation that a brother had raped his sister. Both were under sixteen. The investigating detective suggested that there had been some inappropriate sex play that had

117

resulted in accidental penetration. Those phrases appeared on a number of reports so that the crime could be filed rather than investigated. From personal experience, deliberate and consensual penetration has on occasion proved difficult. The idea that penetration can happen accidentally sounds just a little bit far-fetched to me.

A detective was sitting in the canteen describing, in far too graphic detail for my liking, a nasty rape that he was dealing with. He had a captive audience of impressionable probationers. I tuned out and tried to imagine the detective's version if it had been a lovely rape. My scenario included flowers, chocolates and a pillow under the victim's bum.

Eating, but not particularly enjoying, a cheese sandwich in the police canteen at Kings Heath, I heard a couple of shift officers talking.

"Have you heard about John Dowling?" His mate confirmed he hadn't.

"Well, John was sort of working undercover." I chipped in:

"Not John Dowling, C-Unit?"

"Yeah, is he a mate of yours?"

"A good mate." Well, we did have breakfast together once. We were uniform cops talking about another uniform cop. I could be trusted.

"Well, John went into Boots the chemist on the High Street, and he spoke to the guy in charge of the photo department, you know about the film they develop. John told him to call him out if they received any pictures of any naked women. John could check them out and then maybe seize them for his operation. It turned out that the guy from Boots knew an inspector from the complaints department: he's rowed John right in it."

"No way." I said, having worked out that these two naïve fuckwits were big fans of our friend Squadron Leader Dowling.

"Yes, it turns out that John had forgot to get his operation authorised. So, even though he was doing this in his own time for the love of the job, the chief inspector has threatened to punch John's fucking lights out if he ever goes into Boots again."

"That's unbelievable," I said and meant it.

"Yes. It makes you wonder why we bother at all."

This was a surprising development regarding my fighter pilot compatriot. I knew John had not finished with his adventures and had a feeling that they were going to get even more interesting.

"Wolfie. There's a thief on the shift!" Hughie Friel shouted at me at the end of our third shift of a week of nights together. I knew there was, but I thought I was looking at him. Subconsciously my eyes glanced at his car coat: I could just about make out the outline of my A-Z in his pocket.

"Hughie, how do you know?"

"Well, you know where we leave our snack bags for nights. Halfway up the stairs on the way to our lockers. Well, I've left my bag there for the last three nights, and some fucker has been helping themselves."

This was serious: a usually laid-back Hughie was seething.

"Are you sure?"

"Abso-fucking-lutely certain, and the only reason I'm telling you is that for the last three nights you've not been out of my sight. Don't worry, though, this will all be sorted out tonight: you see if it isn't."

I was glad I was not a suspect, but I was concerned for the thief. Hughie had shotguns that he used for hunting, lots of them.

On Thursday night we paraded at 9.45 pm. Hughie and I were posted to Bravo Zulu 7, and we were scheduled to take 1 am refreshments. Hughie gave me a sort of *High Noon* nod. We went on a patrol of the Maypole area, and it was pretty quiet. At 0.45 am Hughie parked our Zulu car at the top of the car park at Kings Heath police station. We entered through a side door and hid in the collator's office twenty yards from our tuck bags. We'd only waited about five minutes when a blood-curdling scream pierced the building. Hughie shouted. "Got you, you fucker!" and sprinted towards the stairs. I joined him a few seconds later. A young cadet, who was attached to our shift, was puking violently and holding a half-eaten Scotch egg. Between gags and retches, the cadet was trying to find enough air to scream, though he was only managing a kind of mewling, hysterical whimper. Through the tears and vomit, he managed to croak out.

"Sorry, Hughie, what is it? Please, what the fuck is it?" Hughie triumphantly stomped off to fully brief Sergeant Mason, who agreed that the young man had got exactly what he deserved. Mason supportively commented:

"Cheeky little shit, nice one, Hughie." The cadet was sent home as he just could not stop vomiting. Sitting in our police car, I asked Hughie what he had done. He laughed. "Wolfie, some stuff was taken from my bag on the first three nights, sometimes sandwiches, sometimes my apple, but on all three nights, my Scotch egg went. I went to the butcher's and got my mate to put an actual bull's eye inside the Scotch egg, you know, replacing the egg." He took a drag on his fag. "I knew if anyone bit into my Scotch egg, we would hear about it." The poor cadet had bitten so deeply into the bull's eye; it must have exploded in his mouth.

I have always enjoyed a Scotch egg, but since that night, I have been unable to eat one without first slicing it in half to check the contents.

CHAPTER 9

I DON'T LIKE CRICKET

Even though police forces were considerably smaller, certain duties were routinely carried out then, but are not now. Examples include attending every activated alarm, whether it was a house or business premises. Officers and the organisation took pride in a swift and effective attendance. Also, if anyone went on holiday, and informed their local police station, a uniformed police officer would check on their house during their absence. The police visited pubs regularly. Uniformed officers applied the licensing laws. The rowdier the pub, the more police visits they received. In the 1980s, the pubs were open between 12 am to 3 pm, reopened at 6 pm and closed again at 11 pm. Shift officers would only use the breathalyser kits at the scene of a car accident. The drink-driving laws were full of complex stated cases, such as were you in uniform if you were not wearing your hat or tie? Buggered if I knew. Most of us just left breathalysers with the traffic department. They loved that sort of stuff. Drunk drivers were referred to as having had one over the eight. Yep, eight pints of beer was seen as still being fit to drive.

Stray dogs that were handed in were kennelled until their owners collected them or they were taken to the central dog pound by the council. The West Midlands police had a Mounted Branch, and when I was on duty at a football match, and it was getting a little bit squeaky bum time, watching a police horse forcing back 20 or 30 ne'er-do-wells was timely and appreciated. We had an underwater search unit that regularly called out Johnny Mac, utilising the diving skills John learned in the Royal Navy. These departments were nationally recognised for their expertise. The Mounted Branch and the underwater search section no longer exist. As for the police receiving stray dogs, sorry, but there is no longer any room at the inn.

Every police station was staffed, 24 hours a day, usually by a crotchety, seen-it-all, bitter and twisted, just-about-to-retire policeman. Frustrated parents would attend, towing their nine-year-old scamp by his ear, and complain that he kept pulling the arms off his little sister's doll. The office man would read the little chap's horoscope to him, threatening him with a lifetime of penal servitude, unless he started to fucking well behave himself. It was all part of the service.

How could those departments be staffed with what was a significantly smaller workforce? Well, as fit and able-bodied employees, who were not umbilically connected to a computer, we were deployed in the areas of the community that required our actual physical presence. I guess my message to the chief constables of today would be: 'If you have more constables sitting at computers than you have on the streets, then you probably need to make some serious changes.'

If I made a decent arrest, a burglar, robber or anything serious, then the detective inspector would instruct one of his detectives to take the case off the arresting woodentop. The offence and offender would be upgraded to nasty, and with a brusque and condescending "Leave it with us, kid," the prisoner would now be dealt with by a top city detective. As well as nasty rapes, detectives also dealt with nasty wounding's and nasty murders. Detectives were keen to describe their investigations as 'nasty', as it gave their role just a little more gravitas. There was no love lost between shift officers and the CID.

Giving evidence at court was a time to focus and pay attention. Whatever the result, if there was any suggestion of any wrongdoing, you may well end up back in court as a defendant. If convicted and sent to prison, then what followed was a journey directly into *Dante's Fifth Circle of Hell*. The horror stories about the treatment of police officers in jail kept most, but not all, on the straight and narrow.

Malcolm Rudge was a uniformed police constable when he gave evidence at the Magistrates' Court in Birmingham. His prisoner had pleaded not guilty to a public order offence. The incident had taken place in the city centre and Malcolm Rudge, who stands an impressive 6' 8" tall, had been on foot patrol when he saw a man threatening some people at a bus stop in Corporation Street. Malcolm Rudge intervened and arrested the man, whom he frogmarched to Steelhouse Lane police station. The offender was charged and bailed. At the trial, without a witness - and remember this took place long before CCTV - the defence solicitor established that the case against his client was solely reliant on the evidence of PC Rudge. Under cross-examination, Malcolm Rudge confirmed that at no stage of the incident had he been frightened. The defence solicitor addressed the magistrates:

"Before I put forward a motion to dismiss this case, I ask the court for permission to probe this witness as to why, when the whole of Birmingham seemed to be terrified, PC Rudge, alone, was not. I would like this court to find out exactly what sort of man this officer is." The magistrates agreed that this was an acceptable line of questioning. "Officer," the solicitor continued in a nasal and condescending tone, "is it possible for you to think of a situation, real or imagined, that would scare you? Which would, shall we say, have you absolutely quaking in your boots?"

PC Rudge stared down at the bespectacled little man. "Sir. If you were defending me in any court of law in this country, I would be absolutely bloody terrified." The solicitor had no further questions, and his client was convicted.

In the early 80s, a fairly misogynous shift initiation ceremony was routinely conducted. When they joined, policewomen had their arses date-stamped. This involved pulling up their skirt and the station's date-stamp being pressed against their bare bum. For the most part, this was consensual. Indeed, some females insisted on their right to be date-stamped, and they seemed a little put out that their male colleagues were only interested in performing the ceremony on the more attractive female recruits.

While I am on the subject of women, around the same time, a senior officer issued an instruction that, before they were placed in a cell, all female prisoners should have their brassieres removed. This was supposedly done to prevent suicides. Dave Yellowley, my nimble-fingered colleague in basic training, must have been delighted. Brassieres being removed meant that quite a few policemen chose to spend a little more time in the custody block than previously. Each subdivision had a collator, whose job was to provide current intelligence and information to operational police officers. They used an index card system that they maintained. It wasn't exactly cutting-edge, but it worked. The collators must have been a lot more talented than anyone thought because it seems to have taken about 30 officers and staff to replace each one of them in today's police world. The collator at Kings Heath was Malcolm Wright. He monitored the panda cars arriving at the custody suite. Then, depending on the cleavage size, or the attractiveness, of the female prisoner he would burst along the corridor, often knocking people out of the way in order not to miss what he described as the *ceremonial unveiling*. Brassiere removal only lasted a few months before someone with a brain rescinded the original instruction. Dave Yellowley could stand down.

The 1980s were punctuated by some memorable events and PC Hughie Friel, my A-Z thief was responsible for some of them. He was a constable who marched to the beat of his own drum, however offbeat and syncopated that beat was. Despite his quirks, he was actually a talented police driver. In the early hours of the morning, the police airwaves crackled into life, and an excited Hughie called over the radio:

"Bravo Zulu 7 to Control. I am in immediate pursuit of a suspected stolen car, which is travelling at 100mph." Hughie then broadcast the registration, make and model, adding that the car was speeding along the High Street towards Kings Heath police station. The registration number was Felix O'Neill's car, and he was the radio controller. He nearly had a heart attack and screamed down the radio:

"Ram the fucker, Hughie, just ram the fucker!" Felix leapt out of his chair and jumped through the ground-floor controller's window and ran towards the High Street. Was Felix really going to try to chase a car travelling at 100mph in his Dr Martens shoes? Of course, Felix's vehicle was parked safe and sound in the police yard exactly where he'd left it. Hughie was sitting in Bravo Zulu 7, parked opposite the police station, smoking a cigarette and pissing himself laughing.

Some of Hughie's other pranks were slightly more questionable. Hughie Friel happened to be blessed with a rather large cock, and he was quite proud of it. He was not one to blow his own trumpet, but given the size of the thing, that was definitely an option. Hughie saw Ray Siddall sat at a desk at Billesley station. Ray was engrossed in a telephone conversation with a member of the public. Hughie crept up behind Ray, unzipped his fly, then delicately placed his cock on Ray's shoulder. He tapped Ray on the back. Ray Siddall turned and found himself staring at Hughie's pride and joy.

Ray was quick enough to get in a good thwack with a plastic ruler that he'd been holding, then seamlessly carried on with his conversation. I spoke to Ray. He told me that Hughie was a very lucky boy, as he had only just put a cigarette out; otherwise, it would have been extinguished on the tip of Hughie's penis.

Undaunted Hughie continued with his unpleasant stunts. A few weeks later he cut a hole in his trouser pocket and fed his cock through the hole. He positioned himself near a policewoman. Then, while holding a large bundle of papers, he feigned that he was going to do a massive sneeze. He indicated, through head nodding, to the policewoman that she should get a non-existent handkerchief from his pocket. Keen to help, she thrust her hand into his pocket, and took a firm hold of Hughie's cock, which she almost ripped out by the root. I remember thinking that Hughie's penis would one day get him into serious strife. I was wrong, it was actually going to get him out of trouble.

I joined a group of cops one night for a gentlemen's evening, in the lounge of The Red Lion in Kings Heath. Two strippers came out and removed all of their clothes. Sexy, it was not. I can remember their stretch marks a lot more than their ladybits. Steve Groome arrived late, knowing that the girls were a lot more liberal with their favours for the second half of a show, as they were usually drunk. Steve walked in as the ladies were looking for a volunteer.

"Take me, girls. I'm yours," Steve offered. He was wearing white chinos and a Hawaiian shirt which were swiftly removed.

He then lay on his back while one of the strippers sat on his face. I can't recall how cold it was inside the pub, but Steve's manhood was less than impressive. It would not have been out of jealousy that Hughie Friel grabbed a bottle of Tabasco sauce from behind the bar, and emptied it over Steve's cock, and boy, did he scream. The cops exploded with laughter, and the ladies beat a hasty retreat. They didn't mind how short the show was: they had already been paid. Having extricated himself from underneath the stripper and blinked the tears away, a disgruntled Steve Groome used a jug of water and beer towels to extinguish the fire. He joined the rest of us but kept his distance. Steve was trying to work out who the *Tabasco Twat* was. A colossal arse, with a pink G-string, had obscured his vision. Steve felt that he had to do something: his pride and karate qualifications required him to take action. I had reached the ridiculous part of the evening where I was racing Big Brian Bridgewater in a Guinness drinking competition. Steve decided that the biggest bloke in the room was going to have to pay for this. He yelled: "Oi Brian, let's have a scrap. Just you and me."

I was pleased, firstly that I didn't have to fight Groomie, and I could attempt to recover from the pasting that Brian was giving me in the drinking competition. Brian calmly walked across to Steve, who lunged at him. Brian threw all of his 20+ stone in Steve Groome's direction. Steve found himself flat on his back with all of Brian on top of him. I could only see Steve's hands and feet and hear his muffled screams: "Get off me, you fucker. I can't fucking breathe!" Brian waited until Steve had calmed down. We knew this tactic, which was unique to Brian, as being *egged*. Following this incident, Brian bought Steve a whisky which Steve drank at the bar while he considered his next move. Brian and I resumed our drinking competition. Brian was so relaxed it was as if the events of a few moments earlier had never happened.

Twenty minutes later, Steve walked towards us. He was a little drunker, and he looked like he meant serious business.

"Brian. I wasn't ready last time. Let's do it again. Only this time I will say go." He growled. Brian shrugged. "Fair enough, Steve, you say go." They squared up to each other and Steve shouted, "Go!"

Brian egged him again, and that was game over. Steve was going to have to take his martial arts training on to a whole new level.

Late one night, I was sent to a sudden death at an old people's home near the Maypole. An 80-year-old man had passed away. He had a history of heart problems. It was just after midnight, and this was a routine part of being on a shift. I conducted a cursory examination of the deceased. In the absence of any suspicious circumstances, my job was to complete a form for the Coroner's Department. The duty nurse was unpleasantly snapping answers to my fairly routine questions. Finally, after about five minutes, I put my pen down. I told her that I was not going to write another word until she told me what her problem was. She sneered.

"Well, you policemen, you're all the bloody same."

"Actually, we aren't, the only similarity is the uniform,

and to be honest, if you look closely enough... Well, that isn't important right now. What on earth has upset you?"

"I liked the police. I felt reassured just by the sight of the uniform. Until he started coming here."

"Who started coming here? Who are you talking about?"

"That bloody John Dowling... he comes around when he's on nights, pretending he wants a cup of tea, but I know why he comes. He likes to help the old ladies go to the toilet."

I felt nauseous. I completed the sudden death form as quickly as I could. I never had a cup of tea, nor did I help any of the old dears to the toilet. John Dowling appeared to be unravelling.

A police officer that I had the pleasure of working with was John Moore. He was a brilliant fast-response driver, and he had an almost regal way about him. He would announce his presence with a cheery cry of "Greetings!" John was attached to the central traffic department when he was sent to a large house in Lady Byron Lane, Solihull: he had a high-priority message to deliver. When John arrived, a very posh garden party was in full flow. John rang the doorbell a few times. Eventually, the lady of the house answered. John established her identity, which confirmed that she was the correct person to receive the message. Before he could deliver it, though, she spoke to him in a firm voice.

"Officer, please do not stand at my front door, people might see you. Use the tradesmen's entrance at the side of my house." She pointed in the direction that John should go. Feeling extremely put out, John stropped around the house and waited by a door, which actually had a 'Tradesmen's Entrance' sign. John was livid and becoming more and more angry. He was ready to explode. When the front door opened, John noticed that the downstairs was fitted with an expensive beige carpet. Next to the tradesmen's entrance, John saw a flower bed that had been recently watered. John planted his size twelve Dr Martens, welt-deep, next to a well-tended rose bush. After about ten minutes of John listening, over the fence, to plum-in-mouth partygoers comparing the relative merits of Merlot and Rioja, the lady of the house finally deigned to open the tradesmen's entrance door. Before John could speak, she cut him off. "Constable, what on earth is so bloody important that you have come to my house, without an appointment, interrupting my annual garden party?"

"Can we speak inside please?" John asked, his tone insistent.

"If we must," the lady harrumphed. "Follow me." She led John to a drawing room. John was pleased to see that the entirety of the downstairs was carpeted.

"Well, what do you want?" she demanded. John had spent quite long enough with this rude woman.

"Madam." John paused before continuing in double-quick time. "For your information your husband has just been fucking killed in a fucking car crash on the M fucking 42 motorway. Goodbye." There was barely a flicker of emotion at the news. As John marched out of the house, he heard a shriek: he was pretty sure that it was his muddy footprints and not the message, that had caused it.

I worked with John at Kings Heath because he had been moved from the central traffic department. Matters had come to a head for John during a violent staff appraisal with his boss. John tried to throw his superintendent out of the second-floor window at Park Lane police station.

Uniformed officers policed most sporting events. There were only ever a handful of stewards at sporting venues, and the police and the general public usually ignored them. I made regular trips to football matches at Aston Villa, Birmingham City, Coventry City, Wolverhampton Wanderers and West Bromwich Albion. I also policed the Rugby Union matches at Moseley. In the summer I was posted to the cricket for the county and Test matches at Edgbaston. In the first twelve years of my service, I never missed an Edgbaston Test match. I even took a wicket at the England v Pakistan game in 1986. No, I wasn't playing, I just recovered a stump from a drunken spectator at the end of the match. I've still got it. I had a great time at the Test matches. The pre-match briefings were basic: we were told we could have a drink, but not to get too drunk, but most important of all avoid doing anything stupid that could be captured by the BBC cameras and broadcast all over the world. We policed the bars diligently. Particular attention was paid to the Guinness tent, as the women who worked there were absolute stunners.

The police officers on duty at the Test match were drawn from throughout the West Midlands. It was a chance to see colleagues that I'd not seen since I joined. We worked in different areas, not many of which seemed to place too high an emphasis on being smartly turned out. At 8.30 am on the first day of the Test match, Superintendent Nigel Rawson arrived, complete with RAF handlebar moustache. He was the senior officer in charge. Rawson spotted the medal ribbon on my tunic.

"Who are you, son?"

"Wolfie Smith, sir, and what can I do for you?"

"Served in the Army, did you? Good, good. Round up the chaps, I'm going to inspect them before I send them out for their duties." Shit. I was looking at the chaps, and a scruffier bunch I had never seen. The ones who weren't smoking were chomping gum; others allowed their untucked shirts to flap in the morning breeze.

"Is that er, wise, sir?"

"Form the fuckers up, Smith. And that is an order!" Rawson barked. I told the assembled rabble to form three ranks. Surprisingly they did. I shouted:

"Atten-shun!"

Two or three shuffled their feet together in a Pavlovian response triggered by a distant memory from their initial training at Ryton. Mr Rawson started to walk along the ranks. I can only assume that he'd been on some sort of course at the Bramshill Police College and been told that this was the way forward. Mr Rawson was quite lenient with his inspection. He pointed out boots that needed a polish, and the odd officer who needed a haircut. Then Rawson stood in front of the last man in the front rank. The officer looked like he had climbed out of a builders' skip to come to work.

"When was the last time that those trousers were cleaned and pressed, Officer?"

"Well, mate, you have got me there," the officer drawled in a thick Black Country accent, "let's have a think." There was a delay as he tried to recall. He started to think out loud, slowly. "Well. I've got twelve years in the job, so I am going to say," he broke into a smile, "but don't hold me to it... Never."

"Go and get them cleaned," Rawson screamed, "and don't come back until they are!" The Black Country lad shrugged his shoulders, then before leaving went to the police hut to retrieve his raincoat. There were dozens in there, but he would have had no problem recognising his; it would have been different to everyone else's. Raincoat collected, he lit up a cigarette and smoked it near the door of the hut while glaring at Rawson. The superintendent was aware that he was the recipient of a *1,000-yard stare*, so he marched over and challenged the officer. Superintendent Rawson applied a little rank structure reinforcement.

"Have you got anything that you'd like to say before you leave, Constable?"

"Actually, sir, yes, I do."

"Well? Spit it out," snapped Rawson.

Dirty Trousers took a long draw on his cigarette. "Sir, if I called you a cunt, would you discipline me?"

"Yes, I most certainly would!"

"But sir, if I just thought you were a cunt, you couldn't discipline me for that, could you?" Rawson pondered this for a moment and then answered.

"Realistically, Constable, there's not much that I, or anyone else for that matter, can do about what you choose to think."

Dirty Trousers took a final draw on his cigarette, dropped it to the floor, and defiantly extinguished it with his boot. He looked at Rawson and spoke quietly, but loud enough for us to hear:

"Sir, in that case, I think you are a total cunt."

He smiled and walked off. Rawson spent the rest of the day fuming. None of this had been covered in his training course at Bramshill. Two hours later, I answered the phone in the police hut.

"Is Rawson there?" I recognised the Black Country drawl as belonging to Dirty Trousers.

"No, do you have a message for him?"

"Yes, tell the cunt that Sketchleys reckon them trousers, which are the only pair I've got by the way, will be ready to collect on Tuesday." I didn't pass on the message.

CHAPTER 10
NO TWO DAYS THE SAME

In the 80s, there was a clearly drawn battle line between the CID and the rest of us. Detectives were tasked to interview every suspect who was not making a full and frank admission. A denial meant a not-guilty file was required for the prosecuting solicitor's department. A confession meant much less work for everyone. West Midlands detectives had extracted admissions from four of the Birmingham Six, so obtaining confessions from ordinary criminals should not be too difficult. Whenever someone was arrested the question that the CID asked was never, 'Have they done it?' but always, 'Are they admitting it?' Detectives were not shy about letting uniformed officers know just how exceptional they were. A detective inspector crowed after he bollocked me for putting some drugs in the wrong safe. "If a bunch of woodentops had been in charge of that Birmingham Six enquiry, none of them fuckers would have ended up behind bars." With the benefit of hindsight that may not have been such a bad thing.

Detectives worked on the most interesting cases. They were

paid a plain clothes allowance, a detective allowance, and were allowed to claim expenses. They also earned a lot more overtime than their uniform colleagues. Detectives had their own desks with lockable drawers. Their desks were adorned with certificates, awards and photographs of their children, but rarely pictures of their wives. There was no point in letting the attractive new policewoman know that they were off the market. They strutted around the police station wearing suits, cheap silk ties and Old Spice aftershave. Detectives maintained an official diary - a big, green hardback book that contained their best joined-up handwriting. This item was an essential fashion accessory. The detective's pocketbook and diary were submitted every month for examination, along with their overtime and expense claim forms. Expenses were paid cash in hand, and that was money that nobody else needed to know about. The detective chief inspector compared the officers' submissions with the CID time book, the vehicle logbooks and custody records. If everything checked out, the diary and pocketbook would be signed and returned. The first casualty for any errors would be the detective's pocket. Overtime and expense forms would be ripped up and chucked in the bin, and the diary and pocketbook flung back at the detective. The message was clear for the following month - must try harder.

Detective Constable Gerry Davidson was 5' 7", with short, wiry, greying hair brushed cruelly back. His bushy, menacing eyebrows were also brushed back. Not many people messed with Gerry. At 8 pm one Monday evening Gerry was the duty cover and working a 2-10 pm shift. Gerry was based at Kings Heath, so where else would he be but in The Cross Guns pub on the Kings Heath High Street? Gerry, putting the clamp on the licensee, ordered a pint of bitter, a drink that could easily have been named after him. The licensee summoned up all of his courage and stammered:

"Gerry. The missus says there are to be no more free drinks for the CID... we might lose the pub at this rate, with the amount you friggers have been drinking for free. If... if you want a pint, Gerry you'll have to pay for it."

Gerry was standing at the bar with a bunch of regulars who were keen to see the outcome but took care to avoid eye contact with the detective. Gerry didn't have any money, so actually paying for the pint he had ordered wasn't even an option.

"Well. If that's how you feel, Stan, I will take my fucking custom elsewhere. Shove your beer up your arse." Gerry about-faced and stepped smartly out of the pub. He turned the collar of his short, beige raincoat up as a shield from the rain. Though he'd made a good show of departing with dignity, Gerry was deeply embarrassed, and raging. That fucker has just challenged my pocket, thought Gerry. He marched the 400 yards back to Kings Heath police station. Once inside, he spoke to a slightly surprised uniformed police constable who was covering the front office and the cells. Anyone who knew Gerry was working until 10 pm did not expect to see him at 8.15 pm. Instead, they expected to see Gerry 'three sheets to the wind' at 10.15 pm, just before he booked off.

"What's in the cells?" Gerry asked.

"A burglar, a real tough nut. They reckon that he's definitely not having it."

"We'll see about that. Give me the keys." Gerry ambled along the cell passage, unlocked the cell door and demanded:

"Right, twat, what about this burglary?" The prisoner said:

"Wha fugging burgalary?" Gerry dropped the nut on the prisoner, and he followed that up with some well-placed kicks to the face, which was not too tricky as the prisoner had adopted the foetal position on the floor. Each kick was punctuated by a threat, followed by a question. The interview continued for about ten minutes. Gerry left the cell and returned to the front office: he was speckled with blood, none of which was his.

"Fuck me, that's one tough cookie," the out of breath detective announced to the probationer who had just taken over the desk duties. The previous office man, who knew exactly what Gerry was capable of, had invented a commitment and left the station.

"Who is?" asked the probationer.

"That burglar in cell one."

"Gerry, cell one is a breathalyser. The burglar is in cell three. Please tell me that you're joking." Gerry was not joking.

"Kid, don't put my visit on the custody record; his facial injuries are mostly superficial. I'm going home. I've had a really shit night, I'll leave it with you." The probationer looked through the hatch on cell one and phoned for an ambulance.

"John Dowling has only been nicked," a sergeant told a group of us in the canteen. "Can't they just leave him alone?" moaned one of the squadron leader's supporters. In police circles, it can often impress an audience if you appear to have some inside knowledge about a subject, so I thought I would try to do just that.

"Is it to do with the old people's home, by the Maypole?"

"What're you on about, Wolfie? Is there something wrong with you?" The sergeant turned back to the group.

"Do any of you know the old boy on the Yardley Wood Road that John became friendly with?" Someone chipped in with:

"Not the guy who had the Aston Martin DB7, in mint condition, with about three miles on the clock?"

"That's the fella. Well, he passed away, and he had told John that he could have his car when he died. John went around to see the grieving family. He offered his condolences and asked when he could collect the car. Well... they only told him to fuck off!"

One of Dowling's supporters groaned:

"Fuck me. After everything John has done for him. I heard John would go around to his house and sit in that car for hours."

"That's unbelievable," I said and meant it.

"Well," the sergeant continued, "on the day of the funeral John took a couple of lads from Billesley (one of whom was Hughie McGowan), they forced open the garage and pushed John's new car up to the nick. The funeral cortège only bloody drove past Billesley police station. The entire family saw their father's pride and joy being admired by half the West Midlands police Force. They went nuts and have made a formal complaint. John has been arrested, interviewed and suspended."

One of the squadron leader's admirers was livid:

"This will all be sorted out at the Crown Court. John will get

141

his job and his car back. Anyway, John told me in confidence that he was a decorated war hero: he will never be convicted."

John Dowling was found guilty of theft at Birmingham Crown Court. He was sentenced to three years' imprisonment. I never saw John again, though if I had seen him on the front page of *The Sun* newspaper, having been arrested when the police stumbled across his fridge full of missing 'Tinder' dates, I would not have been surprised.

A colleague of everyone's favourite interviewer, Gerry Davidson, was DC John Pestridge. He was known as 'Bosher', and it didn't take me long to work out why. John would be in a pub when either a colleague or a member of the public would annoy him, and believe me, it didn't take much. John, with speed that beggared belief, would flick his slip-on shoe up to his hand. He would catch the toe of the shoe and slam the heel onto the victim's head, hard. John would drop the shoe and be wearing it before the victim hit the ground. To the untrained eye, the victim appeared to have either fainted or been shot by a sniper.

With less than two years in the job, I became the PBO for Moseley village. It meant leaving B-Unit, but there was nothing about a shift to be loyal to, most officers used their shift as a springboard to other departments. Moseley was not some quaint Middle England hamlet - the residents included hippies, prostitutes, tramps, drug dealers, Members of Parliament and William Peter McKenzie, I first met Pete in Moseley he was in his late thirties. Pete was slim, always wore a cowboy hat, a waistcoat and denim jeans. He looked a bit like a wild west Jesus. Peter's lovely wife, Jenny, had a proper job. Peter didn't work, so he drank most days, and The Bull's Head was his watering hole of choice. Pete rolled his own cigarettes; his makings were kept in a pouch, which dangled on his hip like a holster. What made him different, though, was not his outfit, although that was eye-catching enough, it was that he never wore shoes. No matter what the elements threw at him, he never wore anything on his feet except bright blue nail varnish on his toenails. Over the years we became mates. He hailed from Barrow-in-Furness and was always softly spoken when he dispensed his wisdom, usually over a game of backgammon and a pint at The Bull's Head. Eventually, I just had to ask him.

"Pete, why don't you wear shoes?"

"Wolfie, I just don't like them, I haven't worn them for over twenty years."

"Jesus, Pete, I've seen you out in snow and ice, how do you do it?"

Pete took a sip of Old Speckled Hen from his pint glass, then took a drag from his roll-up, before responding.

"Wolfie, I am exactly the same as you if you think about it." I thought about it. I was wearing Dr Martens boots, it was January, and it was freezing. The Feet saw that I wasn't following his rationale. I waited. Pete smiled.

"At night before you get into bed, Wolfie, do you take your shoes and socks off?" I confirmed that I did. Pete finished off his pint.

"Wolfie, the only real difference, then, between you and me is that in the morning I don't put the fuckers on." Pete stood up and walked the few steps to the bar. While waiting to be served, he finished his cigarette, dropped it to the floor and extinguished it with his foot, I shit you not. I spent a lot of time with Pete the Feet when I worked in Moseley; I enjoyed his company enormously.

Hughie and I spent quite a lot of time drinking and playing backgammon in The Bull's Head. Everyone knew we were police officers. Those who liked the police spoke to us; the rest tolerated our presence. One day we had been propping up the bar since about midday. Just after 5 pm a female, who was the spitting image of Millie Tant, the left-wing feminist from the British comic *Viz*, cropped hair, denim boiler suit and toe-capped boots, marched into the pub carrying a clipboard. She made a beeline for Hughie and me, probably because we were among the few who appeared to be employed. Rather brusquely, she said:

"Right, I am doing a sponsored event, and I need you two to sponsor me."

Hughie took a drag on his cigarette then quaffed half of his pint and asked:

"And what exactly would I be sponsoring you for, princess?"

Millie bridled at the misogynist term, but looking for sponsorship she said:

"It's for the rape crisis centre."

"Fair enough, love, you can put me down for two rapes?" Millie smashed her clipboard over Hughie's head.

Later that night, Pat came in and joined us at the bar. He had a right grump on. Pat was Irish in his seventies, stood just over five feet tall, and wore a black cap that I had never seen him without. Pat got stuck into both of us:

"You useless pair of bastards, call yourselves the police. You're a pair of oxygen thieves, that's what you are."

Hughie decided that after his encounter with Millie, he needed to improve his communication skills. He listened to Pat rant on about his flat being burgled, and of course, the fact that the police had done nothing. Hughie asked:

"Pat, what was stolen?"

"Nothing. I don't own anything, my telly was nicked years ago."

"Okay, how much damage did they do?" Hughie asked that question because as a time-served carpenter, he would have probably offered to pop round to Pat's and fix his door or window. Pat just scowled:

"There's no damage, I left a window open, and the feral fuckers just climbed in." Hughie looked confused: he queried why Pat was so angry when nothing was stolen, and no damage caused.

"Jaysus... Hughie, you just don't understand, do you? I make a big pan of stew on a Sunday, and that lasts me all week. I was broken into on Tuesday. The bastards had a good look around. As there was nothing to take, one of the animals did a shit in my pan of stew." Well, that certainly explained the reason for his anger. Hughie pulled out a fiver and bought Pat a pint of mild. Pat was now a lot calmer.

"Thanks, lads. You know what pissed me off the most... I had to throw nearly half the pan of stew away."

Half the pan? I blew a mouthful of Guinness out of my nose and nearly died laughing.

In the centre of Moseley, there was a tiny village green next to the public toilets. Kind-hearted residents would throw bread to the pigeons, and the tramps would fight with the birds for the right to eat it. Chris Taylor, a fellow beat man, christened the homeless drunks 'Cider Gliders' and that name stuck for years. I didn't have a lot of police service, and not being a police driver was probably the reason for my posting. Just on the subject of driving, if you are reading my book hoping for tales about getaway drivers that I nabbed because I used my brilliant driving skills, then you should probably put it down now. I must be one of the few people to leave the British Army without a driving licence, and as they were practically being given away, that took some doing. When I did get around to driving, I was a lot more *Driving Miss Daisy* than *Fast & Furious*.

While I was a bit jealous of those who could drive, there was one occasion when it helped that I couldn't. I saw a known prostitute soliciting in Church Road, Moseley. I was in a double-manned panda car with another policeman. We watched her for 40 minutes, and I kept a log of her activities. During that time, this scantily dressed lady of the night flagged down three vehicles and got into each car, then after ten minutes she was delivered back to her 'beat' and continued her shift. Having gathered the evidence, I approached and made the arrest. That was all fairly standard. The paperwork at the station only took about 30 minutes: if the prostitute was compliant, she was given a cup of tea, charged and bailed to appear before the magistrates. At the station, my partner went to put the kettle on, and I escorted my prisoner into the custody block. The custody sergeant asked me for the details of the arrest. Before I was able to, my prisoner decided to get her retaliation in first. Pointing at me, she spat out:

"Sergeant, it is this dirty, bastard you should be putting in the cells, not me."

The sergeant asked, "That is a very serious allegation, young lady, can you give me some more details?"

"This so-called policeman has been pestering me for sex for months. He is a regular punter, only he doesn't pay, he just shows me his warrant card."

I tried to interject, to plead my innocence; the custody sergeant told me to be quiet. The sergeant asked, "Right, when he picks you up for sex what car does he drive?"

"Sergeant, I am not very good with cars, all I can remember is that it's definitely red. Oh, and he is quite rough and refuses to wear a condom."

"Okay, young lady, how many times has this officer had sex with you in his red car?"

Triumphant, growing in confidence and fairly certain that she had cost me my job: "Ten or twelve times, Sergeant, and I will make a statement."

The custody sergeant asked me for the circumstances surrounding the arrest, which I angrily gave him. He then instructed me to get a policewoman to conduct a search of the prisoner before she was placed in a cell.

The prisoner was not impressed, "A cell? What about this fucker? Is he going to get away scot-free? You always cover things up to look after your own."

The custody sergeant calmly responded. "The officer that you have just made the allegation against is Wolfie Smith: he doesn't own a car, let alone a red one. He doesn't even have a driving licence. Are you seriously suggesting that on ten or twelve occasions he has gone out and stolen red cars with the sole intention of having sex with a common prostitute? Grow up, love."

A policewoman took the prostitute away so that she could be searched.

I said to the custody sergeant, "Thank you, Sergeant Mason, I appreciated that." John Mason, my old B-Unit supervisor said, "No problem, Wolfie, I enjoyed putting that lying trollop in her place."

John Mason, sorry I called you a twat in the first chapter.

To police my beat, I was based at Woodbridge Road. It was a small but fully operational police station. There was a public enquiry counter, three cells, and separate offices for the CID and the PBOs. The single men's quarters' bedrooms were above the police station, and their lounge and kitchen were on the ground floor adjacent to the station. Mark Blackburn had a room, though he mostly stayed at his mum and dads. Hughie McGowan had managed to get shit-faced drunk, in The

Bull's Head, and lost a small fortune to Pete the Feet playing backgammon. Hughie staggered back to the station, then fell up the stairs, and into the single men's quarters. He leant against Mark Blackburn's room door, which had no choice but to open, then he collapsed onto the bed. At 7 am, Mark Blackburn had just finished nights and decided to use his room to get some kip. Mark found his room door open: lying there, snoring loudly on his bed, was a huge, hairy beast of a man. Hughie looked a lot more like *Hagrid* than *Goldilocks*. Mark sort of recognised him, and their conversation went:

"Oi! Get out of my bed. I've just finished work, and I want to get some sleep!"

Hughie gently roused himself, half-sat up and lit a Benson & Hedges.

"It's Mark, isn't it? Mark Blackburn?"

"Yes it is, and I've just finished nights, and now I want to go to bed, mate."

Hughie took a long draw on his cigarette.

"It's your bed," he calmly said, "and sure, I can get up. But even if I do you can't get into it, sorry."

"Why the fuck not?"

"Well, I've just got back from a holiday in Spain, and I think I have picked up a dose of crabs. Sorry, mate."

Hughie smiled, extinguished his cigarette and went back to sleep. Mark drove to his parent's house.

My new sergeant, Nicholas Fisher, was very well educated and a top bloke. His mother and father ran a private school in Edgbaston, and he was the first person that I knew who had a personalised number plate on his car - NF999. Nick talked quite posh and was destined to fly through the ranks. I remember being on mobile patrol one evening with Nick. We both saw a youth snatch a lady's handbag and run off with it. Nick played a lot of squash and was incredibly fit: he chased and caught the robber. Having made the arrest, we took our prisoner to Kings Heath. Nick decided that the streets of Moseley would be a lot safer if we remanded this particular chap (Nick's word) in custody. That meant someone was going to have to go to court the following morning. I explained to Nick that things had not gone too well the last time I tried to remand a prisoner in custody.

"Vince, I will do the remand. Come along, and you can see how it should be done." The following morning, I was sitting with Nick Fisher in the public gallery of Court 1 at the Birmingham Magistrates. The street robber was having a conversation with his solicitor. Our case was first on the list. Proceedings began, and the defendant stood up. The prosecuting solicitor told the court that a police officer would explain the reasons for their objection to bail. A smartly turned out Nick Fisher strode purposefully to the witness box. It was time for me to watch and learn. Nick stood upright and faced the three magistrates. The chairman recognised my sergeant.

"It's young Nicholas, isn't it? Nicholas Fisher?"

"Oh hello, George, how the devil are you?"

"Fine, fine Nicholas... it's nice to see that they've promoted you. My, how you've grown." Christ, this was so different from how my remand application had gone. The magistrate continued.

"How are your mother and father? Well, I hope?"

"They're fine and thank you for asking, George."

"What brings you here today, Nicholas?"

"It's that awful gentleman in the dock." Nick pointed to him. "I caught him last night committing a robbery in Moseley. I'd very much like to remand him in custody, please." The chairman sat upright: he'd heard enough. Without even conferring with the other magistrates, he had made his decision.

"Stand up straight, young man," he said to the defendant, then to the sergeant controlling the dock, "Sergeant, take him to the cells. He is remanded in custody for one month." The defendant and his solicitor shook their heads in disbelief, and I did as well. I was really going to struggle to use any of what I had seen for my next bail objection.

After two years as a pro-con, I was formally appointed as a police constable. I was off shifts and my hours were more flexible. I hoped I could see out the remainder of my service as the Sheriff of Moseley. It was a beautiful thought. As PBOs, we would be deployed at sporting events and public order incidents. For safety reasons, there were only so many officers that could be extracted from the shifts. The Reddings in Moseley was on my beat area, and Moseley Rugby Club was one of the top three teams in the country. I policed most of their home games. Mark Linnett was a friend who played prop forward for Moseley and was also a policeman. Mark was a good man to have on your side on a rugby pitch. He was even more useful to have around as a copper. Mark went on to represent England.

He enjoyed himself when he went on his first tour, perhaps just a little too much.

Mark was at a training camp in Lanzarote with the England squad; it was just a few weeks before the memorable 1990 Grand Slam deciding Calcutta Cup clash with Scotland. Merlene Ottey, the gorgeous, legendary Jamaican sprinter, was also at the training facility. Mark spotted her running outfit drying outside her room. Mark borrowed her kit and shoehorned his muscular frame into it. He then sashayed into the bar where an England team meeting was taking place and reduced the entire gathering to tears. The England squad witnessed a *Mr Incredible* impersonation fourteen years before the film was even made.

The atmosphere was brilliant at The Reddings, especially for the cup games. I enjoyed the corporate and club hospitality on match days, and it was not unheard of for me to get just a little bit squiffy. News of my behaviour had reached the ear of my inspector. I was summoned to his office and given a warning. He told me that he would be at The Reddings on Saturday for the cup match and that I had better be sober for the duration of the fixture. If not, then my time as the Sheriff of Moseley was about to come to an end. The ground at The Reddings was in an appalling state, and there was only one stand worthy of the name. The rest of the stadium consisted of poorly maintained terracing. There were five Portakabins, allowing the occupants a little bit of privacy while spectating.

Determined not to upset my inspector any further, I brushed my uniform, polished my boots and policed the match. The game was in full flow. Frank, a local businessman, sponsored a Portakabin. He popped his head out and shouted:

"Wolfie! Come in and have a drink, son."

"Not today, Frank, my inspector is on my case. I wish I could, but I definitely can't."

I carried on watching the game and was standing next to an elderly lady and a young lad. Twenty minutes later, Frank popped his head out and shouted.

"Quick, Wolfie! You're needed in here, it's urgent."

"Frank, I am not drinking."

"Just get in here, for fuck's sake." I went in, there were fifteen pissed-up blokes and a pissed-up barmaid. I feared the worst.

"It isn't what you think," insisted Frank. He explained that they had done a sweep, and there was £50 in the pot, but there was a problem. The barmaid started to giggle. "Wolfie, this is Beryl. Each of us has had a guess on the number of hairs she has on her nipples, and we cannot agree because some of them are sort of split hairs."

Frank insisted that they needed a decision, and if this was not resolved, it could turn nasty. My English teacher at school told me that it was no good arguing over split hairs - that had meant nothing to me until this moment. To prevent a breach of the peace and with some reluctance, I agreed to adjudicate. Beryl produced her breasts, I concentrated and counted her nipple hairs. There were 23. I recounted: I was nothing if not a professional. I announced the result, someone shouted, "Yes!" and scooped the pot. The rest resignedly accepted my decision. The winner tried to entice me into having a drink. I declined, left the Portakabin and carried on watching the match. The old lady and the young lad were still there. The boy stepped towards the Portakabin that I had just left and asked:

"Is my mum in there, sir?"

"What's your mum's name?" I just knew it was going to be Beryl and of course, it was. I tried to do the right thing and said:

"Son, there's nobody in there by that name." No good was going to come out of him entering that Portakabin. I don't think Beryl had even bothered putting her boobs away.

"Just wait here, I'm sure your mum will see you if you're with me." The three of us carried on watching the match. The old lady decided to pipe up.

"Ooh, Officer, I bet your job's really interesting, and no two days are the same." She was absolutely right.

CHAPTER 11
THE SHERIFF OF MOSELEY

My hours of work, as a PBO, were a lot more comfortable and without four sergeants and an inspector to micromanage me, there was a reasonable amount of wiggle room. Also, the area controllers were under pressure to improve incident response times, so sending a resource who did not have access to a vehicle was never going to be as effective as dispatching a Zulu or a panda. As a bonus and purely to relieve the boredom, you understand, I had a little bit of fun. A woman driving her red Mini pulled up just as I was walking out of Woodbridge Road police station.

"Officer, I need to get to an optician's which is near the Maypole Island. I'm late for my appointment, and I'm a bit lost."

"I am terribly sorry, madam, but you simply cannot get there from here."

"Is there anything you can do to help, please?"

"Don't worry," I reassured her, "just reverse your car for me, that's it... keep going. A bit more." I kept an eye out for the traffic behind her while she backed her car up. "Ah, that's perfect," I said and leant into her window. "Right, drive to the end of the street then turn left onto the Alcester Road. Stay on that road, drive through Kings Heath, and the Maypole Island is about five miles away. It should only take you about twenty minutes."

"Thank you so much, Officer." She sped off to her appointment. I speculated, at what point of her journey she would replay this and wonder why on earth she had to reverse her car twenty yards.

In every area, there is always some obscure street that no one can ever find. In Moseley, it was Louise Lorne Road. It was a side road off another road that looked like a cul-de-sac. One morning I stopped a car for a routine check. The driver did a little bit too much tutting and clucking for my liking. He produced his documents, and everything was in order. I was just about to let him carry on, then I asked:

"Sir, do you know where Louise Lorne Road is?"

"No, I've lived in Moseley for twenty years, Officer, and I've never heard of it." No one ever had.

"Right, it's quite complicated, so you need to listen carefully."

I gave detailed directions to the driver. He sat in his car clutching his documents, nodding along to my instructions, clearly visualising the route as I described it.

"Thank you, Officer." I stood back: he seemed genuinely grateful. He turned his car around and headed towards Louise Lorne Road. I have no idea what he did when he got there.

Another time I was on foot patrol, walking towards Kings Heath, a Labrador dog ran into the road and was clipped by a car. The driver had slammed her brakes on but still struck the poor beast. The dog seemed to be okay: it yelped but ran off before I could get to it. I had seen the whole thing, and the driver couldn't have avoided the collision. The car door opened, and the driver stepped out. She was quite young and on the verge of tears. Any accident that involved a dog was reportable to the police. I tried to reassure the young lady that it was not her fault. I told her that I had seen what had happened. I took her details, then she said:

"Officer, I'm on my way to a job interview," adding, "look at me, I'm a total mess, I didn't need this!"

"Where are you going?"

"Poplar Road, Kings Heath. Please, what's the quickest way from here?"

Aha! I knew just how to cheer her up.

"Carry straight on for about a mile," I said, pointing down the road, "then turn left over the Poodle, right over the Alsatian, when you hit the Golden Retriever, you've arrived." She called me an insensitive prick, got into her car, and drove off.

A letter was delivered to Woodbridge Road police station, addressed to the 'Police Officer in Charge of Woodbridge Road Police Station', but as there wasn't anybody else in the station, I read it. It was a neatly typed formal complaint about a policeman - my mate Mark Blackburn. It was from the Administrator of the Sorrento Maternity Hospital in Wake Green Road. Mark had dealt with a report of criminal damage at the hospital. According to the letter, Mark arrived in his panda car, put his police hat on, then proceeded to upset the four members of the staff that he spoke to. Officious, unpleasant and obnoxious were just some of the words that described the service Mark had dispensed. I laughed, but just as I was about to file the letter in the bin, I noticed that a copy had been sent to Superintendent Walters at Kings Heath police station. Bollocks.

I thought I'd best give Mark the heads-up. I found him slumped on the sofa in the communal lounge at single men's quarters, watching a *Blackadder* video. I handed Mark the letter, he stared at it, then at me, back at the letter, then back at me. The penny was dropping, this was not a wind-up. I could see he was getting angry, but he wasn't saying anything. Finally, the penny dropped. "Right, that's it, Wolfie. That is the last nurse that I am going to fuck. Ever." I had a vision of thousands of sexually frustrated nurses marching through Birmingham begging Mark to reconsider, chanting:

> ♫ *What Do We Want?*
> *Mark Blackburn's Cock...*
> *When Do We Want It?*
> *NOW!* ♫

Warren Nixon was a young policeman who had lived in single men's. He only moved out because he married his sweetheart Heidi. They were perfectly matched, he was 5' 7", and she was slightly smaller. They made a handsome couple. When they returned from their honeymoon, Warren decided to pop into single men's quarters to show off his new bride, and their honeymoon photographs. On most days in single men's there would have been quite a few policemen, plus Kitty the cleaner and Eileen the cook. Some of the residents were actually on Warren's shift and no doubt they would have cooed over the photographs and politely listened to Warren's tales about the wedding and honeymoon. When Warren and Heidi walked in the only person at home was Hughie McGowan. Hughie was sprawled out on that very popular sofa, wearing only a pair of loose-fitting shorts. Hughie was smoking, drinking a can of lager and watching a porno film. Warren tried to find the video remote control, but couldn't as it was in Hughie's hand, and he wasn't switching the film off anytime soon. Undeterred, Warren pressed ahead.

"Hughie, I'd like to introduce you to my wife, Heidi. We've just got married." Hughie, a bit irked at the interruption, looked Warren and Heidi up and down.

"That's grand, Warren, really grand. I bet your wedding was lovely, and in its own way, unique."

Now Heidi had not been impressed with anything she had seen so far and was not overly happy with Hughie's tone, especially the emphasis he had placed on his final word.

"What do you mean by unique?" she challenged. Hughie took a swig from his can and a drag on his cigarette.

"Well," he spluttered through a haze of smoke, "would you look at the size of the two of you. Can I ask, did you stand on top of the wedding cake for the photos?"

Heidi flew at him. Chris Taylor was returning to single men's from another unprofitable visit to Ladbrokes. Through the lounge window he saw the altercation: he said it was like watching a squirrel trying to beat up a grizzly bear.

Brian Bridgewater, an OSU officer, was on a van patrol: ten rufty, tufty, riot-trained officers, patrolling the mean streets of Birmingham, and ready for anything. An Asian controller shouted up:

"Bravo 3! Bravo 3 to the OSU van patrol, are you receiving?"

The keen as mustard sergeant responded:

"Van patrol, we are receiving. Where do you want us, Asif?"

"Can you go immediately to The Red Lion pub, Kings Heath? There is a report of a lot of people fahting." The van erupted. The sergeant needed clarification.

"Asif, please confirm. You are sending us to The Red Lion to a report that people are farting?"

"No! No! No!" Asif yelled down the radio, frustrated. "Not poop-poop fahting! Fisty-fisty fahting!"

Years later, I worked with another Asian Sergeant, Bal Singh. He punctuated his sentences with expressions that were almost correct. There are over 25,000 in everyday use in the English language, and yet Bal seemed to feel that a few more were needed. Examples he created include:

"Ugly? He looked like a wasp chewing a bulldog."

"The pen is mightier than the fork."

"They were so poor, they never even had a poodle to piss on."

"I was trying to take the bull by the horns. After the horse had bolted."

"They were behaving just like the gangsters in that film *Reservoir Ducks*."

"Big? He was built like a shit brick house."

Bal had a hole in the middle of his left ear. The hole was large enough to see through, and it distracted me terribly. When he was talking to me, I would stare through the hole, and couldn't tear my eyes away. I wasn't sure what to make of it and thought it might be something religious. One day Bal was taking over from me in the custody block. I was staring through the hole in his ear.

"Vince, are you staring at my ear?"

"Bal, that hole. Is it religious?"

"No, Vince." Bal smiled at me. "It stops me from getting migraines." I was puzzled.

"Does it work?"

"I think so, but I'm not really sure because I've never actually had one." I remained none the wiser. PC Jack Regan was a mate who worked for Bal: he updated me on the latest 'Balisms'. I shared these gems with John Scott, my superintendent, who found them hilarious. John Scott held a meeting with a group of sergeants who were responsible for Quinton. Mr Scott told the sergeants that he wanted officers to leaflet houses with crime prevention information, adding that the residents needed to be spoken to as well. Bal Singh required clarification:

"So basically, gaffer, you are trying to kill the two people with just the one brick." John Scott blew his tea out through his nose and blamed me. Of all Bal Singh's personal suggestions for acceptance into the *Oxford Dictionary of English Idioms*, the last one that Jack told me about still makes me chuckle. Bal was giving a probationer a good telling-off for repeatedly being late for work. Losing his patience, Bal threatened:

"If you are late once more, you are for the Bob Beamon, yeah the Bob Beamon, and I am not joking." Jack saw the probationer's eyes glaze over. Bal, having discharged his duties as a supervisor, left the room. A puzzled pro-con turned and asked:

"Jack, who the fuck is Bob Beamon, and why have you just fallen off your chair laughing?" Jack did not have to explain anything to me, he knew that I would crack the code. For those not fluent in Bal - at the 1968 Olympic Games, held in Mexico City, Bob Beamon set an incredible world record and won an Olympic gold medal in the long jump. If only Beamon had performed a similar feat in the high jump, Bal's threat might have made sense. Bal Singh's malapropisms were just naturally brilliant. I really miss him, or as he would probably put it, 'Absence has made my hair grow longer.'

Woodbridge Road single men's quarters were the meeting place for some of the lads before a night out. One of the older guys who lived there was Mick Holland. Mick thought the rest of us were lightweights when it came to drinking. Mick was a good-looking guy, six feet tall, intelligent and well built. Mick would return from his drinking crusades covered in blood, rarely his own, evidence that he had inflicted injuries on whatever poor sod Mick thought had crossed that night's *Rubicon*. Mick had quite a lot of success with the ladies. They all seemed to think they could change him. I remember being in the courtyard, at the back of the PBO office at Woodbridge Road, which happened to be just below Mick's room. Hughie McGowan was changing into his motorcycle leathers to go home and having a smoke. We were both disturbed by the noises coming from Mick's room: whatever was going on did not seem to be consensual. Hughie commented:

"Jaysus, Wolfie, the last time I heard a woman making them noises somebody was fucking thumping her." Hughie finished his cigarette and left. I waited a few more minutes trying to decide whether or not to go upstairs and intervene. I heard the woman's voice again.

"Yes. Yes, Mick. Harder, harder, do it harder, yes." Phew. I guess she wasn't getting a kicking after all, and I'd probably saved myself from one by not bursting into Mick's room.

Probably through drink and a degree of isolation, Mick could get quite moody. I was having a pint with Mark Blackburn in The Prince of Wales pub, which was just around the corner from Woodbridge Road. It was a sunny evening, and Mick breezed in. He had the look of a man on a mission, and as this was not just a hobby for him, he was not looking for company. Mark and I didn't distract him. Two men came into the hallway carrying newspapers.

"Get Your *Socialist Worker*!" bellowed one of them, indicating that the newspaper could be purchased from him.

"Cunt!" hollered Mick and head-butted him. The unconscious vendor slid down the wall, blood streaming from his nose, papers strewn everywhere. His fellow socialist was shocked.

"Fucking hell, mate. That was a bit unnecessary."

Thunk! Mick nutted him as well, and he joined his friend on the floor. It all happened in a matter of seconds. Mick finished his pint, shook his head, tutted, then looked around and asked:

"Can't a bloke have a fucking pint in peace?" He gave the casualties a look of contempt as if to say, 'Now look at what you've gone and made me do.' Mick stepped over their bodies and headed off in the direction of The Bull's Head. Mark turned to me.

"Wolfie. I'm glad them *Socialist Worker* blokes came in, otherwise that could have been us lying on the floor."

Mark Blackburn was a valuable companion as he had a car and money. Every time Mark went to an ATM, I was on his shoulder, borrowing funds to continue drinking. I would like to think I paid it all back, but I doubt it. I was usually sitting in his front passenger seat, being driven to that night's venue. Mark was the sort of guy that, if another ten to fifteen people were needed at any function, then Mark was invited. Once word went around where he was going, others would always follow.

Life at single men's quarters was eventful. I did not live there, but it was integral to the station, and it was impossible to escape some of their domestic issues. Like the time that Mick Holland noticed that someone had been stealing his orange juice from the communal fridge, Mick decided that I was the offender. The word around the campfire was that a *fatwa* had been placed on my life. I waited until 9 pm one night, gathered up my courage, and went into the single quarters' lounge. I confronted Mick. I denied taking his orange juice and offered to fight the lunatic. Mick, quite incredibly, declined my offer. He was a terrifying fucker, and I knew he wasn't scared of me.

I can only assume that I caught him during a mellow period between his drinking sessions and am lucky to still be alive. I found out Hughie McGowan had been drinking Mick's frigging orange juice.

I did find time to do some police work while I was on my beat. PC Chris Pritchard, a colleague from my old B-Unit shift, was working nights and on foot patrol in Kingswood Road, Moseley. Chris stopped two lads who were messing about on a big road roller, the sort of vehicle that flattened tarmac. One of them told Chris it belonged to his uncle. Chris tried to check the vehicle on the Police National Computer. Both lads realised the game was up and sprinted off. Chris, who was quite fit, chased, rugby-tackled and held onto one of them. That was the last thing Chris remembered before waking up two days later in the hospital.

The detectives at Woodbridge Road, Colin Abbotts and John Davies, were the CID role models that Johnny Mac was to uniformed officers. They took it upon themselves to round up all the usual local suspects, but without success. I spent a bit of time in Moseley's pubs and met a guy in The Fighting Cocks who broached the subject of Chris's assault. Because of his distinctive looks - he was dark-skinned, had shoulder-length hair and eyes like Marty Feldman - I knew he was not one of the offenders. I figured he knew something, but he didn't just want to offer up his information too quickly: that would have made him a *grass*. I chose to visit The Fighting Cocks pub a little more than usual. One night Marty was drunk. I manipulated our conversation around to the assault on the policeman. In a drunken state, he agreed to a game of Hangman based on the name of one of the offenders. I had to give him a one-pound note for each incorrect guess. He peeled a beer mat and scribbled on it.

It cost me £6, but I guessed the name of the offender for an extra £4 he also gave me his address. I was so excited that I went to work early the next day. I was posted to a 2 pm-10 pm shift and went straight to see Detective Sergeant Stu Bruce. He was in charge of the CID at Woodbridge Road. DS Bruce was not very friendly: he was short, stocky, and had cropped swept-back hair. I told him everything I knew, except the name of my informant: I had learned that much in my short time in the police. DS Bruce probed me:

"Is your informant tried and tested, son?" Having been a policeman for just over two years, how could the answer to that question have ever been yes?

"He certainly is, Sergeant." DS Bruce instructed me to get someone else to assist, adding that he would arrest the suspect at 6 pm. At 5 pm I was in the CID office with Chris Taylor waiting for Sergeant Bruce who eventually strolled in, as pissed as a parrot, at 9.30 pm. I gently enquired why he had not turned up at 6 pm. Gently, because DS Bruce could be pretty violent when stone-cold sober and alcohol in no way improved his mood or humour. He glared at us, swaying slightly, and then stormed off. As he left the room, he turned and waved a finger in our general direction.

"Both of you be here at 5 pm tomorrow. And don't be fucking late."

The following day, a sober DS Bruce arrived on time. Chris Taylor and I accompanied him on the short journey to the suspect's house. An elderly lady, who was busy making that evening's tea, opened the front door. My suspect was sitting at a table waiting for his food. When he stood up, I could see why Chris Pritchard had spent two days in the hospital, he was 6' 4" and built like a brick shithouse - *note for Bal Singh: that is the accepted version of that expression*. I arrested, cautioned and handcuffed the suspect. Driving back to the station, DS Bruce looked in the rear-view mirror and spoke to my prisoner.

"Listen, mate, this is probably just a complete load of bollocks. We just need to go through the motions at the nick."

I felt gutted. I knew my information was right, and Stu Bruce was royally pissing all over my chips. I held my tongue, but DS Bruce didn't.

"Cheer up," he said to the giant in the handcuffs, "you'll be back home and tucking into your tea in a few minutes." Thank you, Sergeant Bruce, another dagger through my investigative heart. The prisoner shifted uncomfortably in his seat, then whimpered in a delicate Scottish accent:

"Why do you keep saying that this has got nothing to do with me? I hit the copper, and I knew what I did was wrong. I'll tell you exactly what happened and who I was with. I know I will get a kicking, and I deserve it."

He sat back in his seat and stared out of the window. Wow,

the actus reus, and the mens rea all in a legally admissible confession. DS Bruce nearly crashed the car. Never mind a kicking, I could have kissed my prisoner. Sergeant Bruce hadn't finished his cross-examination:

"This is all very interesting, Jock. But why the fuck are you admitting something we probably can't prove?" There was quite a pause before the prisoner finally said.

"Because that copper did nothing wrong." My prisoner was as good as his word. He explained exactly what had happened. The bit that Chris Pritchard had not been able to remember was that while he was desperately holding onto his prisoner, his mate ran back and punched Chris so hard on the side of the head, he knocked him out. My prisoner, who had delivered the punch, named his accomplice. I arrested the second offender the following morning. Both suspects were charged with wounding. Neither had any previous convictions: they were both given custodial sentences. My prisoner never received a kicking. To be fair to Stu Bruce, unlike most detectives, he never tried to claim any credit for the arrest and conviction. That was proper police work. I really enjoyed that.

CHAPTER 12
BACK TO THE FUTURE

In May 1982 Hughie McGowan, my best mate, drew a pretty short straw and was posted to Lloyd House security. He did not want to go. It was a posting that PCs were usually given when they only had a few months left in the job. Hughie's role was to stand at the entrance of the police headquarters and deter unwelcome visitors. It didn't take long for Hughie to be known by most of the senior officers who worked at Lloyd House: most liked him, but one senior officer was less than enamoured.

It was 8 pm on a Wednesday night, and Hughie was on duty deterring visitors just as he had been for the previous two weeks. He was standing over a WPC who was sitting at a desk reading *The Sun* newspaper. Hughie was ogling the breasts on page three. Assistant Chief Constable Ken Davies, whose factory settings had been set to unpleasant, strode into the reception and barked:

"McGowan! Where are the keys to my office?"

Hughie walked the few paces to the key cabinet and handed the ACC his office keys, then he returned to his previous position. As the WPC had moved on from page three, Hughie now ogled the WPC's breasts. An hour later Mr Davies returned to the reception, and a brief, unpleasant exchange took place between him and PC McGowan, following which Mr Davies stormed off. After his shift, Hughie handed his pocketbook to his sergeant and was expecting it to be returned to him on Monday night, after his weekend off. Hughie's pocketbook, unusually, contained details of a conversation. Hughie's sergeant read the entry:

Wednesday 12 May 1982
1345hrs. On duty Lloyd House Security.
2000hrs. ACC Ken Davies attended security counter and demanded the keys to his office, which he snatched from me as I handed them to him.
2100hrs. ACC Davies returned to the front office. He said:
'McGowan, my office was open, you idiot - I did not need the keys.'
I replied, 'Sir, you asked me for the keys, you did not ask me if your office was open.' ACC Davies started to rant. 'McGowan, you are an Irish idiot, I would post you somewhere else, but there is nowhere lower for you to go.'
The ACC moved closer to me in a menacing manner. I could smell alcohol on his breath. I formed the opinion that he was drunk. He stormed off in the direction of the car park. I hope he is not going to drive his car in that state.
2200hrs. Off Duty.

Hughie had written up the incident in his pocketbook, just as he had been trained to. Hughie's sergeant's face dropped, and he changed his grip on the pocketbook to reduce the number of fingerprints he was leaving. Needing to offload this problem, he made his way to his inspector's office. Hughie had the weekend off and returned to work at 9.30 pm on Monday to begin his night shift. Upon arrival he was called into Assistant Chief Constable Smith's office, Hughie was invited to sit down and offered a coffee, both of which he declined. ACC Smith explained that Ken Davies had been terribly busy and was under a lot of pressure. Mr Smith produced Hughie's pocketbook and placed it on the desk between them, then asked if Hughie wished to make a formal complaint about the assistant chief constable's behaviour? Hughie thought carefully.

"Sir," leaning in conspiratorially, "I have had quite a few of them complaints myself. Mr Davies is probably a man of good character. This could even be his first offence. I think on this occasion he should be let off with a warning." Mr Smith explained that as Hughie did not wish to make a complaint, Mr Davies would like to speak to him and was waiting in the adjoining office. Davies had adjusted his factory settings to almost agreeable. Hughie was still on his guard and again declined the offer of a seat and coffee. Mr Davies spoke.

"Hughie," he said sympathetically, "you're not happy here at Lloyd House, are you?"

"You could say that, sir." Through gritted teeth, the ACC said, "Hughie, call me Ken," then asked, "if I could arrange for you to work anywhere in the West Midlands, on any shift, where would you choose?"

"A-Unit, Acocks Green." Hughie replied without hesitation. He had loads of mates there, and it was closer to home. Hughie added, "If that's okay with you... Ken." The ACC winced.

"Right, then McGowan." Davies's personal settings now

reset to their factory default. "You start tomorrow, and you can have the rest of the night off. Is there anything else?"

Hughie smiled, ignored the offer of a handshake and left. Now that was how to use a pocketbook.

I stayed on my beat in Moseley for the next few years and was working there in 1983 when police forces were called on to assist with the massive public order problems that surrounded the miners' dispute. The overtime was plentiful, and there was no shortage of volunteers. It was policemen only, so to plug the operational gaps back on division, policewomen worked as much overtime as they wanted. I went on eight trips all over England: the accommodation was a little bit basic, as was the food: it was a no-star all-inclusive holiday. On the upside, I was away with my mates and being well paid.

Initially, there was some excellent banter between the strikers and the police. We were just a group of cops away from our regular duties; most cops sympathised with the plight of the miners, so we shared our snack bags with them. To battle the boredom we spent almost all of our spare time playing cards for cash. I benefited from having spent nearly six years in the British Army studying the intricacies of three-card brag. On four of my miners' trips, I doubled my overtime with the profits I made at the card table. The B Division always sent two public order vans to police whatever colliery we were posted to. We split into the 'Glees and the Glums'. The Glees drank, gambled and tried to fornicate with the local females. The Glums moaned about our behaviour.

In July 1983, I was posted to St George's Barracks in Sutton Coldfield for ten days. That was the same barracks that I had attended before joining the Army: it had not changed one little bit. Our team's role was to police the pickets protesting outside the Keresley pit in Warwickshire. I was on this adventure with Andy Crowson, Mark Blackburn, Chris Taylor, Hughie Friel, Mick Holland and Dave McClughen. Andy jumped into the van and took a seat over the wheel arch and at 6' 3", this meant he spent a week with his knees up by his ears. We had no public order kit. Other police forces did, but we had nothing. We formed up as a squad, and a superintendent from Warwickshire told us to get into our public order kit. Most of us didn't move, what was the point? Mick Holland, sounding unusually helpful, piped up.

"It's okay, lads. I'll get it." I thought he had lost his mind. Mick popped into the van and collected a metal bin lid which, until this trip, had resided outside the single men's quarters at Woodbridge Road.

"What the fuck is that?" asked the superintendent. Mick, with a big, cheesy grin said:

"This, mate, is our public order kit... all of it."

"West Mids wankers," muttered the senior officer as he walked off.

We didn't see many females, and most that we encountered were hostile. They supported the miners, and we were very much the enemy. Our driver pulled over next to a newsagent's shop in a remote village. Most of us went into the shop to buy newspapers, pop, sweets and fags. On the counter was a big red bucket for contributions to the striking miners. The young lady serving was fairly unpleasant. Whenever someone asked if she had something, her answer was a snappy and rude "NO." Just to let us know where her allegiance lay when she handed the officers any change, she tapped the bucket, indicating where it should be deposited. I was with Dave McClughen in the queue. When it was his turn, he asked the disagreeable young lady.

"Excuse me... I don't suppose you have any gorms in the shop, do you?"

True to form, the shop assistant immediately snapped, "NO."

"That's because you are fucking gormless, love." Said Clug.

We walked out of the shop giggling, we didn't purchase any provisions, but it was worth it.

The hours we worked on this trip were strange. Our shift started at midnight, so most of us went to the bar and had a drink before work. Some played cards, some watched films and others just dossed about. Mick Holland launched himself into a drinking frenzy. The barmaid was quite attractive, but not very friendly. Undeterred Mick spent the night trying to chat her up. At midnight we climbed into our van. I was in the back corner seat, sharing the double seat; to my right was Hughie Friel, and next to him, totally pissed, was Mick Holland. We set off in the van to our holding location. After twenty minutes, Hughie offered me a cigarette. I have never smoked, and Hughie knew that. Hughie was insistent, pointing to the packet he was offering. There was something written on the cigarette packet.

I held it up to the tiny interior light. Hughie had written, Mick is having a wank. I looked past Hughie: sure enough, there was Mick Holland absolutely hammered with his dick in his hand, he was giving the bishop the bashing of a lifetime. The following morning, we finished work, a full night on standby, sleeping in the sweaty, smelly van. At 9 am, we were tucking into our breakfast. Mick Holland leant over the table.

"Wolfie," he said, "did you see that fit barmaid last night?"

"Yes, Mick, why?"

"I fucked her, you know," he boasted.

"I know Mick, I think I saw you." I winked at Hughie.

If anyone tried to sleep in the police van during the day, they were loudly asked, "Do You Want to Buy A Battleship?" Mark Blackburn was the unfortunate victim who had drifted off. He appeared to be having an erotic dream, a load of cooing, with a little bit of lip-curling (the other sort). I shouted the question at Mark and, annoyed at the intrusion, he remained in a sulk for the rest of the morning. We were on our way to a school that had been opened to provide hot meals for the police. The same female serving assistant had been there most days, and she seemed to have taken a bit of shine to Mark. Some days she had even given Mark an extra sausage which was, I suppose, some sort of Freudian foreplay. As we walked in, she saw Mark, who had still not entirely recovered from the battleship question. Mark took his food and was about to shuffle off.

"What's the matter, love? Has the cat got your tongue today?"

Mark turned and asked.

"Are you doing anything tonight?"

"No," she said, and her face lit up like a pinball table. She hopefully asked, "Why?"

Mark crushed her with, "Well, brush your teeth, they're a disgrace." I cringed and sat down next to Mark. I thought his remark was a bit over the top and told him so. Mark stuck his fork into his solitary sausage then looked back at the serving assistant.

"Wolfie, have a look at her. She's got a face that looks about as appealing as the inside of a shit smuggler's duffel bag."

On one of the early miners' trips, I was based at the Proteus Training camp in Nottingham. There was a massive gathering of strikers, union stewards, miners and police. There were a substantial number of press and people with the National Council for Civil Liberties tabards. Looking back, I am not sure whether I created a media headline about the possibility that soldiers were assisting the police on the picket lines. This is what happened:

Our coach parked a short distance away from our designated location. Inspector Stuart Harris instructed me:

"Wolfie, you were in the Army... form up the lads and march them into position."

I gave it the full Army drill sergeant, bellowing:

"A Left...A Left...A Left...Right...Left."

Our twenty officers looked impressive. A single body of men marching through the crowd. Once in position, I screamed:

"The Second Battalion of the Parachute Regiment... Halt!" I

stage-whispered to Inspector Harris, "Sorry, Captain."

"Wolfie," Inspector Harris whispered in my ear, "if the shit hits the fan over this, you are on your fucking own."

Over the next few days, the media suggested that Maggie Thatcher was deploying soldiers dressed as policemen to assist with the policing of the miners' strike. I really don't think she was.

The strike dragged on: police officers became wealthier, while the miners were starved into submission. Their initial commitment had long since disappeared. At first, there were battles, but in the end, with the hostility and spirit completely drained from them, the strikers would arrive at their colliery and mumble, "Scab," to claim their strike pay allowance. Then with their heads bowed and shoulders slumped, they went home.

In December 1983, I remarried. The money I earned on the miners' strike comfortably paid for the entire event. Johnnie Mac was my best man. My dad stole my brother's wallet the night before my wedding, which left Anthony skint for the weekend. Dad also appropriated the decorative *Last of the Summer Wine* hotel room key fob. The manager of the hotel noticed the fob was missing as we were climbing into a taxi. He ran out of the hotel and ran towards our taxi. My father instructed the driver to put his foot down, and we made a clean getaway.

CHAPTER 13
SCHOOL VISITS

After my miners' sojourn, I went back to police my beat in Moseley. These were the days before the police had dedicated school liaison officers. As a permanent beat officer, it was part of my job to visit the schools on my patch and speak to the children. A *Say No to Strangers* campaign was delivered to the schools by the police. The message came with a video and quite a catchy song. You can find it on YouTube. Kids loved it - even I quite liked it. One of the junior schools in my area was St Martin de Porres. I visited the school to deliver the message and just could not help myself. I was singing the song on my way up the path, I didn't think anyone was listening, so I changed the lyrics to make the song slightly more impactive. My version of the song went:

> ♫ *Say No to Strangers,*
> *They'll try and be your chum,*
> *Say No to strangers,*
> *They'll stick it up your bum.* ♫

I added a little jump at the end of the verse that looked like I was trying to avoid anal penetration - be it accidental or deliberate. I sniggered. Oh, the cleverness of me. Well, if the original song was catchy, the two or three children who watched my performance were hooked. In modern parlance, my song and dance routine went viral. Within fifteen minutes, dozens of kids in the playground were singing my song - they also included my little jump at the end. I hadn't even started my official visit but was concerned and thought that I might have to start looking for another job.

That morning, I was sitting in the headmaster's office, and not enjoying a cup of coffee. I was desperately hoping he couldn't hear the children in the playground singing. The refrains of the tune mixed with giggles floated in through his window. Finally, he snapped:

"PC Smith. It may be best if you allow my teachers to deliver the Say No to Strangers message to the children. There has to be some other area of bloody police work that you can be getting on with. Goodbye." He snatched my half-finished cup of coffee and pointed to the door. I never went back.

A year later, I met a class of children at Queensbridge School in Moseley. This was a large secondary modern school with a catchment area that included Balsall Heath, Moseley and Kings Heath. I had dealt with some of the kids from the school for some quite serious offences. Some of these children had their own, Say Hello to Strangers campaign, often adding, "This is a knife, now give me your wallet."

The headmaster thought that it might be a positive move for

the children to have an informal chat with a uniformed police officer. It was 11 am, and I was in a classroom with 25 children. The teacher went for a smoke break and just let me get on with it. The kids were great, it was going well. An Asian lad was sat on his own in the corner of the classroom. I could see he was covered in rubbish and he stank.

"What's happened to him?" I asked the class.

"Go on, Asif," a fat skinhead encouraged, "tell him. This is brilliant, man." Asif found his voice.

"What I do like is wind up the teachers, you know. Push their buttons and really annoy them." The skinhead encouraged him to continue. "Anyway, the deputy head comes into class this morning, and I was doing a number on him. Usually, I stop, you know before he explodes. Well, I must have sort of misjudged it. He picked me up and carried me like a rolled-up carpet along the corridor and down the stairs. He took me out of the back door to where the kitchens are. There are these massive, round industrial bins, right. He focking javelined me into one! It was full of slops," he blurted. "I waited in the bin; I didn't want to get out in case he killed me. Then I heard an ambulance coming." I asked if the ambulance crew had helped him out of the bin. "The ambulance wasn't for me. It was for the deputy. They took him away. He was having some sort of mental breakdown."

"What did you do then?" I asked, trying not to laugh.

"I came to my classroom to see you." I mentally crossed Queensbridge off my son's list of prospective schools.

In 1984, a permanent beat officer named PC Pete Monckton was on duty and strolling around his patch, in Kings Norton, without a care in the world. His police helmet was at its usual jaunty angle. Pete, like all beat officers, knew his area; and didn't care too much about what was happening elsewhere. Pete's casual attitude meant that some sergeants enjoyed giving him crappy jobs - just to wipe the smile off his face. This particular day, his police radio chirped up, he was sent to a report of an incident on the railway track near to Kings Norton police station. Pete questioned being sent.

"Sergeant... isn't that a job for the British Transport Police?"

"Monckton, we both know it is, but they haven't got anyone to send, so I'm sending you. Get on with it."

Twenty minutes later, PC Monckton radioed Control.

"Sarge, I'm on the railway track. Just to update the log... It was a train versus a pedestrian. For your information, I am with the train driver. Oh, and I'm also with the deceased."

"The deceased Monckton... the bloody deceased, may I remind you that you are not medically qualified to pronounce life extinct. Do your job and render first aid."

"Yeah, no problem, what sort of first aid would you suggest?"

"Well, Monckton, I suggest at the very least you try mouth-to-mouth resuscitation." There was a pause while PC Monckton mulled this instruction over.

"Righto, Sarge, I will have a good look around, and if I find the head, I will definitely give that a go."

I was now a part of a Community Action Team (CAT) responsible for Balsall Heath: twelve officers and two sergeants. Also part of the team was PC Les Yeomans, a handsome, rough-looking Brummie, with jet-black, centre-parted hair, and some serious facial scarring around his eyes. Les swore a lot; we all swore, but Les swore a lot. I can still picture him in his usual pose, hands on hips, wearing the new police NATO sweater, and screaming abuse at any member of the public who did not immediately comply with whatever instruction he was yelling.

Looking at life in the rear-view mirror, this was a strange time. If it was quiet on nights, I could pop into the front office and have a look at who was currently off sick. Sickness reports were attached to a clipboard that was hung up on the wall. Not exactly confidential in those days, was it? One morning I did just that and went through the sickness reports, I saw that Les Yeomans was off work with a sore throat. I amended the illness to make it far more exciting and exotic. I had no reason to think about my actions for seven years.

It's worth returning to Hughie Friel, his career took an unfortunate turn around this time. Having finished his shift at 10 pm, Hughie set off for a pint, at Tally Ho, the police club. He drove a Range Rover quite possibly the most bedraggled car in the country. He arrived at 10.30 pm. Phil, the manager, had already put the towels on and was busy counting that night's takings. Hughie asked for a pint of lager, and there were still a few people milling about. Phil was in a lousy mood and refused to serve Hughie, who was less than impressed. Hughie took a drag on his cigarette and glared at the barman.

"Phil, if I do not get a pint, I will destroy that fucking bowling green." Hughie pointed over his shoulder, with his thumb, in the direction of the bowling green. Now the bowling green to which he was referring was pristine. Visitors to Tally Ho would comment that it resembled a well-brushed snooker table. Phil was not to be swayed.

"The bar's closed, Hughie," Phil insisted. "You are not getting served, so why don't you just fuck off?" Hughie fucked off.

The morning after this exchange, the bowling green did not look quite so perfect. Someone had driven over the grass, performed a figure of eight manoeuvre, and then thrown in a handbrake turn just for good measure. The bowling green looked like it had been the subject of a terrorist mortar attack. To the untrained eye, it looked a lot like a Range Rover had driven over the bowling green. The untrained eye's opinion was of minor importance. What was of major importance was the forensic scientist's expert opinion. Having examined Hughie's car and recovered masses of the unique grass and soil mixture, which could only be found on the bowling green at Tally Ho, embedded in the tyre tread of all four tyres. His expert view was that Hughie's Range Rover was responsible for all of the damage that had been caused. Hughie was arrested, interviewed and charged. Hughie was suspended from work until his trial. At the Magistrates' Court Hughie was tried and convicted. Following his conviction, Hughie was sacked so he lodged an appeal, and some months later, his appeal was heard at the Crown Court.

Hughie accepted every shred of evidence the prosecution

had. He even admitted making the threat to damage the bowling green. He explained that he had jokingly made the threat to Phil, the bar manager, and then went to the toilet for a number two - I remember the jury laughed at that. He said he always parked his car directly outside the club entrance and left his keys in the ignition. Hughie added that he did this because it was a police club and, "If you cannot trust the people at a police club, then who can you trust?" His barrister asked Hughie if he could explain to the jury what he thought had happened on that fateful night. Hughie said that he had remembered something since his original trial. He explained that there must have been someone in the bar who had heard his threat to Phil. Someone who bore him a grudge, possibly because Hughie probably had a sexual relationship with that person's wife, or fiancée, or mother, or sister. When the real culprit saw Hughie go to the toilet, they seized the opportunity to drive Hughie's car over the bowling green, then return it to nearly the same spot that he had left it. He said that it was done maliciously so that he would be blamed for the damage. Hughie was asked if he could estimate how many colleagues could have taken umbrage regarding his inappropriate sexual activities. Hughie shrugged as if to say, how long is a piece of string? Amazingly Hughie was acquitted.

Following his return to work, Hughie ambled into the police payday disco at Tally Ho. I asked the DJ to play *An Innocent Man*, by Billy Joel for him. Phil, the bar manager, looked totally pissed off. I spoke to Hughie and asked him how the hell he had got away with it. Hughie laughed, pointed to his groin, and said that his cock had often dropped him in the shit, but on this occasion, he was delighted that it was able to get him out of it. Three months after being reinstated, Hughie was breathalysed and convicted of driving his car while drunk and sacked again. I tried, but failed, to catch him before he left the police. Not to say goodbye or anything. I just wanted to get my A-Z back from the crazy bastard.

Friday night and I was posted to a van patrol working 10 pm-2 am. We had a uniformed sergeant, eight uniformed officers, and Les Yeomans driving the marked police van - aggressively. We were driving away from Birmingham, and as it was 11.30 pm, loads of people were also leaving the city. Les was turning right off the Pershore Road. The back of our van was slightly sticking out into the dual carriageway. One of the cars driving out of the city beeped its horn.

"Who the fuck was that?!" Les exploded. Mick Hazelwood, who could actually see nothing as he was sitting in a police van that had blacked-out windows, told Les that a Red Sierra was responsible. In 1985 almost every other car was a Red Sierra. Les launched himself into action. Blue lights and two-tone audible warnings were deployed as we rejoined, but mostly ignored, the other vehicles on the road. A hundred yards in front of us was a Red Sierra. What were the chances? The driver of the Sierra, who was oblivious to our pursuit, pulled onto a garage forecourt by the Selly Park Tavern. He nipped into the garage. Our van skidded to a halt on the forecourt and stopped about an inch behind the offending Sierra. Les burst from the police van and slammed the van door shut.

We exploded with laughter, but what would Les do? As Les approached the Sierra, I could see an Asian man watching from the garage. Les climbed into the car, did a wheel spin on the forecourt, and drove off. The driver must have left his keys in the ignition. We were buckled with laughter, but then the bemused Asian approached. Our sergeant locked the doors of the van, then clambered into the back to hide with the rest of us. We stuffed our hands in our mouths to stifle the giggles. I never understood why police vans had blacked-out windows: perhaps it was for this very situation. Meanwhile, the confused Asian man was gently tapping on our van.

"Excuse me. That copper has just stolen my car, mate, what's happening? I've got to pick up a fare from Edgbaston in twenty minutes." We said nothing. What could we say? We waited while the man stood by our van, only feet away from nine grown men giggling like schoolgirls and shushing each other. Ten minutes later, his Sierra skidded onto the forecourt. Les exploded from the car and did not allow the cabbie to speak. He shouted and poked him several times in the chest; he told him he was lucky as he was going to let him off with a verbal warning. Then Les climbed back into our van and drove off into the night, leaving the cabbie standing on the forecourt, trying to piece together the events of the last ten minutes.

Woodbridge Road station, having been flattened, was rebuilt, and its official opening was scheduled to take place on 14 February 1986. The guest of honour was to be Edwin Shore, the Chairman of the West Midlands police Authority. He was not a popular choice, as he had gone on record with his view that 'Police rent allowance is a tax-free perk and should be withdrawn.' I embarked on a personal crusade to recruit a replacement guest of honour. I spoke to some local shopkeepers and Mr Luker, from the bakery next door, told me he was in touch with an elderly lady, Amy Jones, whose father had been a sergeant at the original Woodbridge police station. He added that Amy had lived in the station as a child. She sounded perfect. I checked her availability, and, although she was in a wheelchair, she said that she would be delighted to be the guest of honour.

Mr Shore, however, was not prepared to surrender the spotlight that easily. He requested that Amy's deceased father's police record should be examined, to ensure that his character assessment was exemplary. I searched the dusty cellars at the police headquarters, Lloyd House, and located Sergeant Jones's entire service record. It was all contained on one sheet of A3 paper. Not only was his career unblemished; Sergeant Jones had been awarded two Police Authority commendations in the late 1880s. One was for arresting a pickpocket, and the other was for stopping a runaway horse in Moseley village.

Amy was the focal point of the media when she formally cut the ribbon and opened the new police station. Mr Shore took a back seat. I counted this as a minor victory for my colleagues. There's a lesson here: don't be a dick to the people who work for you.

On 22 June 1986, the World Cup was being played in Mexico. England had reached the quarter-finals and been drawn to play against Argentina. The war over the ownership of the Falkland Islands meant there was an unpleasant backdrop to the fixture. With ten other officers, I was posted to a public order van: we were on standby at Bournville Lane, just in case there was any trouble. Then it happened. Diego Maradona, with all the skills of an Olympic volleyball player, 'spiked' the ball into our net. The referee missed the handball, and a goal was awarded. Then it was 'Off at Haydock' in pubs all around the country. The Beeches pub in Northfield, Birmingham really went for it, and we were dispatched to quell the riot. There were ten of us. I still remember our sergeant's motivational speech just before we all leapt from the van:

"Get stuck in, ladies," he growled, "these fuckers are all wind and piss. Never forget what Sir Winston Churchill said. We will fight them in the Beeches. That's right, the fucking Beeches. Charge." I reckon he had waited his whole life to deliver that line.

We separated into two groups: half entered the lounge, I went into the bar. For reasons I have never understood I was called an Argentinian-loving cunt. I knew precisely why the locals were so frustrated: there was a complete absence of anything Argentinian to vent their anger on. No restaurants, no vehicles and, worst of all, no actual Argentinians. In the absence of anything that they could patriotically destroy, the police were going to bear the brunt. We arrested the ten rowdiest. I explained to one of the detained that the offending player's name was actually Diego Maradona and not Dago

Motherfucker. The offenders were all charged.

Four months later the officers who had dealt with the incident were summoned to the Magistrates' Court as some of the defendants were intending to plead not guilty. At court, there was a bit of a stand-off (Mexican?) between the defendants' solicitors and the CPS. A full hour of horse-trading went on, charges were reduced, and all but one agreed to plead guilty to something. My prisoner was scheduled to plead guilty. I was just about to leave when one of the officers, who had dealt with events in the lounge, told me that the prisoner who was going to be tried would be worth watching. He piqued my interest, so I sat with him at the back of the court and waited. There was little prospect of my being called as a witness: I could relax.

The defendant, a tattooed dimwit, was sitting snarling in the dock. The hearing started, and the arresting officer winked at the policeman sitting next to me as he took the witness stand. He took the oath, introduced himself and asked the magistrates if he could refer to his pocketbook when he gave evidence. The magistrates, as usual, asked the officer when he made his notes up. *A point of law here* - if notes are made contemporaneously, then the officer must be allowed to refer to them. If they are completed after the event, then they have to be made as soon as possible, and then, with the permission of the court, they can be referred to. The officer stated that he had completed his notes at the time. This caused the magistrates to confer. After a few minutes, the chairman addressed the policeman:

"Officer. At the time, there was a full-scale riot going on. The court will allow you to refer to your pocketbook. But, in the opinion of this bench, you have damaged your own credibility."

The officer shrugged, took his pocketbook from the breast pocket of his tunic and began to give his evidence. He read out the date, the time, and who was with him. He continued to read from his pocketbook.

"As the van approached the Beeches pub, I could hear shouting and glasses being smashed. I entered the lounge, where I saw the defendant. He was standing on a table with his shirt off," the officer continued. "He," and he looked up to point at the accused, "was screaming, 'Come on, I will fucking kill the lot of you.' I said, get off the table, you will only get yourself into serious trouble. The defendant jumped off the table, picked up an empty bottle of Newcastle Brown Ale. He smashed the bottle and pointed the jagged end at me. He was no more than ten feet from me."

The defendant's solicitor interrupted.

"Did he say anything to you, Officer?"

"Yes he did, he said, 'What are you writing in that little book, you cunt?' Your Worships, it was at this juncture that I put my pocketbook and pen away and arrested the defendant for committing an offence under Section 5 of the Public Order Act."

CHAPTER 14
A HOLIDAY WITH HUGHIE

In January 1988 I was on weekly leave when I heard, on a local radio news broadcast, that a man been had been stabbed in Moseley. The police were treating the attack as attempted murder. The victim was in the hospital and not expected to live. An incident room was being set up at Woodbridge Road police station. This nasty enquiry was a matter for the CID. I had not been called in to assist.

A Home Office Large Enquiry System (HOLMES) computer suite had been set up on the first floor of the new Woodbridge Road station. Detectives arrived regularly to investigate serious crimes. They turned up in their flashy suits, wearing silk ties and cheap aftershave, and were far too important to speak to the local police officers. I needed to strike back on behalf of the woodentops. The gents' toilet was directly opposite my office. I had a plan. I used a cigarette lighter to heat the soap dispenser nozzle. Once molten, I altered its angle from squirt-onto-hand to splurt-onto-expensive-silk-tie. It worked a treat. Detectives would strut along the corridor, glance with contempt in the direction of my office, then stride into the toilet. A few minutes later I would hear, "Oh, for fuck's sake!" or "Jesus fucking wept!" Whatever cheap industrial hand cleaner being used by the police was impossible to remove from a silk tie. My childish campaign went on for years.

Female detectives didn't get off lightly either. I dimmed the lighting by removing a bulb from their toilet, then expertly placed cling film over the toilet bowl with sufficient sag to not be detected. The result was that several ladies had to go home for a complete change of outfit.

Getting back to the attempted murder, on this particular Friday, I had a dental appointment booked, and that involved me taking three buses to get to the Maypole area of Birmingham. The route took me through Moseley village. I broke my journey and popped into Woodbridge Road station, just to be nosey. There was a lot of activity, loads of busy detectives swanning around like they owned the place: confirmation that a police incident room was indeed being set up. I walked, uninvited, into the empty briefing room. There was a whiteboard with just one name written on it, Michael Walsh, and a half-dozen addresses attributed to him. He was the only suspect, and his arrest appeared to be a priority. I found a detective sergeant that I sort of knew. I had a quick check of his tie, it was silk and unblemished. I told him that I knew Walsh pretty well and that stabbing somebody was well out of character for him. He laughed and dismissed my assessment: he said that showed just how little I knew about 'Mad' Micky Walsh. He made it crystal-clear that I was not required to assist the investigation, and as it was my leave day, suggested that I should go home. I hoped his overtime would be sufficient to pay for a couple of new silk ties. I went to see my dentist. I returned to Moseley to catch my connecting bus home and, as I was about to get onto the 11C Outer Circle bus, Micky Walsh was getting off it. I let the bus go, and I arrested and cautioned Mr Walsh.

"Wolfie," he blubbered, "I had to stab him. He sank his teeth into my nose and wouldn't let go! What else could I do?" We walked the short distance to Woodbridge Road police station. At the station a lot more cars had arrived: I guessed by a lack of visible staff that everyone in the incident room was being briefed. I lodged my distraught prisoner with the office man, who made him a cup of tea and gave him a ginger nut biscuit. I went upstairs and found an empty office. There was something I had to do first, it only took five minutes.

Then I took a deep breath and knocked on the briefing room door.

"Enter!" the DCI shouted angrily. I walked into the briefing room. The sergeant I had been talking to earlier leant in to brief the DCI:

"That's Wolfie Smith," he said, loud enough for me to hear, "the prick I was telling you about earlier, boss."

I looked around, there were at least 30 detectives in the room. I made a mental note to buy shares in silk ties. The only female in the incident room was absent, following a visit to the toilet: she had to go home to get changed, apparently. The DCI pointed to me:

"Son, you shouldn't interrupt a briefing unless it's important. Now I'm going to assume it's not, so sit at the back of the room and listen. Who knows, you might actually learn something."

"But sir," I started.

"Sit down, twat," the DCI finished.

I sat down. The briefing continued; the victim had been repeatedly stabbed. Michael Walsh was a violent psychopath who would probably not be captured alive. Safety was of paramount importance. Six officers would attend each targeted address, dog handlers and firearms officers were on standby. I waited. With his staff briefed, it was time for the DCI to humiliate the only woodentop in the room. He turned to me, and 30 silk ties, with varying degrees of damage, also stared at me.

"Right, son, I know you are the beat man that knows Micky Walsh so what earth-shattering news do you have? Did Micky use to steal women's knickers off washing lines when he was a kid? Please, tell." He opened his hands wide, suggesting that I should now share my information with the class.

"Do you know where Michael Walsh is now, sir?"

"No," the DCI said and made a show of looking around the room. "Nobody does. That is why we are all here, you knob. Do you know where he is?" He was enjoying this. Internally I smiled.

"Yes, sir... Actually, he's downstairs. I have just arrested him on suspicion of attempted murder."

The DCI stopped smiling. He made his final attempt to shoot me down in flames. "Constable, get your pocketbook out and read me Walsh's reply to the caution, when you arrested him." He didn't think for one second that I would be able to comply. I produced my pocketbook and read:

"Wolfie, I had to stab him. He sank his teeth into my nose..." The DCI stopped me in full flow. "Okay, okay, enough. Go and write up your statement: you can interview Walsh under the supervision of DC Colin Abbotts. Right, I need to speak to the incident room staff so can you leave us for a few minutes, thank you... Wolfie." 26 of the 30 detectives were stood down. They were not happy, with me, as a weekend's overtime had just disappeared down the gurgler. I interviewed Micky Walsh, who made a detailed admission. Walsh was charged and received a lengthy custodial sentence, and the victim made a full recovery.

In July 1988, I was on a family holiday with my wife and my eight-year-old son Peter. We were enjoying fourteen days in Fuengirola on the Costa del Sol and sharing a villa with Hughie McGowan and his wife, Yvonne. The McGowan's took the opportunity to embark upon a fortnight's domestic dispute. The weather was fantastic, and we had a private pool. Hughie and I played a bit of golf, drank beer and relaxed. I never even tried to keep up with the amount of alcohol that Hughie was putting away. Hughie had turned a social pastime into an endurance event. One night, during a temporary ceasefire in the McGowan domestic hostilities, we all went out to a British pub in Benalmádena. They served cold San Miguel and had a karaoke machine, hardly British, but it was rather pleasant. Then I saw a man in the pub I recognised.

"Hughie, can you see that bloke in the corner? The one with the suntan, wearing the pink cardigan." Hughie subtly clocked him and then turned back to me.

"Wolfie, we're not the fucking fashion police. Anyway, it's your round."

"Hughie! It's Ronnie Knight." Hughie looked confused.

"The piano player?"

"Hughie, I don't even think there is a piano player called Ronnie Knight. It's Ronnie Knight, the armed bank robber, Britain's most wanted criminal."

Ronnie was sitting with a few people, and a particularly attractive blonde lady was paying him a lot of attention. She looked a bit like Ronnie's ex-wife, Babs Windsor, but was at least 30 years younger. Ronnie owned the bar, which meant that his young floozy was allowed more turns on the karaoke than anybody else. To the patrons' dismay, it was becoming apparent that Ronnie was most definitely not with her for her singing ability. I didn't want to intrude, but I did want a picture of him if I could get one. I had an idea.

"Peter, go and ask that man if we can have a photo taken with him." Who could refuse the request of my smart, polite, eight-year-old son? Well, it turned out that Ronnie Knight could. Peter came back within seconds.

"He told me to piss off, Dad." I went across to have a word with Mr Knight. It was pretty quiet in the pub as Ronnie's girlfriend had just finished dismembering Gloria Gaynor's *I Will Survive*. Silence reigned, I suspect because the patrons didn't want to applaud or encourage her in any way.

"Excuse me, Ronnie, can we have a photograph taken with you?"

"No, you can't, fuck off." Charming.

"I see. I suppose your fingerprints are out of the question."

"I fucking knew you two were the Old Bill." He laughed and agreed to have his picture taken with us. His only request was that I didn't sell it to *The Sun* newspaper. Seven years later, in 1995, Ronnie Knight was sentenced to eleven years in prison for his part in the 1983 six million pound armed robbery at the Security Express headquarters in Shoreditch, London. He admitted handling some of the proceeds, but he denied taking part in the theft. I never sold the photo.

On 3 January 1989, at the ripe old age of 33, I finally took my driving test. I was not confident about my chances. I attended in full uniform. I gambled everything on my examiner being pro-police. I took my truncheon and handcuffs out of my trouser pockets and placed them on the back seat of the car. I said:

"Christ, I am on a 2-10 later and what a tour of duty I had yesterday. I wouldn't be surprised if my driving isn't up to much today." I smiled pathetically; my examiner maintained the obligatory professional silence.

"In your own time, Mr Smith, drive out of the compound and watch out for the other cars." I waited and allowed the other drivers to drive away first. I then used the clutch, engaged first gear, and applied the accelerator. Nothing. I had forgotten to turn the engine on.

"I bet you thought you were in a Rolls Royce for a second there," I joked.

The examiner looked out of his window and tutted. 25 minutes later, I had finished.

"You have passed," the examiner said somewhat reluctantly, I thought.

"Was there anything that I could have improved on?" The examiner looked me straight in the eye. "Oh yes, most things," he said and walked back to the test centre.

On 15 April 1989, I was on duty at Villa Park for the FA Cup semi-final. It was a 3 pm kick off. I was posted to the Holte End, which was split to separate the Everton and Norwich City supporters. It was a warm, sunny day, and both sets of fans were in great spirits, especially those from Norwich, their green and yellow colours and Norfolk accents, were not usually a part of an FA Cup semi-final's make-up. Realistically Norwich did not expect to win, but in an FA Cup tie, you never knew.

I knew exactly what could happen in an FA Cup game, because on 5 February 1972 I was one of 14,313 spectators who crammed into Edgar Street, the home ground of Hereford United, for their FA Cup tie against the mighty Newcastle United. This was Hereford's seventh match in the Cup that season: our cup run started in November. The level of excitement in the town was at fever pitch. I had queued for hours with my friends to get a ticket for the game. In addition to the spectators inside the ground, hundreds more had climbed trees and pylons to see the match. Hereford had battled hard, but an 82nd-minute goal from Newcastle's Malcolm 'Supermac' Macdonald looked like it was going to win the game for the Division One side. As

Hereford fans, we responded with a foul and offensive chant:

> ♫ *Super Mac...*
> *Superstar...*
> *He wears frilly knickers,*
> *And a padded bra.* ♫

What happened next became a part of football folklore.

"Oh, what a goal! Radford is the scorer, the crowd are on the pitch. What a tremendous shot by Ronnie Radford," said John Motson on Match of the Day. Ricky George scored Hereford's winner in extra time. The whole of Hereford was ecstatic, and for me, football was never quite as good again. By the way, the week after Hereford United beat them, Newcastle went to Old Trafford and beat Manchester United 2-0.

Back at Villa Park, lots of fans brought transistor radios for updates on other games, or just to listen to the commentary of the match they were watching. Both semi-finals kicked off at the same time, and it was not long after the Villa Park game had started that fans and the police began to get updates from the other semi-final at Hillsborough between Liverpool and Nottingham Forest. The word 'fatalities' became a part of the news updates. By the time the Everton game finished, with a comfortable win for the Merseysiders, I remember that 15 people were believed to have died. That number would rise to the now famous 96.

The 46,553 spectators who watched the semi-final at Villa Park saw a football match and went home after it had finished. The same could not be said about the fans at Hillsborough.

There was a dark cloud hanging over English football. The game was to change forever. Graham Kelly, the voice of the Football Association, did his best to dignify events and proceedings. He could only work with the information that he was given by those in authority. People that he had no reason to question. After limited initial disclosure, the authorities blamed the Liverpool fans for just about everything.

The following day dozens of officers from the West Midlands were seconded to the Hillsborough Inquiry. I was not selected and was jealous of the officers who were. Why was the West Midlands police chosen to head this enquiry? Possibly because we were a large police force with a proven record of investigating major incidents and had secured the convictions of the Birmingham Six. We also had a robust Serious Crime Squad, so what could go wrong? Within two years, their credentials were not quite so impressive.

In August 1989, the Chief Constable, Geoffrey Dear, disbanded the Serious Crime Squad. Then in March 1991, the Birmingham Six were released and received apologies and millions of pounds in compensation for their mistreatment and wrongful convictions. Perhaps the West Midlands police were not quite as good at serious crime and major incident investigation as they thought. Detectives who had dined out for years on their pivotal roles in nailing the Birmingham Bombers reflected and remembered that they had only actually made the tea for the incident room staff.

In September 1989, a brothel was operating in Edgbaston Road, Balsall Heath. Our team, led by a chief inspector, with a sergeant and eight police constables, were ready to strike and close down this den of iniquity. Accompanying our team was a reporter and a photographer from the *Birmingham Evening Mail*. We were trying to hit a 3 pm newspaper deadline. At 2.45 pm a brand new red Sierra - see, I told you there were loads of them, turned up and the smartly dressed driver walked to the target address. We waited five minutes, and then the chief inspector called the strike. I hope this amount of time was arbitrary and that the chief inspector had no personal knowledge of how long it takes a punter to get into a compromising position with a prostitute in a brothel. We barged through the front door.

In the lounge, two topless women were stoned, kissing, singing and painting the walls. They were utterly oblivious to our entrance, presence and subsequent departure. In a downstairs bedroom, a prostitute was entertaining three Asian males: this did not involve cash and was purely recreational. Upstairs in the main bedroom the man, no longer wearing his suit, was *up to his nuts*, and with two crisp £10 notes on the floor, our mission was complete. Our sergeant physically pulled the punter out of the prostitute. Desperate to cross the finishing line, the punter continued to hump fresh air. I remember thinking that was never going to get the job done. The press requested that we brought everyone down the fire escape so that they could photograph proceedings: we were happy to oblige. The chief inspector had a vision of the Crown that comes with a promotion to superintendent.

While the press photographer was taking pictures, an Asian man at the top of the fire escape screamed out:

"Any fucker who takes my photograph will get their fucking head knocked off!" There was a pause: most of us knew what the response would have been if the senior officer and the press had not been there. I was busy internally drafting a response, something that would be firm with authority, and yet impress the *Birmingham Evening Mail*'s one million readers. While my reply was still being mentally proofread, I was almost deafened by Les Yeomans:

"Oi, cunt! If any fucker's swede is coming off his fucking shoulders, it will be your fucking fucker!" The photographer actually captured the moment. Les was predictive talking, two decades before the rest of us were predictive texting. I then heard the slamming of car doors, as the press and an embarrassed senior officer departed and left it with us.

CHAPTER 15
OUT OF THE CLOSET

In 1990 I was still in uniform working the same area but had moved to Woodbridge Road police station. The Sheriff of Moseley had returned. There had been some boundary and area changes, and also some advances in technology. All personal police records had been transferred onto a computer. Everything was input, printed out, then sent to each officer to sign and confirm as accurate. One morning the thick brown envelopes were delivered to our office: the data included next of kin, courses, awards, qualifications and sickness records, all pretty basic stuff. Then, like children with their school reports, we sat in the canteen and scrutinised our packages. Anything incorrect, which enhanced our personal data, would remain unchallenged, but anything detrimental, no matter how trivial, would be ferociously contested. It wasn't long before Les Yeomans exploded:

"That's fucking it." He sprang to his feet. With his personal record crumpled in his fist, rage in his eyes and murder in his heart, he declared, "I'm off to see admin, some fucker is going to pay for this." The vast empire that would become Human

Resources was still years away from creation. Les marched off to the admin office, and some of us followed. When we caught up with Les, he was shaking a spotty sixteen-year-old Youth Training Scheme lad by the throat. "Are you responsible for this, you twat?" Les mashed the sickness section of his computer printout into the youth's face. It was highly unlikely that the poor lad that Les was shouting at was responsible for the cheese and tomato sandwiches he'd brought in for his lunch. Dropping the whimpering teenager to the floor, Les jabbed a finger at a sickness entry dating back to 1984, that stated that he had been off work for fourteen days with 'vaginal warts'. Everything became clear. That was the entry that I had changed all those years before. With a Christian name of Lesley, it wasn't picked up in the migration onto computer. Les spent a good ten minutes chasing the terrified teenager around the office. I decided that it was not the right time to confess. Les remained none the wiser until, one night in September 2010, I made a full and frank admission. Les was still pretty angry, even though it was 26 years later.

In 1990 something else changed in the police: training took on a far more invasive role. All police trainers completed a residential training course at Harrogate. They became informed and, having seen the light, they returned to their respective police forces intending to put right all of the wrongs that had been pointed out to them. They were now *training ninja assassins*, armed with *buzzword daggers* to drive through the hearts of the unenlightened. The rest of us just thought that their course had consisted of having had their brains drilled out, and an intelligent dog being allowed to shit in the hole. More officers seemed to get into trouble on training courses than on the streets. Most classes started the same way: we would sit in a circle and introduce ourselves. Because of the sheer size of our force, it was unlikely that I would know everyone, or possibly even anyone on any course. We were all somewhat guarded. Only the naïve or the stupid ever actually opened up. One Monday morning, I was on a constable's refresher course. Twelve of us sat in a circle, one instructor talking and the other busy writing. What was he writing? Christ knows: no one had even spoken.

"Good morning, I'm Bob," said the talking trainer, "my colleague is Dave who will be taking notes during the lessons. This is only for our benefit, and there's nothing for you to worry about." All twelve of us were worried. "Starting in a clockwise direction, can you introduce yourselves? Names, length of service, marital status, that sort of thing." I had been before and had deliberately taken a seat in the middle, ensuring that I would not have to go first. The first victim gave his name, adding that he was married and had 12 years in the job. The introductions continued until the fourth officer took a deep breath, stood up, and said:

"My name is George." A slight tremor in his voice. "I've got 8 years service, and I'm not married. I've never said this before, but for some reason, I feel strong enough to say it today. I am gay. There it is, I've said it." George blew out a deep breath, sat down and stared intently at his shoes. Dave's writing hand was a blur he was scribbling for all he was worth. There was a murmur from the group, but Bob insisted that the introductions continued. Then it was my turn:

"I'm Wolfie Smith. I have got just over ten years in the job. My marital status is currently on a life support machine." Some of my classmates smiled, but Bob looked unimpressed and thought that I might not be taking the course seriously. George continued to stare at his feet. The penultimate officer seemed to be getting more and more agitated: as his turn approached his legs twitched, and he was scratching his head nervously. He stood up to introduce himself, he took a huge breath, exhaled, and with his voice shaking, he spoke:

"Gents, I'm Simon," he began, falteringly. "I have been in the police for 14 years. I am married, and I have three children." He raised his palm to indicate that he had not finished speaking. "Because George has shown such courage today. I have also found the strength to end the lie that I have been living all of my life. My name is Simon. I am gay. And I am proud to be gay."

Dave was scribbling at such a speed that his pen was not visible to the naked eye. I thought it possible that his notebook would catch fire. There was a stunned silence. Simon was now sobbing, and the trainers were in a state of shock. Nobody spoke. Finally, George stood up and addressed the group.

"For fuck's sake, I was only joking. I'm really sorry, Simon." The talking trainer took charge.

"Right. No one speaks or leaves this classroom. I'll be back shortly."

Dave the scribe did not have anything to write, although he could have written: 'PC Smith has just pissed himself laughing'.

We waited for twenty minutes, then Bob returned to the class with an angry, red faced superintendent, who addressed all of us:

"I'll keep this short. This course never happened. Go back to your areas, and report to whatever twat is unfortunate enough to be in charge of you. Get up and go. Now." We all stood up to leave. Bob whispered quickly into the ear of the superintendent, who made one more announcement:

"Wait," he called out, "the really clever fucker, with the first name George, can make his way to my office, now!"

The entire course had lasted 25 minutes.

In June 1991. I was one of six beat officers sat in our office at Woodbridge Road, drinking tea and chatting. Richard Davies, another member of our team, burst in and screamed:

"You're all anti-Semitic, racist bastards. I'm reporting this, and you lot are deep in the fucking shit." Then he stormed off. We looked at each other and had no idea what he was talking about. Richard was on our team, he was really well liked. Richard had been trying for years to get an attachment to the Mounted Branch. Frustratingly, it looked like it was never going to happen.

"Wolfie," an unusually rattled Brian Bridgewater fumed, "if he talks to me like that again, I will fucking knock him out." An hour later, Inspector Pete Hood turned up. He put his police hat on after he parked his car and left it on as he entered the station. This was ominous: Pete Hood was a fair and practical bloke. He looked at our group and selected Brian; he told the rest of us to wait in our office, adding that we were not to discuss the incident. It was not hard to comply, as we had no idea what he was talking about. Brian was with Pete Hood for ten minutes, then they both came back to our office. Inspector Hood stood in the doorway and glanced around the room, muttered, "Wankers," then left. Brian walked into our office, looking a bit shocked.

"You're not going to believe this," he said. Brian explained. There was a popular television programme on ITV called *Spitting Image*: it ripped the piss out of celebrities, politicians and sports stars. It was hilarious, poor old Steve Davies, the snooker player, was slaughtered every week. His problem was that he needed a nickname, something similar to what his rivals had: 'Whirlwind' Jimmy White and Alex 'Hurricane' Higgins. The Spitting Image programme decided that his snooker name should be, Steve 'Interesting' Davies. As it was an amusing fit, someone decided to insert the word interesting into Richard Davies's name, so he became Richard 'Interesting' Davies. In time it became abbreviated to Interesting Davies, and finally to 'ID'. On the morning Richard exploded he could hear that we were talking about him, and thought that he was being referred to as a Yid. Now there were two things about Richard that none of us knew, and before this, they were of absolutely no importance. Firstly, Richard was Jewish, and secondly, his middle name was Israel.

The police had a funny way of defusing potential racist allegations. Within a few weeks, Richard Israel Interesting Davies started an attachment to the Mounted Branch.

In 1992 a new inspector was put in charge of our team. I must have looked too happy or been smiling too much. Anyway, she took one look at the cut of my jib and decided that I was the finest candidate for shift work that she had met in a long time. There was no discussion and no appeal process. It was made clear to me that if I felt really strongly that I had suffered an injustice, then I could always go to the toilet and have a little cry. I was abruptly flung onto D-Unit at Belgrave Road. My new inspector was Phil Walsh, who had been an excellent detective sergeant, before he had been promoted. If he had investigated his new shift member to see what I was bringing to the team, well, he was going to be pretty disappointed.

The first mistake I made was presenting him with an annual leave request on my first day, and he took that as a personal insult. The shift pattern had not changed since I joined. It was tiring, but at least I was now a panda car driver. That meant that when it was cold and quiet on nights, I could have a crafty little power nap with the car heater on. Over the years, purely through repetition and osmosis, I learned how to do my job. I had also worked out how to *skive to survive*, not a trait that my supervision was ever impressed with. Mr Walsh did not speak to me for my first three months on his shift. On parade, he just checked and signed my pocketbook and dropped it on the table in front of me. So that was how it was going to be, then. I started working hard and became a competent panda driver, which was not as difficult as I feared. The time went really quick, and I actually enjoyed myself. Eventually, after five months, Mr Walsh had to speak to me, as it was time for my appraisal. A few pleasantries were exchanged to start with. Then he ripped into me:

"Do you know why I don't like you?" I told him I had no idea, so he explained. "Some people try really hard to do this job and are useless at it, and they always will be. You don't even try and are actually quite good. Just think how much better you could be if you actually made a bit of an effort, you lazy cunt." I briefly contemplated going to the toilet for a little cry. Sensing this, Mr Walsh offered some support:

"Oh by the way, if you're looking for sympathy, you'll find it between shit and syphilis in any decent dictionary." Then he added something that changed my career. "Keep grafting the way you are, then come and see me in three months and we will discuss your future. However, if your work rate drops, I will sack you. Understood?"

I understood.

I started to get the occasional nod on parade for my arrests, and as time passed, hostilities ceased, and we were on speaking terms. We were both warned to attend Birmingham Magistrates' court. I was still emotionally scarred from my first court experience and told Mr Walsh the details on the car ride to Birmingham. I was scheduled to follow him into the witness box. He gave evidence for over an hour. My brain was working overtime. What could be taking so long? Finally, Mr Walsh walked out of the court looking, for him anyway, pretty flustered. The court usher called out:

"Police Constable Vincent Smith." Shit. I was going to have

to give evidence. I walked past Mr Walsh trying to read his expression, desperate for a nod, a smile or a wink. Nothing. As I brushed past him, he whispered:

"Well, that's fucked it." My legs wobbled. I shuffled to the witness box, stuttered through the oath, and introduced myself. I started mentally rehearsing the words of the formal police caution, just in case. The prosecuting solicitor asked me to confirm that I had been on duty with Mr Walsh on the day in question. There was a short pause then he added, "Neither the defence nor I have any questions for you, Officer. You may stand down." In a daze I left the court. I could see Mr Walsh waiting for me. He was sitting on one of the stone benches, which made sense, as he couldn't stand because he was laughing so much.

Later that day, Mr Walsh called me into his office and mapped out my career. He told me to make an application for the CID, which would definitely be unsuccessful. That I should then take and pass the Sergeant's exam, and make a successful application to join the CID. He added that when I eventually became a detective, I should try to get all of my cases to court and let the magistrates or a jury make decisions of guilt or innocence. He added that too many coppers think they have the right to decide what should happen with their cases. The final piece of advice he gave me, once my case was put before a court, my job was finished: it was up to the court to decide the outcome. I never forgot what he said. Looking back, Mr Walsh gave me the kick up the backside that I needed.

In 1992 I watched a film with my son Peter, and that film changed his life. I enjoyed the movie; Peter watched it again and again. After four days and countless viewings, he decided that when he grew up, he was going to be a jet fighter pilot. The film was, of course, *Top Gun*. I didn't have the heart to tell Peter that there was no one to whom he was related that had the jet fighter pilot's gene and that he was going to have to complete the full four years' training. Peter's focus and commitment never wavered, and after he left university, he became a fighter pilot. I told this story to a mate years later, who said that it was a good job that my son did not get inspired by the film *Star Wars*. Otherwise, he might now be a Wookiee. Still, it shows what you can do when you knuckle down and aim for something. When I look back, it's nice to think that my son and I, purely by chance, both started working hard at the same time.

On the afternoon of Sunday, 5 July 1992, I was busy getting drunk in the Acorn pub, Winson Green. It was a christening celebration for a friend of mine, Peter O'Dowd's, son Pierre. The licensee of the pub, Chris Stapleton, was both arranging and playing the live music. Chris announced that a twelve-year-old lad was about to make his musical debut onstage:

"So everybody... can you please put your hands together for, Peter." There was a loud cheer. On the stage, to my astonishment, was my son, Peter, belting out a Jerry Lee Lewis number on the piano.

"Can you not frigging sing, son?" someone shouted. I couldn't identify the heckler but stopped looking when a young girl, around the same age as my son, jumped onto the stage and sang along with him. She was fantastic and was the older sister of Pierre.

Just after midnight on 18 November 1993, a school minibus crashed on the M40. A teacher and twelve children died as a result of that collision. The last child to die was Charlene O'Dowd - the little girl who had joined my son onstage. I went to the funeral in Kidderminster; I struggled to cope. I was sitting in the church with Hughie. As a distraction, I wrote out Rudyard Kipling's poem *If* on the back of his funeral mass card. The grief was raw. Hughie and I joined the family for an after service celebration of Charlene's life. Incredibly, Peter O'Dowd who, for his own reasons, had given up drinking ten years previous remained sober for the funeral. Hughie and I needed to numb our pain. We left the function, found the roughest pub in Balsall Heath, and went on a bender. We started on the locals, scattering pool balls and knocking over drinks: we just wanted a fight, needing to feel some physical pain to relieve our emotional anguish. Still wearing suits and black ties, the patrons probably worked out that we were in a self-destruct mode and decided, on this occasion, to just leave us alone.

God bless you, Charlene O'Dowd. Rest in Peace.

Before I made a successful CID application, I was posted to the Divisional Crime Support Unit (DCSU) at Edward Road, Balsall Heath. The station was a big old Victorian house that had been refurbished to accommodate various police squads. The rear courtyard was a secure area where police vehicles were parked. My detective sergeant was Derek Whitehouse, he was an ex-Royal Marine, and, although he had left the Marines, the Marines would always be a part of him. Derek encouraged me to learn and recite his favourite poem, *Vitae Lampada*. Derek told me that as I was studying for the Sergeant's exam, it would be my job to ensure that our team's actions were mostly legal. A bespectacled, wispy bearded, graduate looking probationer wandered into our office with a question; Derek did not like graduates. Derek was busy plotting the execution of a search warrant in Sparkbrook and working out how we could cause as much havoc as legally possible. Derek paused, looking the nerd up and down.

"Do you want something, Sonny?" he growled. The graduate nodded.

"Sarge," he whined, "what's the difference between an arrest by a police officer and a citizen's arrest? You know an arrest made by a member of the public. It's for a project." I expected this to be referred to me and went to answer; Derek raised his hand and stopped me. He faced the probationer.

"In essence," he said, with authority, "they are very similar. But if a criminal is lucky enough to get arrested by a member of the public, then they don't usually get a searing pain in their bollocks. Anything else?"

Derek was a natural leader and not someone to be trifled with. I did see Derek punched to the ground on one occasion. The guy who knocked him down was a pretty tough cookie. How tough? Well, a few years later, at a Coroner's inquest, his family insisted that it took at least eight prison officers to murder him while he was on remand.

On the same team was Tony Taylor, an experienced detective, who had his own way of working. He had an informant who produced enough intelligence to keep us busy all day, every day. Tony was different from the other detectives. He always had a two-day stubble, and for some strange reason, he wore a red and white tea towel around his neck: he looked like a middle eastern terrorist. Tony would go missing for days, then breeze into the office, and declare "*Bonjour, Derik*", to our sergeant, who would go nuts. Tony had to be left to his own devices, top notch information meant quality prisoners which resulted in loads of overtime. Tony had a couple of interests that he managed to fit around his job: he played a game of squash every day and had a keen eye for antiques, old furniture and artefacts. Tony could often be found rooting through builders' skips outside police stations, rescuing discarded police furniture, which he repaired and sold.

Another thing about Tony, he was the only police officer that I ever met who was even more terrified of giving evidence at court than I was. Having worked undercover on an investigation, the defence barrister had absolutely ripped him into little pieces in the witness box. Whenever the possibility of a court attendance loomed, Tony used the medical scheme to see a consultant about some minor ailment. His consultant would promptly schedule a medical procedure, the details of which Tony relayed to the CPS. Tony would be stood down as a witness. As the operation date approached, Tony without any fuss would just cancel the operation. Clever.

Tony was a regular visitor to the Biddle & Webb auction house, which is just off the Ladywood Middleway near to Birmingham city centre. Tony and I were out and about in an unmarked car. At 9.15 am, we were parked outside Biddle & Webb waiting for it to open. Over the radio, details were broadcast of an armed robbery at a post office in Sparkbrook. Being keen, I suggested that we should at least make towards the area. Tony was having none of it, and as I was in the passenger seat, he had cast the deciding vote. I listened to the radio for updates. The description of the offender was circulated: An Afro-Caribbean male, six feet tall, with glasses, and wearing a combat jacket. The robber had jumped into his getaway car and was chased by the police. Initially, he managed to lose them. We never moved. Tony kept checking his watch. The cops kept finding and losing the suspect. Given the sightings, with every follow and loss, he seemed to be trying to find us.

The offender's car was no more than a hundred yards away and directly in front of us. We never moved. A six-foot-tall, Afro-Caribbean male, with glasses and wearing a combat jacket ran past us. Tony sighed, and finally, we moved. We gave chase, and as we played squash most days, we were quite fit. We followed the suspect through an alleyway, which leads to Digbeth, just opposite the police station. The suspect turned left and ran into a Nat West bank. I did not know it, but the Nat West had been a hugely profitable place for him to visit on previous occasions; that was not the case on this day, though. As Tony and I chased him into the bank, I saw the suspect's heels as he ran up some stairs. Tony went to follow. I stopped him because I had actually been to the bank the week before: I knew that the upstairs area was totally secure. We waited at the bottom of the stairs and when the thief ran back down, we tackled and arrested him. Fortunately, for us, the armed part of the robbery at the post office was two weightlifting bars that had been taped together and placed in a carrier bag, to look like a shotgun, but we had no way of knowing that. Jubilant, we took our prisoner to Acocks Green police station and lodged him in the cell block. Tony and I went into the CID office to brag about our heroic arrest.

The local Detective Sergeant Tom Kenny tried to not look too impressed and told me to make him a cup of tea. Tony Taylor was delighted: he had worked out that this arrest would result in our working the weekend, and that we would rake in a boatload of overtime. I made Tom Kenny his tea and went to put his cup on his desk. In that anal way that some people try to protect their workspace from tea stains, Tom Kenny slid a recent Midlands Crime Intelligence circulation under his cup. This was an internal document that contained CCTV photographs of suspects committing offences. There were pictures of our prisoner committing three armed robberies at the Nat West bank in Sheldon. I quickly swapped the MCI for some plain paper and left. I showed it to Tony, who mentally upgraded his family's annual holiday. The offender was a well-spoken, courteous law student, who had never been in trouble with the police. He came from a decent family in Solihull. His mother was a surgeon, and his father an anaesthetist.

Tony had a different way of dealing with suspects.

Instead of threats and unpleasantness, Tony tried sympathy, understanding and kindness. Tony bought the suspect, whom I shall call Dwayne because that is his name, McDonald's meals, *The Times* newspaper and a law magazine. Tony wanted admissions, but he also wanted Dwayne to admit the offences at court so that he would not have to give evidence. Tony's interview was genuinely kind and caring. Dwayne gave an incredibly detailed account of the four robberies that he had committed. I watched how Tony Taylor approached interviewing. There was more than one way to skin a cat, it seemed. Dwayne made one request, before his mum found them: could we please dispose of all of his copies of *Big Jugs*, which were hidden under his bed? There was no shortage of volunteers for that job. Dwayne pleaded guilty at Crown Court and was sentenced to six years imprisonment for the robberies he had committed. Tony Taylor was delighted, not about the sentence, but the guilty plea meant that he did not have to attend court.

Our intelligence officer was a huge man-mountain called Les Gough. He must have weighed twenty stone, and Les could punch hard, really hard. Les treated our teams' police vehicles like his own personal carpool, and once he had car keys in his hand, no one was ever going to get them from him. It pissed us all off, more than just a little. On the Monday after our heroic arrest, Tony Taylor told me to be outside my house at precisely 4.30 am on Tuesday morning. At light o'clock the next day he collected me, and we drove to Edward Road. En route, he told me that I did not have the security clearance to be briefed until we arrived at the nick. Fair enough, this must be important.

At the station, Tony led me to one of our crime cars, a silver four-door Ford Escort. As per usual, I sat in the front passenger seat. Tony handed me half of a two-pound bag of flour, a funnel, and a rag. Then Tony showed me how to pour the powder into the air vents on the dashboard. We filled the vents, then wiped down the car, leaving no trace of our actions. Tony pointed all the vents towards the driver's seat and set the control to maximum blow.

Tony had briefed our Detective Inspector, John 'Bosher' Pestridge, who spoke to Les Gough when he came on duty. Bosher told Les to drop some papers off at Lloyd House. When Les saw car keys on one of our desks, he grabbed them and said to us that he was doing a job for the boss, and added that if we wanted the car, then we could all just fuck off. We protested, Les squealed with delight and plodded off to the car pound.

As Les approached the car, the entire DCSU was watching through the first-floor windows: there must have been over 30 officers and staff, all waiting in anticipation. Les wore spectacles and was in plain clothes. Come to think of it, I don't think police uniform has ever been made in his size, if he'd turned up at the police stores, they would have had to wallpaper him in a blue flock. We had a perfect side-on view. Les gunned the engine, the flour exploded like an airbag. The entire car interior was instantly white. It looked like someone had Tippexed the windows. Les roared, then tried to escape the blizzard inside the car. He fell out of the car and looked like a pissed-up snowman. Then he blindly groped his way back to his feet using the car for leverage. Les was looking for the culprits but couldn't see anything. He realised why and removed his glasses. Les Gough stood like Everest, white from head to toe, except for two perfectly round circles where his glasses had been. Barely able to breathe for laughing, we ducked down at the windows. Les, still yelling curses at the courtyard, stomped towards our office, leaving a thick, white smoke trail behind him. He was going to punch someone really, really, really hard. By the time Les walked into our office, we were back at our desks. Though he looked hilarious no one laughed. Tony had positioned himself next to the fire escape door. Les stared at him, he was reasonably sure that Tony was responsible, but looking for some sort of confirmation before he dismantled him. Tony was fifteen feet from Les. Tony made eye contact with Les. There was a hush in the office before Tony asked Les: "Everything all right, flower?" That was enough. Les roared and advanced on Tony, turning over a desk that was in his path. Tony burst through the fire escape giggling his head off and fled; he didn't come back to work for four days. I really enjoyed my time with Tony Taylor. I learned a hell of a lot from him.

While working for Derek Whitehouse, I became qualified to Sergeant. Promotion was a three-part process - a theory exam and a practical exam, followed by a promotion board. I passed both exams and then sat before a panel of two senior officers and a Federation representative. I gave reasonably straightforward answers to the questions I was asked. It was all going fine until the chairman's final question, which I thought was a bit loaded:

"PC Smith, what would you say is your greatest weakness?"

If I had answered honestly, I would never have been promoted. So I told the board that my greatest weakness was that I just had too many strengths. I passed and was put on a list of successful constables waiting for a sergeant's vacancy, somewhere in the West Midlands.

CHAPTER 16
GET IN THE HOLE AND A PAIN IN THE ARSE

I contacted Warwickshire police in 1994. My informant suggested the name of a possible suspect responsible for a recent murder in Nuneaton. I was keen to demonstrate that crime investigation was an arena where I could shine. My time as a detective constable could be limited, as my promotion was imminent. In 1994 my *snout* fell into the category of being thoroughly tried and tested. I drafted an intelligence log, which I needed to deliver into the hands of the Warwickshire detectives. All that I required was the operational name to complete my report. I rang the incident room in Nuneaton. I spoke to a police constable, who could not have been less interested in what I had to say. I asked:

"Can you tell me the operational name for the Carol Wardell murder enquiry?"

"Do you have a pen?"

I confirmed that I had and waited. There was a pause; I heard the sound of shuffling papers. He was not in any rush.

"Right. The official operational name for the Carol Wardell murder is... the Nuneaton Murder." That could not be right: each police force generated random unique operational names for staffing and budgets.

"Okay. So what will be the operational name if there is another murder in Nuneaton this year?"

"Well, I suppose the operational name for that extremely unlikely occurrence will likely be, the other fucking Nuneaton murder." He put the phone down. I managed to get the information to the detectives later that day; though well intended it did not assist the investigation, and that probably explains the officer's attitude. Warwickshire police encouraged their suspect Gordon Wardell to take part in an appeal to the public for information and witnesses. Mr Wardell's performance was woeful and probably helped convict him.

A few weeks later I read in a newspaper:

Gordon Wardell was remanded in custody for eight days when he appeared in court charged with murdering his wife Carol, a building society manager. Mr Wardell, 41, was also accused of burglary at the Woolwich Building Society office in Nuneaton, Warwickshire, where his wife worked, and with stealing more than £14,000.

There was no application for bail during his five-minute appearance before Nuneaton magistrates, and reporting restrictions were not lifted. Mr Wardell stood in the dock and was flanked by two plain-clothed police officers. He spoke only three times to confirm his name, age, and address. Wardell was charged with murdering his wife at Meriden or elsewhere on

11 or 12 September 1994 and with a burglary at the Woolwich Building Society office in Nuneaton on 12 September 1994

The body of 38-year-old Mrs Wardell was found dumped in a lay-by near Nuneaton on 12 September 1994. She had been asphyxiated. On the 21 December 1995, Wardell was convicted of murder, and ordered to serve a minimum of 18 years' imprisonment.

On Sunday 24 September 1995, I was part of a four-ball golf team playing in a charity event at the Forest of Arden Golf Course. Steve Rooney, a friend from Moseley Golf Club, Billy Doyle, a licensee, and Hughie McGowan, made up the quartet. Steve was the only decent golfer. I wasn't too bad, but Billy and Hughie's golf swings would not have been out of place in an All-Ireland hurling final. It was a serious golf competition with some decent prizes, none of which our team would be winning. It was only by allowing Steve to tee off at the first hole that we were able to bluff our way onto the course. After only a few holes, Steve bailed from his serious approach, relaxed and enjoyed the Sunday morning stroll, which realistically was all it was ever going to be. The reason the event was so popular was that the 31st Ryder Cup was being played at Oak Hill in the USA at the same time. The competition was on a knife-edge, with the Americans leading 9-7 going into the final day's singles matches. On Saturday, the second day of the Ryder Cup, Costantino Rocca had a hole-in-one at the 6th hole, which was only the fourth ace in Ryder Cup history.

Our golf was finished just after midday, so we adjourned

to a large marquee bar and started drinking. The competition prizes were to be awarded at 6 pm. A charity auction was scheduled to be the final event of the day: being curious, we had a look at the items in the auction. Billy saw a football signed by the 1982 Aston Villa European cup winning team. Billy commented that the football would look great behind the bar of his pub. Inside the marquee, a TV had been set up to show the last day of the Ryder Cup. To avoid disturbing the golfers at the Forest of Arden, the sound had been muted, but at least we could see what was happening. Loads of fellow competitors decided that the marquee was an excellent place to spend that Sunday afternoon. Hughie, if not the best golfer, was off quite a low handicap when it came to drinking.

The 18th hole at the Forest of Arden is the course's signature hole, a 211-yard par 3 with a water hazard in front of the green. To generate further revenue for the charity, anyone could place a live bet on any player to hit the green from the tee. Hughie watched the action for a while and then started to place bets. When Hughie joined us in the marquee, he looked pretty pleased with himself and told us he was winning a small fortune.

At about 4 pm Howard Clark was on the 11th tee at Oak Hills, and he hit a hole-in-one. There was a cheer in the marquee, and a few minutes later, Hughie came in to see if he was missing anything. Hughie sat down and started to count the his winnings. Hughie looked up at the television and Sky Sports were showing a replay of Costantino Rocca's hole-in-one the previous day. Hughie said:

"I saw that yesterday, that was some fecking shot. I don't

think there will be a hole-in-one today." Hughie carried on counting his winnings. Steve, Billy and I, from the microglances we gave one another, all had the same idea. It was still in the embryonic stage, and we had to proceed with the utmost caution. I nodded at Billy, who picked up the baton and ran with it.

"I wouldn't be so sure about that, Hughie: there is a shedload of quality golfers playing in that Ryder Cup thing." Hughie stopped counting his money, put his bookie's hat on for a few seconds, and made a decision:

"Billy, I will give you ten to one there will not be a hole-in-one today at the Ryder Cup, will you take the bet?" Hughie was staring at Billy; so were Steve and I, but we were nodding.

"Hughie put me down for £20, to win £200." As the Irish do, they spat on their hands, and a firm handshake sealed the deal.

Hughie popped out to place bets on the 18th green challenge but came in to sit with us more often, ensuring that Billy did not make a run for it. The four of us were looking up at the silent screen when Sky Sports obliged. They showed Howard Clark on the 11th tee hit what three of us already knew was the sweetest strike of his career. Steve Rooney jumped up and shouted, "Get in the hole!" The golf ball obeyed Steve's instruction. Only three people in the marquee erupted when the ball fell into the hole, but we made enough noise to fool the now head-in-hands Hughie who was distraught. If only Hughie had looked up at the screen, he would have seen that Howard Clark was now playing the 14th hole. Hughie kept offering all sorts of bets that afternoon, to try to recoup his losses, but there were no takers. We carried on drinking.

The auction started. I asked Billy when he was going to 'fess up to Hughie. Billy said probably at the end of the night, but he intended to enjoy Hughie's pain for as long as possible. The Aston Villa football came up for auction. I had almost no money left. Billy said he would pass, and Steve Rooney, as a Birmingham City fan, declared he would prefer to bid for a steaming hot elephant turd. Hughie wasn't with us. The bidding for the football started, and quickly it was up to £120, then the bidding stalled. From the back of the marquee Hughie McGowan's loud Irish voice shouted:

"Two hundred pounds and let that be the fucking end of it!" Hughie marched up to the stage with a handful of £20 notes. He counted out £200 and collected the football. Hughie walked over to join a stunned Billy, Steve and me. Hughie threw the ball to Billy, and said:

"Put that behind your bar, Billy, and that's me and you quits." I think Hughie then went off to the toilet for a little cry. Billy turned to Steve and me:

"Hughie can never know what has happened here today. Otherwise, he will murder the fucking three of us." We never told Hughie, but we did tell everyone else. Years later the subject cropped up in the pub. Hughie said that it was Steve Rooney's actions that had annoyed him the most. Hughie explained that every time he thought about what had happened, all he could remember was Steve Rooney shouting, "Get in the hole!"

"I'll give him get in the fucking hole when I see him." I had a quiet word with Steve.

The first time I had the pleasure of working with DC Paul 'Punchy' Waldron was during Christmas in 1995. We were the CID duty cover for the Birmingham South area and paired up for the week, 7 nights, 9 hours a night, working from 10 pm to 7 am with responsibility for the serious crime incidents in our area. Punchy, as the senior detective, insisted that he would be doing all the driving, and boy, that suited me. Over the years Punchy and I had the occasional fallout but never about who was going to be driving. He was nicknamed Punchy because of a legend, probably created by him, that he had thumped a couple of sergeants early on in his service.

Punchy had been a detective for years, long before I stepped into the fold, and had served on national and regional crime squads. He could be trusted to deliver results whenever possible, and with Punchy, it was usually possible. He was just over 6 feet tall, well built, and his blond hair was swept back. Punchy always looked smart and professional. He could more than look after himself. He was confident, and that sometimes came across as cocky. Impressively I never saw him panic, and never saw him take a backward step, ever.

In the early 1980s, Paul Waldron was a detective working at Queens Road. His detective inspector was a fearsome character, Jim Murphy, who was from whatever the education system that preceded *old school* was called. Murphy ran the CID at Queens Road with a rod of iron. Punchy was a young, thrusting detective keen to make his mark and impress. He lived a hectic life, which mostly revolved around the job. DI Murphy insisted that his staff were punctual. The early turn shift started promptly at 8.00 am, and his detectives swiftly found out that they were better off reporting sick than being late. One morning Punchy arrived at Queens Road in a bit of a flap. It was 8.10 am, and he was late. He was simultaneously tying his shoelaces and trying to button his shirt as he burst into the station. In the CID office, Punchy saw his sergeant who was sitting ominously shaking his head. He told Punchy to go upstairs and wait outside Mr Murphy's office, adding that he was not to enter until he was called in.

The DI's office was at the end of a corridor. Even the unflappable Punchy was having a bit of a twitch. He knew better than to make up some flimsy excuse. Mr Murphy would just attack him. No, he thought, it was better to just take this one on the chin. The inspector's door was slightly ajar: Punchy could hear a noise coming from inside. After listening for a few seconds, Punchy, being a detective, deduced it was definitely the sound of a cock being sucked. Through the small gap, Punchy could see the legs of the CID typist, who was kneeling by Jim Murphy's chair. Fucking hell, thought Punchy, I was only ten minutes late, I hope he doesn't call me in to finish him off. After a few minutes, a post-orgasmic shout emanated from the office, which almost cut the police station in half.

"Waldron. Get your arse in here. Now."

Punchy entered as the typist exited: she was wiping her mouth with a tissue. Punchy wasn't the only one going to be taking it on the chin that morning. The detective inspector was smiling: he delivered his bollocking.

"Punchy. See what you can get when you bother to get to

work on time. Don't be fucking late again."

Getting back to our week of nights, our duties included giving advice and guidance to the shift. Every arrested prisoner that was going to be dealt with by the morning CID was accompanied by a paperwork package. Also, we drafted a night-note that included briefing points for the morning CID. That note was always sought out and read by senior management, a bunch of people who read it out of curiosity. If anything significant had happened during the night, they wouldn't have to read about it, they would have been called out to deal with it. The area detective inspector allocated the investigation packages to their detective sergeants, whose teams continued the enquiries and deal with the prisoners. The prisoner packages had better be right: if not, I would receive the dreaded 10 am phone call ordering my immediate return to complete or explain my actions. After just two hours' sleep this was not a call that I wanted, but just not answering my phone was not an option: I might find myself deposited back onto the four-shift pattern that I had only just escaped from.

At 3 am on our first night, Punchy and I were in a CID car and parked up in the multicultural area of Sparkhill. The police radio was unusually quiet. Punchy explained that sometimes it was better to park up and listen, rather than race around the patch, the way that most panda car drivers did. I guess our covert car was a lot more conspicuous than we thought. A huge bloke came running out of an entry between some terraced houses. He was carrying a big metal pole, and screaming while he charged at us, like some kind of horseless medieval jouster. I yelled out as I pointed at the man, now 30 yards away and closing fast. Punchy said nothing he started the police car and smoothly drove away. So much for the fearless Punchy, I had heard about. Punchy drove about 50 yards and braked sharply. I looked at Punchy. He was staring in the rear-view mirror: he squinted through one eye for accuracy and biting his lower lip in concentration. Just as smoothly as he had pulled away, Punchy selected reverse and accelerated clean through our would-be attacker. There was an almighty thud, and I saw the nutter cartwheeling out of sight over a small garden wall. Though we searched, we never found the man, or his pole, and are still none the wiser about the reason for his behaviour. "Cheeky cunt," declared Punchy, shaking his head. We resumed our patrol. This set the tone for the week.

The following night was Christmas Eve. A local villain had been arrested and was not happy. Over our police radio, the prisoner could be heard hurling abuse at the uniformed officers in the custody suite at Acocks Green. We attended to offer our assistance. When we arrived, the prisoner was refusing, point blank, to go into a cell. Punchy brushed past the officers and squared up to the thug. Punchy told him that he could either walk into the cell, or we would grab a leg and a wing each, and fucking throw him in. It let the wind out of his sails. As the reluctant inmate walked to a cell, he spoke to Punchy.

"Young coppers these days, eh, Punch," he muttered, "they really are as soft as shite," Punchy agreed. Unfortunately, this episode meant that we had missed a call for the CID to attend an address in Kings Heath. A female was claiming that her ex-boyfriend had raped her. Both parties were still at the address and were drunk. By missing the call, we allowed the duty inspector, two sergeants, three policewomen, and three policemen the opportunity to moan about our absence. We arrived ten minutes after everyone else. The duty inspector was one of identical twins that, amazingly, were both uniformed inspectors in the police. The general consensus was that one of them was a good bloke while the other was a twat. Punchy had no problem confusing them as he thought that they were both twats. As we arrived, the inspector tried to show off in front of his shift.

"Right. Where have you two wankers been?" Punchy defiantly responded.

"We've been assisting that fucking infant, that you put in charge of the custody suite at Acocks Green." The inspector actually harrumphed. I didn't think people really did that. To reassert his authority, he tried to sum up events.

"Right. It's Punchy, isn't it? I think we can sort this out in double-quick time. Ex-bird has popped round, and ex-boyfriend has given her one. She thinks their relationship is back on. He's told her it's not. She reckons if that's how he feels, then she's been raped. It's a simple misunderstanding. Have a quick word, would you, Punchy? Sort her out, and we can all get off in time for a Christmas morning with our families. I have a female officer with her, and a male officer with him, okay?" The inspector looked around at a bank of nodding uniformed faces.

"Whoa, there," said Punchy, "has she told you that she has been raped... sir?"

"Yes, but.... "

"Hold on," interrupted Punchy, who turned to the rest of the shift. "What about you lot? Has she told you that she's been raped?" They all nodded.

"Ladies and gents," said Punchy, with the commanding authority that had so far eluded the inspector, "this is now officially a rape enquiry." The inspector bridled.

"I'm the senior officer here. I will make the decisions, Waldron."

"No, you won't. I will be briefing the early turn CID about this matter." Punchy allowed a long pause before adding the obligatory "sir". The inspector desperately tried to reclaim some degree of authority:

"Have it your way, Waldron, but I will be consulted."

"Wrong again, sir." Punchy was shaking his head. "I am the senior detective here. Oh, and there are at least three crime scenes that need to be guarded."

"Three scenes, Waldron, three scenes? He has only shagged her once."

"Were you off the day they taught law at Ryton? She's a scene, he's a scene, and where they shagged is also a scene. I will tell your staff what to do, and my decisions will not be based on a show of fucking hands. Is that okay... sir?"

I was impressed. Punchy had just won a battle I wouldn't even have known how to fight. The duty inspector had shrunk. An invisible referee stopped the bout to prevent him from taking any further punishment; he retreated to the sanctuary of the inspector's office at Kings Heath police station. In the meantime, the job was done precisely the way Punchy wanted. The inspector walked around the station, wishing every officer a Happy Christmas, apart from Punchy.

On 14 February 1996, I was invited to the chief constable's office to see Ron Hadfield, so that he could formally promote twenty of his constables to the rank of Sergeant. Ron Hadfield was known, behind his back, as 'Biffo' - Big Ignorant Fucker from Oldham, which was a bit cruel, although in fairness, he was not small, he could be quite rude, and he did come from Oldham. Ron told us that he doubted that he would make Sergeant in today's politically correct climate. After the meeting, I went with some friends to Highbury, Arsenal's ground, to see Aston Villa play in the first leg of the League Cup semi-final. The Villa managed a 2-2 draw and went on to win the League Cup that year. I was never promoted again, and Aston Villa has not won anything since. That was the year we both peaked, it seems.

I was working nights on my last week as a detective constable: it was pretty quiet, and I had no partner. I was scheduled to start as a sergeant at Rose Road, Harborne, at 7 am the following Monday. I had been to the station, but never actually driven there, and as it was on a neighbouring division, I thought I would pop over and take a look at the place. Armed with another new A-Z, I set off in the early hours of Friday morning. Traffic was light, I had all the time in the world. I never found the police station. I don't think I even got close. The area of Harborne, where the station was, had loads of streets with large, terraced Victorian houses. The roads all looked the same to me. I drove around, but my hardly reliable system of ever-decreasing circles failed. I couldn't ask anyone at Belgrave Road for directions, they all knew that I was being promoted, and to where I was being posted. In my head I could hear the tale being retold for years: 'Did you ever meet Wolfie Smith? Somehow he managed to get himself promoted, and he couldn't even find the nick where he was supposed to work from. What a wanker.'

On Saturday morning, I set off to find Rose Road; my now well-thumbed A-Z was folded onto the relevant page and highlighted. It went even worse than the day before. I found Quinton and Kidderminster, but not Rose Road. Oh dear.

On Monday, 27 May 1996, I set off from home at 5 am for my first day as a sergeant: Rose Road should have only been a 25-minute drive. I had to arrive for a shift parade time of 6.45 am. With only fifteen minutes to spare, and no sign of the nick, I had become desperate. I called in at a petrol station which, mercifully, was quiet. With a facial expression that had been set to 'Please for the love of Christ, help me', I asked the lady serving:

"Sorry to trouble you, but is there a police station anywhere near here?"

There was a delay while the woman, who could see my police shirt and tie, wondered if I was taking the piss. She smiled. She then pointed over her shoulder.

"Like you don't know, it's about 100 yards down the road, Mr Policeman. What are you lot like? Always taking the bleeding

Mickey." I thanked her and gave her a cheeky wink: if the police station was that close, she might think I was just having a laugh and not a total fuckwit. I parked in the car park at the front of the station, and the first person I saw was Steve Groome, who was a sergeant on my new shift.

"Yo, Wolfie, great to see you, welcome to A-Unit: did you have any trouble finding the place." Oh my God. This was the area that Steve worked. Had he seen me driving around, like an idiot, trying to locate the nick for the last two nights?

"Sorry, Steve, what do you mean?" I bluffed.

"Wolfie, can you believe some fuckers really struggle to find Rosie Road?" With a straight bat, I swatted that one away.

"Steve, it's a police station, how can anyone not find a police station?" Phew.

I was posted to A-Unit at Rose Road on the F2 subdivision. Paul Figures was my shift inspector: he was a boss who supported his troops and a really nice and genuine guy. Rose Road was brand new and had a disabled access facility fitted to the station entrance. A large, metal button activated the automatic opening of the station's door. Steve Groome was never going to just push the button. He used a roundhouse kick and smashed the box. Yes, Steve managed to disable a disabled door facility. Impressive. I wasn't surprised by Steve's actions. In police terminology, he had previous. Ten years before, Steve and I were in a car park trying to exit Bournville Lane police station. The barrier did not always automatically lift, and it was common knowledge that brushing a car's fire extinguisher along the ground near the exit would trigger the barrier. This was done dozens of times a day. Steve tried to do it with a little more panache than most: he hurled the fire extinguisher at the critical area. The extinguisher missed its target, did a Barnes Wallis, and demolished the driver's door of a parked car.

I turned up on my new shift with three stripes on my arm. I felt about as comfortable as a pair of underpants in a sock drawer. The officers on my shift knew each other well, and in some cases for years. Trust was never going to be given just because I had been promoted: I was going to have to earn it. The sergeants and there were four of us, took it in turns being in charge of the custody block, a tour of duty that was usually quite mundane, but it still had its moments. Steve Groome was the custody sergeant when a detained prostitute was kicking her cell door. Steve unlocked the cell, walked in and put his hand up to pacify her, with some eloquently presented speech, that would probably have started with an introduction of, 'Oi... fucker,' when she swung her stiletto and stuck the heel clean through the palm of his hand. It was off to the Accident Hospital for Steve. I replaced him in the custody suite.

I was the custody sergeant when a mother came to the station with some food for her son. He was detained for drugs offences. Nothing unusual in that, but she wanted to hand a bag of Walkers Salt and Vinegar crisps to him personally. Initially, I thought her primary concern was that I was going to eat the fuckers, but something did not feel right. I took Mum into an interview room, opened the packet and poured the contents onto a table. There were some crisps, not many, it was a Walkers bag after all, but the bag also contained cannabis resin, Rizla cigarette papers, a lighter, plus a little bit of cocaine. The crisp packet had been neatly resealed probably with the use of an iron. I arrested her for attempting to supply drugs to her son. In order not to split the family unit up totally, I put her in the next cell to her boy. Pleasingly, having made the arrest under the Police and Criminal Evidence Act, I could not be the custody sergeant for my own prisoner. I was allowed to go home early.

Legend has it that one custody sergeant had his own way of dispensing justice. Almost every prisoner smoked, and they were allowed to keep their cigarettes, but to get a light, they had to request one from the custody staff. This sergeant purchased two disposable lighters, a red one and a blue one. If the prisoner was polite:

"Officer, is it possible I could have a light, please?" Then, through the cell hatch, he would light their cigarette with his blue lighter, no problem. Other prisoners were not so well mannered: "Oi, fat cunt! Give me a fucking light, you prick." It was the red lighter for them. A bit of fiddling with a pair of pliers ensured that it produced an impressive, six-inch flame. These unpleasant twats had their cigarettes lit as well as their facial hair singed at the same time.

February 1997. What the fuck is it? A huge lump the size of half a tennis ball had grown on my back, just above my arse. It was painful and appeared to be doubling in size every 24 hours. My doctor diagnosed a pilonidal sinus (a hair had grown backwards and become infected). I required an immediate operation to remove the lump and clean out the infected area. Could this be connected with ripping my arse hairs out in 1979, to repay the twat who had burnt my hand when I made the tea? My consultant graphically explained that an ice cream scoop sized area would be removed, and the wound left open, to allow it to heal from the inside. I was booked into the Priory Hospital in Edgbaston, five-star treatment. I had a single room, a basket of fruit, and *The Times* newspaper. However, I did have to go through the discomfort of the operation. Lying in bed, coming around from the procedure, I pulled the red emergency cord for assistance. A nurse arrived almost immediately - well, it was a private hospital. I told her that I desperately needed to go to the toilet. The nurse popped out and returned with a cardboard contraption, which she handed to me.

"Look, nurse, I need to have a Scooby-Doo, and that thing will catch around one tenth of what is about to come flying out of my arse."

"Mister Smith," she said firmly, "that is all you're getting. If you try to go to the toilet, then you will probably collapse, as you have not yet fully recovered from the anaesthetic."

She left my room. I went to the toilet, but a few minutes later, I was pulling the emergency cord again. The nurse returned with, 'I told you so' written all over her face.

"Well, what's the problem now, Mister Smith, is it the anaesthetic?" I was sitting on the toilet. I shook my head.

"No nurse, the anaesthetic was fine. The operation was fine. My shit was fine. They are the problem." I pointed at two blood saturated tampons on the floor. They had fallen from my operational wound when I dropped the stylish elasticated surgical pants to use the toilet. The nurse sighed:

"Mister Smith, we need to plug the wound after surgery, and tampons are designed to do exactly what is required. I cannot see what your problem is."

"My problem, nurse, is that I am a 40-year-old heterosexual male, who has just seen two blood soaked tampons fall from my arse and hit the floor with a splat. I never consented to this." The nurse smiled, which I thought was a strange reaction to my complaint.

"Well, Mister Smith, as a 40-year-old heterosexual male, you need to be aware that your consultant has prescribed Voltarol, a rather powerful painkiller to be taken post-operatively, and that would be about now." Confused, I asked:

"What has that got to do with anything, nurse?"

"Well, Mister Smith, Voltarol is administered by way of a suppository. The manufacturers recommend, and I quote, 'it should be placed deep into the rectum'. If you would like to go back to your bed and get on all fours. I will go and pop some gloves on to assist with the insertion."

Karma can be such a bitch.

CHAPTER 17
THE FRENCH CONNECTION

My recovery from the operation was going well, although I would probably be mentally scarred for life from the trauma of the Voltarol insertion. I was off work, and it was going to be some weeks before I was able to return to duty. Out of the blue, my chief inspector rang me. She asked if I fancied a swift return to non-confrontational duties as the sergeant in charge of the intelligence cell at Rose Road. She believed the cell contained some talented officers, but without a leader, they were fractious. This was a reasonable offer: I thought it could be a route back to the CID. I agreed to do the job and returned to work months before I was fully fit. My team consisted of three other policemen: Chalkie White, Phil Jackson and Bob Paterson. The other guys had years of experience working in intelligence; I had none. Chalkie took time out to teach me how to use the police intelligence systems, which helped me become a more independent investigator.

'Operation Jolson' was an ongoing police investigation and the Harborne CID were desperate to identify a gang of suspects who had robbed mostly, but not exclusively, university students living in Harborne. The offenders had worked out that the students had received their student loans. It was September 1997. The offenders were becoming increasingly violent. Offences that started with "What are you looking at? Give me your watch," in no time had escalated to "Give me your watch, your wallet, and the PIN number for your bank card." Things took a turn for the worse when the robberies started to include kidnapping and assault. "Watch, wallet, PIN number. Right, get into our car, have a beating, get held in a house until after midnight, then we will reuse your bank card."

This investigation had fallen into the quite nasty category.

The CID had no leads, and the offences continued. The only clue was a partial registration number from the offender's vehicle. It was believed to contain the letter A and the numbers 1 and 9. Enquiries with the DVLA produced over 20,000 possible matches. Chalkie said that all attempts to find any similar incidents, connected to the scant car details known, had failed. He suggested that I tried to identify the vehicle as a victim and not as a suspect vehicle. It took a couple of days, but I found a car whose number plate started with A19: the vehicle was registered to an address that was only a fifteen-minute drive from our area. The day after one of our offences that car had been reported stolen, then interestingly, when it was recovered it was re-registered in the name of the owner's wife. The vehicle I traced had a personalised registration plate. It wasn't much, but we didn't have anything else. My suggestion brought hoots of derision from the Rose Road CID. "As if some dozy bastard is going to commit 28 robberies in his own car with a personalised number plate." That was one of the more constructive comments.

I arrived at work on a Monday morning and was told that the car that I had traced was being surveilled to see if it could belong to the suspects. DS Alan 'Shaky' Shakespeare, who was one of the many who had mocked my suggestion, worked with the force surveillance unit for the day. When he returned to Rose Road at 9.30 pm, he confidently stated that the people who had been with the car all day were definitely not connected to our enquiry. Shaky was experienced and, quite rightly, had a lot more support from DI Chris Pretty and DCI Barry Simpson than I had. The decision to pull the plug on this line of enquiry was all but made. Then I pointed out that not one of the offences linked to this series had been committed on a Monday.

The surveillance operation continued. The following night the surveillance team arrested four offenders committing a robbery on a terrified student, who was cornered in a telephone box in Harborne. The vehicle with the personalised plate was recovered at the scene. None of the four arrested had been in trouble before. Their ages ranged from the youngest, 17, to the 27-year-old driver, Roy. Shaky decided that he wanted to deal with the driver as he now had a feel for him. At 10 pm a detective popped into the cell block to have a quick word with Roy.

"What's going on, Officer?"

"Son," said the detective, "let me tell you the rules."

"Great, the rules, I definitely need to know the rules. I've never been, you know, arrested before."

"The rules are very simple," smiled the detective, stepping closer. "if you tell just one fucking lie tomorrow in your interview, you will be going to prison for fifteen years. Goodnight, Roy."

Apparently, Roy cried all night and then admitted all 28 offences, during his first interview. Shaky drip-fed the DCI with his prisoner's admissions over the next three days, which kept him on the overtime gravy train. I wanted to get back on the CID, and DI Chris Pretty knew how keen I was. He had a decent team of sergeants, but it didn't do him any harm to have someone as enthusiastic as me on his substitutes' bench. I was tasked to interview one of the suspects who admitted but minimised his involvement; I took the opportunity to ask why no offences took place on a Saturday or a Monday. He said that he wasn't allowed out on a Saturday, because his mum thought it was too dangerous. He added that Roy had to babysit for his kid on a Monday. One of the victims, who had been traumatised by his robbery, had to be seen again. He had been in no condition to make a statement on the night of his attack. An address where he had been held was possibly identified, but we really needed confirmation.

I went to meet the victim. I was with my old mate, now a detective, Mark Blackburn. The victim, a 25-year-old man, asked if we could blindfold him en route to replicate the original circumstances. What a good idea. We did but were glad that it was his suggestion and not ours. As we led the victim up a path to a bungalow, he piped up.

"There should be a handrail there," he said, pointing. There was. As we went through the front door, he stopped and said, "The lounge is directly in front of me." His breathing became pronounced. He continued with his commentary.

"As I walk into the lounge, there's a settee on my right. On the wall, above the settee, there is a ticking clock." He was right on both counts. Unaided, he made his way to the sofa and sat down. It was quite impressive to watch. He had cognitively taken himself back to the night of his robbery. He was focused and seemed determined to remember every detail. He took a few deep breaths. Mark and I didn't make a sound: we didn't want to break his concentration. After a short pause, he continued. "There's a coffee table near my knees," he said, reaching out to confirm with his hands that it was there, 'They made me sign some of my Nat West cheques on that."

The victim pointed to the place where he remembered the television was, adding that there should be some videos next to it. I kept checking his blindfold as a part of me thought this was some giant wind-up. Although the young man seemed to be doing a fantastic job, maybe Shaky was paying me back for challenging his original thoughts about the suspects' vehicle. Regardless, Mark was busy jotting down the comments made by this incredibly valuable witness.

"In the pile of videos, you'll find one of Roy 'Chubby' Brown's. You know, the comedian? They put a film on, then one of them said, 'He can't see a movie. Put a comedian on for him,' so they did." On top of the pile of videos, smiling at me from a videocassette case, with his thumbs-up and wearing that stupid flying helmet, was Roy Chubby Brown. Britain's most offensive comic had just become a vital piece of evidence.

The defendant I interviewed pleaded not guilty and elected to be tried at the Crown Court. The other three offenders pleaded guilty and had to wait for the conclusion of the trial to be sentenced. In court, numerous students, a blind man, and the man dealt with by Mark Blackburn and myself, all gave disturbing evidence of their treatment. My defendant was found guilty. He joined his co-accused in the dock: they all stood nervously waiting to hear their fate. The public gallery and the jury area were filled with the victims and their families. Some detectives were disappointed that one of the offenders had pleaded not guilty. I wasn't, I was delighted that the Crown Court judge had the opportunity to see and hear from the victims. This was reflected in the severity of the prison sentences that he passed. Roy, the driver, was sentenced to fifteen years; the other three received substantial jail time.

I was still on the CID substitutes' bench and working in the intelligence cell when Justin Tuzzio was arrested for a series of street robberies. Another sergeant was lined up to deal with him but was struggling because he had a court commitment. I moved in like a shot. Tuzzio should have been detained at my home station Rose Road, but someone had set fire to the cell block, so he was lodged at West Bromwich. During that week, I was at work at 7 am and didn't get home until well after 2 am. I had never worked at West Bromwich, and it was always more difficult being away from my home station. However, for the only time in my police career, I saw a prisoner who had been arrested for bestiality. I don't know what type of crimes they investigated at West Brom, but this seemed to rouse almost no interest with the custody staff. I was absolutely fascinated. The suspect was a white male in his fifties and looked a lot like *Worzel Gummidge*. From what I could gather, the man's wife no longer understood him.

Worzel had, over a few weeks, taken to stroking and talking to a horse in a field near his house. He felt that the two had connected. He took their relationship, literally, to the next level and purchased a stepladder from his local B&Q. According to the arresting officer, Worzel with his trousers around his ankles was stood on the third step of the ladder, facing away from the stepladder, and having intercourse with the horse. I suppose this union must have been consensual, as the horse could have just trotted off. Worzel was interviewed. I was sitting nearby, pretending to read some statements the duty inspector, and the custody sergeant needed to hear the outcome of the interview.

"Officer," the inspector asked while glaring at Worzel with contempt, "what did the dirty fucker say during his interview?" The dirty fucker looked down and stared at a hole in his sock. He knew better than to challenge the inspector's character evaluation.

"Sir, the suspect has agreed with all of the circumstances, but he denies full penetration. Technically, it's a denial."

"Look, son," the inspector exploded. "It's just not fucking possible for a human to fully penetrate a horse. Have you seen the size of their cocks?"

He turned to glare at the prisoner. "Charge the twat." The twat was charged.

Getting back to Justin Tuzzio, as a prolific offender, he was often targeted by the police. Following his many arrests, Tuzzio never commented during his interviews and was rarely charged. On this occasion, he had in his pocket a roughly drawn map of two police areas. The area where I worked had a big tick on it while the area adjacent had a big red cross. Was he targeting the F2 subdivision? I asked Tuzzio's solicitor about the map. After her consultation with Tuzzio, her explanation surprised me. Frustrated at a repeated response of 'No comment', the sergeant dealing with him made all sorts of threats about what would happen to Justin if he committed another offence on his patch. Before leaving the station, Tuzzio was handed the map, indicating where he could and could not commit offences. Well, that was a different approach.

I decided to use the Tony Taylor interview technique. Tuzzio was angry and unpleasant. I told his solicitor that his first interview would take place at 11 am the following day. The next morning I brought Tuzzio a McDonald's Big Mac meal and a football magazine. I allowed his girlfriend to speak to him, albeit briefly, through the cell hatch. What could I lose?

Justin Tuzzio, in the presence of his solicitor, gave the most detailed account of each offence he had committed. He was able to recall the place and the dialogue between himself and his victims. I realised how significant the quality of his admissions would be at any trial. So whenever he faltered or became vague about an offence, I refused to accept his account as being an admission. Justin Tuzzio admitted 23 street robberies. My chief inspector was disappointed, with me, for not including the three vague admissions as charges. Offence clearances were important but in the absence of any supporting evidence such as property recovered, CCTV or independent witnesses, the quality and the integrity of the admissions, to me, were of paramount importance. Tuzzio was sentenced to ten years' imprisonment. Following his release, he committed further street robberies and was arrested. Interestingly he refused to leave his cell to be interviewed. He was sentenced to life imprisonment. While dealing with Tuzzio, I arrived home at 2 am. My wife called downstairs:

"Vince, check out ITV Teletext page 333." That was how we received news updates in those days.

"I'm knackered," I moaned, "do I have to?"

"Just look at the page, you knob. It's about the police, just read it." I resigned myself to having to read the news before I was allowed to tuck into my sleeping draught of choice, four cans of Carlsberg lager. I muttered that it would be some item about someone I had probably never even heard of. Page 333 Teletext read:

PC John Patrick McAnneny, 47 years of age, a serving West Midlands police officer from Steelhouse Lane police station, was arrested earlier today. A boat, which he was single-handedly sailing, was unable to land in the UK, due to appalling weather conditions. The boat was forced to return to France, where the boat was seized and searched by the French Police. Over a million pounds worth of cannabis was recovered, and McAnneny was arrested.

The first time I read it, I took in that it was about Johnny Mac and that a million pounds worth of drugs had been recovered. I initially thought, well done, John, you super-sleuth. Then I went through the item again, and the gravity of the message finally hit home. I couldn't believe it then, and I sometimes struggle to accept it now.

This snippet of news was followed a few months later by the following newspaper report:

PC John McAnneny, who was based at Birmingham's Steelhouse Lane police station, was sacked for discreditable conduct following a police disciplinary hearing, at the force's Lloyd House headquarters in the city. The officer, who had 24 years service with the West Midlands police force, had written to the Chief Constable, Mr Edward Crew, admitting the charge from his prison cell in France, where he is waiting to go on trial. About 440lb of cannabis resin with an estimated street value of one million pounds was seized from the craft after a four-month operation, codenamed Baskit, by the Birmingham branch of the Customs and Excise National Investigation Service.

Fucking hell. Johnny Mac was the best man at my second wedding. I had always wondered why my bridesmaids were Colombian. John was sent to prison for nine years. He had the misfortune to be incarcerated during the World Cup, which was played in France: you may recall that the English fans ran riot. It was the wrong time to be a Brit in any part of France, let alone a maximum-security prison. I did write to John while he was on remand. Remembering how shit he was at paperwork, I suggested the only way he could be acquitted was if he was allowed to prepare the court file himself. I always thought that Johnny Mac looked a lot like the actor Gene Hackman. *The French Connection* made Gene Hackman's career, but I guess a French connection destroyed John's.

I finally said goodbye to the CID substitutes' bench in the summer of 1997. Having passed a detective sergeant's board, I now had my own team of detectives. I first met Keith Bristow later that year. I was based in a police bungalow adjacent to the City Hospital in Winson Green. I was born in that hospital. It had taken me precisely 41 years to travel absolutely nowhere. I was policing the actual place of my birth. However, things were not good. Between our ten man team, we had one phone, two cars, one computer and one toilet. No one was happy, so a meeting with senior management was arranged. Dave Harbon, an experienced detective on my team, gave me some advice:

"Vinnie, two things you need to remember before this meeting. Firstly, if you stand up to be counted, you will be counted. Secondly, if you stand in the firing line, you will get fucking shot." Wise words, indeed, Dave. Superintendent Bristow, the deputy commander of our area, came down to discuss our issues. He opened proceedings.

"Sergeant Smith. This is your team. Now, what exactly do you need? If you ask for something that I can provide for you, then I will."

"Sir, for starters, this building is not fit for purpose." I paused. Mr Bristow was braced like a batsman waiting for a 90mph delivery. I continued. "But what we really need down here, what would really help us do our job, is a helicopter."

"A helicopter, Vince. Really. Are you sure?"

"Well, what we actually need is another CID car. But we've already asked for that and been told that there's no chance. I figure, rather than not having a car, I would rather not have a helicopter." He laughed. We established that everything about our working conditions was dreadful, but our bleating was never going to change anything. We carried on working and just produced results.

The pace of work was ramped up a notch, and everyone carried a substantial workload. Our daily plans and appointments could go out of the window if we had to react to a shooting, rape or murder. I enjoyed working for my Detective Inspector, Chris Pretty. He had been an officer in the Army and was respectfully referred to as 'The Captain'. As long as I worked hard and was loyal, he would look after me. He gave me support on the occasions that I needed it.

I was out with some colleagues in a pub in Harborne and had a bit too much to drink. I approached the bar to buy a round of drinks. An attractive lady was sat on a bar stool. Without any charm or expectation, I started talking to her. It was all rather pleasant until a man tapped me on the shoulder.

"Oi twat," he snapped, "that's my fucking wife you're chatting up."

Now I didn't think I had been chatting anyone up and said so, only what came out was:

"Fair enough, why don't we continue this discussion in the car park and the winner can take your wife home." Maybe I was onto something: I got the impression that his wife didn't have a problem with my suggestion. We launched ourselves at each other. The place was full of policemen, so we were swiftly separated. It was time for me to go home.

I booked on at Rose Road the following day. Bob Patterson, from the intelligence cell, took me to one side and told me that the Captain wanted to see me as soon as I came in. Bob warned me that it was to do with my behaviour at the Green Man pub. I feared the worst, took a deep breath and knocked on my inspector's door. Mr Pretty was sitting at his desk.

"Is everything okay, sir?" I asked tentatively.

"Fine, Sergeant, everything is just fine. Come in, close the door and take a seat."

I sat down. There was a lengthy, awkward silence while the Captain was writing minutes on a crime report. He would write a few lines, pause, look around the room and then continue writing. The only sound was the scratching of his fountain pen, and the chink of his teacup being placed onto its saucer. Finally, after what seemed like an hour, the Captain spoke.

"Sergeant, do you know what absolutely guarantees that I enjoy my weekends when I am not at work?" I had no idea and said so.

"A quality bottle of red wine on a Saturday evening, and a bottle of white wine with my dinner on a Sunday." I waited for him to continue. He didn't, so I piped up.

"Will there be anything else, sir?"

"No, no, Sergeant, you can go now. By the way, I'm actually off this weekend. Oh yes, just one other thing... about last night, do not ever behave like that again while you are working for me. Do you understand?" I nodded.

Then he half-smiled and said, "Carry on please, Sergeant, and close the door behind you."

Three hours before that exchange took place, the man I had argued with, who happened to be a solicitor, attended Rose Road to make an official complaint about me. He insisted on seeing Mr Pretty, who listened patiently for nearly five minutes. The solicitor outlined the case against me. He suggested that my sacking would be an appropriate punishment. The Captain put forward the case for my defence.

"You were on licensed premises when you met a man who was a bit drunk. Well, that's hardly unique, is it? You met Detective Sergeant Smith, possibly the hardest-working detective in the West Midlands police Force." *I wasn't, by the way, but for the purpose of that conversation, I was.* Mr Pretty continued. "You had a verbal altercation with Sergeant Smith, who left the pub and went home. A very sensible decision, in my opinion." The Captain paused, took a sip of tea, and gleaned from the solicitor's body language that his summary of events was not going to be challenged. "Now, your wife isn't here to make a complaint, so perhaps, it is only your pride that has been dented. My sergeant will not be sacked. I will speak to him, but, as far as you are concerned, sir, this matter is now concluded. I will show you the way out of the station."

The Captain had an enjoyable weekend with a bottle of Cabernet Sauvignon on Saturday, and a chilled Pinot Grigio on Sunday, with the compliments of Victoria Wines and my credit card. At least I still had a job.

CHAPTER 18
MURDER ON THE DANCE FLOOR

The area that I was responsible for included Her Majesty's Prison Birmingham, Winson Green. This was a tough time for the prison. Several scathing news stories had put the jail under the media spotlight. The scale of drug dealing, assaults and deaths at the prison were a problem. The relationship between the police and the prison will never fully recover from the Birmingham Six issues of the 1970s. Fourteen prison officers were charged and tried for assaulting the Birmingham Six. The prison staff maintained the prisoners had all been beaten up by the police long before they arrived at the jail.

The prison liaison officer, Graham Price, was an experienced detective. Graham resolved most issues himself and only referred an investigation to the CID if he had no choice. The Governor of the prison relied heavily on Graham's experience. During that period, the Home Secretary was briefed about all critical incidents that occurred at the prison.

Back in the mid-70s, Graham Price was a fresh-faced young officer posted to Belgrave Road police station. With only twelve months' service, Graham was already a panda driver. He was working a night shift driving his single manned Austin Allegro around Balsall Heath. At about 10.30 pm, a drunken Irishman flagged Graham down. The drunk was mumbling something about having been burgled. Graham was dragged out of his police car and ushered along the street; he tried to contact the controller but could not get a response. As he cajoled young Graham along, the Irishman was becoming increasingly aggressive. When they arrived at the Irishman's ground-floor flat, Graham was propelled into it with a firm shove between the shoulder blades. He surveyed the scene.

"Jesus H Fucking Christ," Graham sympathised. "They have left your place in a right state." The flat had been ransacked. It looked like every piece of furniture had been turned over, and a dustbin emptied onto the floor.

"What the feck are you talking about?" the Irishman snapped, as he advanced on Graham. "They've only taken my feckin' television." Having inadvertently insulted the man's home, Graham was now confident that he was about to be assaulted. He figured he'd take the initiative. Once the Irishman came into range, Graham threw a 'Hail Mary' uppercut. More through luck than any pugilistic skill, it connected flush with the drunk's chin, and he dropped like a sack of spuds - no racial slur intended. With his would-be assailant now incapacitated, Graham tried again to get some response from his piece-of-shit radio. Nothing. He checked for a telephone in the flat: no joy. The Irishman was motionless.

"Come on, mate, we can sort this out, get up." Nothing. Graham checked for vital signs of life. Nothing. This was worrying. Graham was still wearing his flat hat, and he could feel beads of sweat trickling down his neck. Oh my God, he thought, I've killed somebody, and I'm still in my probation. If only the controller had heard me when I first radioed in. Fuck.

Graham had no idea what he should do. During the ten weeks at the Police Training Centre, there hadn't been a lesson which included instructions about how to dispose of the body of someone that you had just murdered. Graham was not a big bloke, and it was with some difficulty that he managed to get the corpse onto his shoulder. PC Price staggered the short distance to his panda car and dumped the body onto the back seat. Incredibly there was no one about. To buy some time, Graham drove around Balsall Heath in an aimless daze. He was well-liked, but his shift would not dispose of the body and pretend that this hadn't happened. Other options raced through his mind. Perhaps he could find a fatal car accident, and maybe nobody would notice him dumping an already dead body into it. What about dropping the corpse onto a railway line or in a river? As he drove through the dark streets of Balsall Heath, Graham's thoughts were shattered by the sound of his police radio crackling.

"Bravo 1, Bravo 1 to PC Price. Status update and location." Shit. Graham Price was out of time.

"You fucking bastard!" Graham shouted, angrily at the object that he blamed for his predicament, his police radio.

Then Graham felt a tidal wave of relief rush over him, as a pair of gnarled hands snaked around his headrest and began tightening around his throat.

"Who are you calling a feckin' bastard?" Graham was able to pull his police car over and then restrain and arrest the drunk. The Irishman spent six hours in a cell, after which he was allowed to leave: the custody sergeant told Graham to drop him home. En route, the Irishman apologised for his behaviour. But because he had been totally hammered, it was all a bit of a blur, so he couldn't remember much. In stark contrast, Graham Price could remember every little detail, and he was never going to forget it. I'd like to think that everything else that came Graham's way in his long and distinguished police career must have seemed pretty straightforward.

As a new detective sergeant with my own team, I had a lot to learn. What I lacked in experience I would like to think that I made up for with effort. I worked with some seasoned detectives, but it was also a time when a lot of trainee investigators were being processed. Everyone was busy, but most of the pressure was self-induced, as we all desperately wanted to successfully investigate crimes. In the CID, anyone who was useless stood out like a pregnant pole-vaulter.

John Davies was the Crown prosecutor responsible for my area: all of our investigations were submitted to him. John was an easy guy to fall out with. He sent CPS memos that were rude, written in block capitals and in green ink. Looking around my colleagues' desks, I saw a number of his missives:

they were easy to spot. My initial thought about the first green volley I received was: I should buy a baseball bat and drive to his office and teach him some manners. After a few weeks, I sat down with John to discuss some of my team's investigations. I realised then that all he wanted to do was improve the quality of the cases that were put before the courts. It was John who pointed out that he was the prosecutor and that the police were only the investigators. John was sharp. He had a brilliant, practical legal mind, and he was just what I needed. John could cut through all the rubbish and see a case for what it could be if only the police would work with him. The reason he was so blunt was that his advice had often been ignored. I ended up looking forward to his memos. I worked with John on every case in my last ten years with the West Midlands police. I have included the details of some of those cases in this book. We developed an excellent working relationship. I attended High Court appeals long after I had retired, just because John asked me to.

While I was on leave, there had been yet another suspicious death in the prison. Paul Mason was found dead in his cell. It appeared to be suicide. Mason had a ligature around his neck, and his cellmate had tried but been unable to save him. Detectives Dave Harbon and Andy Bentley liaised with Graham Price and the governor of the prison, then interviewed Mason's cellmate, Kevin McAteer, who said that Mason was scheduled to make an application for bail the following day. According to McAteer, Mason feared that he was not going to be granted bail, which was why he took his own life. It was a long way from satisfactory, but there was no evidence to contradict McAteer's account. McAteer was moved to HMP Liverpool. The enquiry remained with my team. I picked it up when I returned to work. When I examined the papers, I discovered two things: that in 1986 Paul Mason had stolen my Ford Mondeo from outside my house in Solihull; and two months before Mason's death another cellmate of McAteer's had attempted suicide. On that occasion, McAteer had been able to intervene and save his cellmate's life.

A couple of weeks after Mason's death, DI Pretty received a telephone call from the prison liaison officer based at HMP Liverpool. McAteer wanted to speak to a detective. DC Shane Saunders and I set off to HMP Liverpool, to collect McAteer and take him to Copy Lane police station for an interview. We managed to get lost on the way. The directions that we were given never made any reference to Aintree racecourse, possibly the most significant landmark in the country. As we circumnavigated Aintree, again, Shane with an excellent impression of Peter O'Sullevan (the Grand National commentator) said:

"And they cross the Melling Road... for the second and final time."

McAteer had legal representation in his interview. I cautioned him, and asked what he wanted to say about the death of Paul Mason. For a full 45 minutes, McAteer gave a detailed and harrowing account of how he had murdered Mason and then checked to ensure that Mason was dead before pushing the cell alarm. McAteer admitted pretending to render first aid when the prison officers rushed into the cell, adding that he was now haunted by what he had done. It was unnerving. There were no questions to be put to him: he explained everything.

Richard Comerford had been the cellmate of McAteer's two months before Mason's death and had made a suicide attempt in strikingly similar circumstances. Initially, he claimed McAteer had saved his life. Then changed that account six months later and made a further statement that McAteer had actually tried to murder him. Comerford was not a credible witness: he had given contradictory accounts and his heroin addiction was slowly killing him. Though warned to attend the Crown Court, I didn't think he would even turn up.

There was no other evidence, apart from McAteer's admission. McAteer appeared before Birmingham Crown Court, charged with murder, and entered a plea of not guilty. He claimed that he had simply invented his confession and now wished to retract it. At a conference with John Davies and David Jones QC, the only item for discussion was the interview. Mr Jones wanted to read the transcript of the interview to the jury, which is standard court procedure. I was desperate for the interview tape to be played. I knew how incredibly powerful it was. I asked Mr Jones to at least listen to it before he made his final decision. The trial was scheduled to commence the following Monday. Mr Jones said that he was driving to Scotland for the weekend, but would try to listen to the interview on his journey. Fair enough, I couldn't ask more than that.

The following Monday, I arrived at Birmingham Crown Court bright and early. Mr Jones, who bears a striking resemblance to Rumpole of the Bailey, came bustling past Crown Court security. I asked him:

"Well, Mr Jones, what do you think?"

"I'm going to see the judge. I'm going to make an application to play the tape to the jury." I was delighted. In the foyer of the court, a very smart young man wearing a suit, shirt and tie approached me.

"Sergeant Smith, don't you recognise me?"

"No, can I help you?" I was reasonably sure I didn't know this lad.

"It's Roger, Roger Comerford." He gave me a firm handshake, then he explained his transformation. "I'm off the gear and have been for months."

From a prosecution perspective, this was getting better. Roger Comerford was an impressive witness. I watched the jury when the tape of McAteer's interview was played. I counted five jurors who were crying. Following the trial the press reported:

Birmingham Mail 14 May 2001:

A serving prisoner was jailed for life today after being convicted of murdering his cellmate by forcing him to hang himself. Kevin McAteer, 30, became irritated by Paul Mason's behaviour as the 22-year-old came off heroin and forced him to stand on a chair and put his head in a noose made from bedsheets. McAteer kicked the chair away and then watched for five minutes as the 'colour drained' from his cellmate's face,

Birmingham Crown Court heard. Sentencing him to life in prison, Mr Justice Rougier said.

'You are not just a criminal you are an evil man,' the Judge said. 'This was a most callous and heartless murder of a young man who had troubles of his own. 'You decided to kill him for no better reason than he interfered with your comfort.' The court heard McAteer had numerous convictions and at the time of the murder, in October last year, was serving a six-year sentence at Birmingham Prison for a post office robbery in Shrewsbury. Earlier, the jury was told how McAteer threatened to slash Mason's throat with a razor blade unless he hanged himself. David Jones, prosecuting, said McAteer had become irritated by his cellmate's behaviour as he struggled with the effects of "cold turkey," he told how the defendant discovered three of his phone cards in a box belonging to his cellmate. Mr Jones said: 'Mr Mason twitched a lot, writhed because of pains. It was irritating to Mr McAteer. McAteer was angry because he was blundering around.

'The motive for this murder is three phone cards and the fact this man irritated him,' Mr Jones added. Two months earlier, McAteer persuaded remand prisoner Richard Comerford that a suicide bid would boost his chances of getting bail when he next appeared in court. Comerford survived, the court heard. McAteer, of Littleton Road, Salford, Manchester, had denied murder.

In July 1999, at the age of 69, my father died in hospital following a short battle with cancer. Most of his brothers had died of lung cancer, so when Dad was diagnosed with the same illness, he just gave up. He died within three weeks. Dad had always been entertaining in the pub. He had an encyclopaedic knowledge of boxing, which is hardly surprising, as he had stolen every boxing book that Redditch Library had ever put on their shelves. Dad enjoyed poetry, mostly Kipling, and some monologues, including *The Green Eye of the Little Yellow God* and *The Cremation of Sam McGee*. He often flawlessly recited these poems in the bar and was rewarded by the patrons who bought him beer. I have him to thank for my appreciation of poetry. Dad spent his last years as a drunk, shoplifting 'Parker' ballpoint pens from WH Smith's. They were quite easy to slide up the cuff of his sleeve apparently. Also, according to Dad, the lady that worked behind that counter had a wonky eye. Dad sheepishly handed out the pens as birthday or Christmas presents. My father spent every penny he ever had on beer and cigarettes. But he was still my dad.

Anthony and I went to Dad's flat. We filled five bin bags with his worldly belongings and dumped them in a nearby skip. It was all quite sad, really. It was time to make arrangements for my father's funeral. We decided to split the cost but had no idea how much that was going to be. Anthony asked if I would mind allowing him to make the arrangements. He said that I had dealt with most things as his elder brother, and it was time for him to step up to the plate. That was just fine with me. Anthony phoned the Redditch funeral directors, Thomas Brothers, and gave a brief explanation of our position and asked for a quote. The director then suggested the funeral package that would be the most appropriate and quoted a price. This caused Anthony to take a deep breath and sit down. Anthony shook his head.

"How much?" The director repeated the figure, and my brother became even more agitated. I quietly asked him for the amount, but he waved me away: this was his time, and he was dealing with this. My brother waited and cleared his throat. "Can we get one thing clear here, mate, we are burying my dad, not Princess fucking Diana. Trim the cars, the flowers, the casket lining, coffin handles and give me a better price." We were waiting for the funeral director to respond. Five minutes later, my brother confirmed, "Yes, I am still here." My brother listened intently and then replied, "Fifteen hundred quid, is that really the best that you can do?"

I sensed that the funeral director was not overly impressed with my brother's attitude. There was another pause, then my brother angrily barked.

"You what? Do I have a suggestion? Well, actually yes, I do. Do you know where the Arrow Valley Lake is?" Anthony waited for confirmation that he did. "No, mate, I'm not thinking about a waterside service. What I'm actually thinking is sticking my dad into a couple of bin bags... driving him to the lake and then with 'A-one, A-two and A-jolly good three', chucking the fucker in. How much will that cost?" Anthony held the phone out: I could hear the dialling tone. My brother opened up:

"I wouldn't mind paying for this, Vince, but Dad never gave a toss about anyone but himself." My brother was shaking his head. Then quietly he added, "Vince, everyone knew about the state of our house, and exactly what we did and didn't have.

Before you left the Army... I was in a science lesson, the teacher really liked me. She was teaching the class about electricity. She walked across the classroom and pointed to a light switch. She said, 'Can anyone tell me what actually happens when this light is switched on?' There was silence: we didn't have many kids in my class who answered the teacher's questions. Trying to coax a response, she encouraged: 'Come on, anyone, anyone at all, just have a guess.' She could see that I probably had some idea and said, 'Anthony Smith, what happens when I turn on the light?' Before I could speak, some kid from the back of my class chipped in, 'Fuck all happens in his house, Miss, he hasn't got electricity.' The class exploded with laughter, it really hurt Vince. It still fucking hurts."

There was nothing I could say. I knew how things had been, we just didn't talk about it. Ant added, "What pisses me off the most, I found out years later that they were not allowed to turn off the electricity if there were kids living in a house. Dad would have known that... he just couldn't be bothered." My brother hardly smoked at all, maybe a couple of cigarettes a year. He lit one up. "There are a lot of dark corners in a house at night, when you are alone and have no electricity. Wondering when or even if your dad was going to come home." I put the kettle on. I rang Thomas Brothers, I told them that £1,500 was acceptable, and, to be fair, they did a decent job on the day.

In May 2000, I was in the intelligence cell in Rose Road and looking for an officer who worked there. I asked WPC Jill Richmond if she knew his whereabouts. Jill and I had never really liked each other. Jill said that she couldn't help me, which was just about par for the course, I mischievously chipped in:

"I'll try one of the other hospital wards, then." Jill started screeching for her Federation rep. She was not happy, and she was going to make a formal complaint about me. I was going to be kicked off the CID and sacked. The following day I was called in to see Chris Pretty. He told me to sit down and listen: he made it clear that I was not to speak.

"Right, Vince, Jill and her Fed rep have been in. She's kicking up a fuss over you mentioning her sickness record in public." The Captain, like a school headmaster, pointed to stop me interrupting before continuing. "Now, I have no interest in what you actually said, or what you meant. Jill is coming back in 30 minutes... so just be here and apologise. This matter will go away, and we can all get on with our day jobs. Now fuck off and come back in half an hour." Well, that was charming. What about my side of the story?

As ordered, 30 minutes later, I knocked on my detective inspector's door. I walked in. Mr Pretty was sitting behind his desk; Jill and her Fed rep were already seated. In the absence of any other chairs, I assumed I was to stand and deliver my apology. The Captain gave me a *Paddington Bear* hard stare, a clear message that I was not to fuck about.

"Ah, Detective Sergeant Smith. It's good of you to join us. This is WPC Richmond and her Federation rep. I believe you have something to say to Jill?" I had known both of these clowns for over three years, so the introductions were unnecessary. Jill Richmond smirked. She was going to enjoy this.

"Jill, if I mentioned anything last night that caused you any offence, I would like to apologise. Also, if I said anything which you felt was about your sickness record in public, then again, I apologise." Jill was beaming. Chris Pretty was nodding; this was just what he had ordered. Then I chummed the water with:

"But Jill, most of all I would like to apologise for calling you fat."

"Fat? You didn't call me fat."

"Are you sure? I could have sworn I called you fat."

"You never called me fat." She was frothing at the mouth. "Are you calling me fat now?" She was losing it.

"Oh," I said calmly, "if I never called you fat, then I withdraw that part of my apology. But I was pretty sure I called you fat, though, Jill."

"Sir. He keeps calling me fat," Jill was screeching at Mr Pretty. "Please make him stop." The Captain, trying to calm things down, said:

"Jill, you have had an apology for the other matters, about which you have complained. But if Sergeant Smith never called you, you know... the F-word last night, then I think we can all move on. Jill, you need to get a cup of tea and calm down." Jill was almost in tears. I went to follow her out of the office. Mr Pretty stopped me.

"No, not you, Sergeant Smith," he hissed. "You can fucking sit down. You are going to be here for some time."

I tried to remember the Victoria Wines price list and if there were any special offers on a bottle of vintage port.

At 7.30 am on Monday, 1 October 2001, I was at home when

my new Detective Inspector, Bob Kearns, called me. He told me that a two-year-old boy, Tyrese Gayle, had been found dead in a house, in Magdala Street in Winson Green. Bob added that a post-mortem was about to be conducted, but even at this stage, it looked suspicious. Bob Kearns phoned me as soon as the autopsy was finished. He confirmed that Tyrese had died as a result of massive internal injuries, consistent with being kicked or punched.

Belroy Blake and Tyrese's mother had separated, and Blake had set up home with his new girlfriend in Magdala Street. Blake's house was a two-up two-down, 1920s terrace; significantly, the stairs in the house were rather steep. The first accounts by Tyrese's father and his new girlfriend were that the child had fallen down the stairs and died.

I arrested them both on suspicion of murder. There were only four officers available to work on the enquiry, detectives Russ McCall, Chris Rigby and myself. We also had WPC Liz Devaney: it was her first day on the CID. There was an awful lot of work to be done; the four of us were going to be busy. Both suspects had solicitors, and by the afternoon, initial interviews had been conducted. Russ and I interviewed Blake, who replied, 'No comment' to everything we asked him. Chris and Liz interviewed Blake's girlfriend. She was a lot more talkative and answered questions, but she kept changing her account. By 7 pm with nothing from Belroy Blake, I stopped the interviews. One of the first officers at the scene was PC Nathan Grix. In the initial confusion at the scene, an officer remembered hearing Nathan talking about the Heimlich manoeuvre. Bob

Kearns decided that Nathan needed to be spoken to as a matter of urgency. In case Nathan was responsible for some of the injuries that had been highlighted by the post mortem. I needed Nathan's explanation in person. I took Russ McCall with me. Now, Russ and Nathan did not really get on, but this was no time to accommodate personal likes and dislikes.

Nathan Grix was an ex-soldier and a no-nonsense type of copper; we arrived at his home at 8 pm. Nathan and Russ exchanged looks. The dining room was sparsely furnished and had been stripped for redecoration. There was a table with an ashtray on it. Nathan and his wife were taking harsh draws on the cigarettes they were smoking. The three of us sat down while Mrs Grix withdrew to the kitchen to make some tea. Nathan and Russ continued to express their dislike of each other through glances. I didn't have time for this. I was just about to ask the critical question when a chocolate Labrador joined us.

Nathan burst into life.

"*Bon garçon s'allonger,*" he said to the dog. Nathan took another aggressive draw on his cigarette, and continued his conversation with the Labrador. "*Couchez-vous, garçon, juste coucher.*"

"Nathan, what's going on?" This was weird.

"It's French, Sarge." Like that explained anything. Looking for, and offering a simple explanation, "Oh, the dog is French?" Nathan shook his head. "No, we just talk French to the dog." I was baffled. I looked at Russ, who was about to explode with laughter. Nathan's wife returned with a pot of tea and said:

"Allez, garçon, allez dans la cuisine," to the Labrador.

Nathan confirmed that he had not performed any medical procedures on Tyrese that morning. I took his statement, and that was my job done. On the way back to the police station, I was quietly reflecting on the surreal encounter with Nathan.

"What was going on in that house?" I asked Russ.

Russ blew out an exaggerated Gallic sigh, then said:

"From the little bit of French I can remember from school, I think they were telling the dog to get in the kitchen, Sarge."

The suspects remained in custody overnight. The following morning I drove to CPS to get advice from John Davies. John told me not to make the mistake of assuming that it was the child's father who had delivered the fatal blow. That it could possibly have been his girlfriend. Given the amount of force used, I asked John how a slightly built female could be responsible. John slid his chair back and raised his right foot. He then slammed his heel down, demonstrating how the injuries could have happened. An excellent point: I never forgot it.

We resumed the interviews. Blake continued to exercise his right of silence, while his girlfriend tied herself in knots trying to maintain her differing accounts. She was told that her boyfriend had not spoken since his arrest. She didn't believe us: why should she? At her request, we played Blake's 'No comment' interview to her. She asked for a consultation with her solicitor, after which she started to untie her knots. She said that she had not even been at home when Tyrese died, and had only lied at the request of her boyfriend. She gave an address at which she had been partying all night. She was sure that there was a CCTV camera on the outside of the building. I was lucky that Dave Harbon was back at work. Dave shot off to the address, and we waited for his update. It came within the hour.

"Vinnie, she is bang on. She went into a flat at 10 pm looking like a princess. At 6 am, she left in a hurry looking totally partied out." Dave Harbon was a talented detective in any enquiry, whether it was mundane or murder: he seamlessly went through the gears and just produced results.

Russ and I conducted a further interview with Belroy Blake. When confronted with his girlfriend's account, he admitted that he was responsible for the death of his son. He wouldn't elaborate any further and apologised. I declined his offer to shake my hand at the end of the interview. This case was now a matter for the Crown Court. At an early hearing, Belroy Blake entered a plea of guilty to manslaughter but denied murder. My chief superintendent thought that Blake's plea should be accepted. I disagreed, but more importantly, so did John Davies. I prepared for a murder trial. The team did well, but the efforts of Liz Devaney on her first two days on the CID were astonishing.

Around this time, as a detective sergeant, working in a pretty busy area, Trevor Wiggan was a frequent flyer and regularly arrested for all manner of offences. I dealt with him on numerous occasions, so much so that whenever I worked overtime, my four-year-old twin stepsons, Marcus and Josef, would ask me if I had been dealing with Trevor again. They often asked how he was doing and if he was in prison. It saved me explaining the details of a procession of prisoners, so I just went along with it. I gave them regular updates on Trevor's criminality. On a Sunday in February 2002, I was working with Dave Harbon, and following a hectic Saturday night, we had a lot of work to do. I noticed that Trevor Wiggan was in custody, again, but on this occasion, the CID would not have to deal with him. I also saw something else. Dave Harbon and I took a break in Winson Green, near to the scene of the previous night's shooting. I popped into a corner shop. At 5 pm, Dave dropped me off at Rose Road, and I went to the custody suite. A mate, Loz Meechan, who I had joined with, was the custody sergeant. I told him that I needed to see Trevor Wiggan about a personal matter.

"Watch him, Vinnie," he warned me, "he's in a foul mood and already had a go at some of my staff."

"Trevor and me go back a long way, Loz, it'll be fine, trust me."

Loz shrugged and handed me the cell key. I walked along the corridor, opened Trevor's cell and went in. True to his usual form, Trevor started on me.

"What the fuck are you doing? I haven't been nicked for a CID matter, why don't you just leave me alone? Hang on... what are you holding behind your back, you cunt?"

I held out a strawberry jam tart.

"Trevor, it's your birthday today. Everyone should get a cake on their birthday." I handed it to him. He was almost tearful.

"Thank you, Mr Smith, I always liked you." I returned the cell key to Loz.

"How was he?" Loz enquired.

"Happy, Loz, it's his birthday today, so why wouldn't he be happy?"

Thirteen years later, in 2015, my wife was at work and phoned me. She let me know that a blast from my past was in custody. And that she was going to deal with him. Yes, it was Trevor Wiggan. My wife went to get Trevor from his cell. He was his usual unpleasant, snarling and swearing self.

"Right, before you kick off, Trevor, I think you know my husband? He worked at Rose Road and dealt with you loads of times, and he has told me all about you. Do you remember Detective Sergeant Vince Smith?" Trevor melted and asked:

"Did you know, Miss, years ago he gave me a cake in my cell on my birthday?" Trevor hugged my wife. He was interviewed and admitted every offence for which he had been arrested. The custody sergeant nearly fell off his stool in shock when my wife updated him. Trevor Wiggan never admitted anything, ever.

In 2002, I was preparing a full file for the murder of Tyrese Gayle; I met up with John Davies on a weekly basis, and every fortnight with Melbourne Inman QC, the barrister that John had selected to lead the prosecution.

At 3.30 am on 4 March, Gladstone Johnson was shot and killed while he was standing on the dance floor at the West Indian

Federation Club. *Murder on the Dancefloor*, a song by Sophie Ellis-Bextor, is still her bestselling single. The song peaked at number two in the UK singles chart; it became Europe's most popular song of 2002. It was still in the charts when Gladstone Johnson was murdered.

The police press release and appeal regarding Gladstone Johnson's murder:

A father who was gunned down in front of his girlfriend in an execution-style killing was acquitted of the murder of a man outside a city nightclub two years ago. Dad-of-two Gladstone Johnson, 34, was shot several times at close range, as he stood on the dance floor of the West Indian Federation Club in the early hours of Monday morning. Police revealed that Johnson had gone to the club in Winson Green Road, Winson Green, with girlfriend Maggie, in her 20s and from Wolverhampton. She was standing nearby when a black man opened fire as he approached him. Det Chief Insp Graeme Pallister, leading the murder inquiry, said he believed Johnson was specifically targeted, although a motive for the crime was not revealed. And he today appealed for people in the club at the time to come forward to help police trace his killers. Johnson, who preferred to be called Wayne, was looking after his daughter who was visiting him from Jamaica for six months. He also has a ten-month-old baby boy. Det Chief Insp Pallister said: 'He was deliberately targeted and shot more than once. I believe the person or person's involved intended to kill him. Firing a weapon in such a crowded and confined environment is extremely dangerous, and it certainly looks clear he was targeted. 'Maggie is in pieces. She is extremely distraught and upset. His daughter is also obviously extremely upset and distraught at the death of her father.' Det Chief Insp Pallister said that police had not seen a huge number of people at the club at the time come forward following earlier appeals. And he said it was too early to say whether the shooting would trigger reprisals.

Johnson's murder investigation was going to be difficult. A circumstantial evidence case was built around a group of Jamaican nationals. Intelligence suggested that they had received an instruction from their gang leader to execute Johnson. The reason? Johnson had claimed the police had intercepted the gang's drug mules, whereas their enquiries led them to believe that Johnson had kept the drugs and their proceeds for himself. The gang leader was not required to apply any beyond a reasonable doubt test. Johnson's punishment was a death sentence.

Gunshot residue was vital, and when the original four defendants were reduced to one, Kirk Robinson alone was scheduled to stand trial for murder. It was the residue recovered from his clothing that was the critical evidence against him. Through a series of interviews, all of Robinson's accounts were proved to be false. He denied his presence at the scene, even though there was compelling evidence that he was there. Following Robinson's arrest, a firearm was found hidden in the toilet cistern in his house. The trial was scheduled to take place in early 2003.

Understandably, as Belroy Blake's trial approached there was a build-up of tension between Blake's family and the mother of Tyrese's family. The natural divide in the public gallery kept the families apart, but on the first day of the trial, it was apparent that there was a real possibility that the families could start fighting. I was summoned to see the trial judge. The inspector in charge of Crown Court security was already there when I arrived. The inspector said he intended to deploy a serial of OSU to police the public gallery for the duration of the trial. This did not sit comfortably with the judge, who thought it could be seen as both oppressive and distracting. The judge asked if I could suggest another option. I said:

"Sir, the families at this trial are not violent people. They are just angry and upset about the death of Tyrese. Eight uniformed officers guarding them is more likely to aggravate the situation." The judge said:

"I accept that Sergeant Smith, but we have to do something. I will not allow their behaviour to escalate into violence. Not in my court."

"Sir, with your permission, DC Harbon and myself will speak to the families. We know them. They will be told that if they want to remain in the public gallery and watch the trial, then they will have to behave. Anyone that does not will be removed, on your instructions, and not allowed to return. DC Harbon and I will be here for the trial, we will just be a lot more visible than normal. The judge mulled this over for a few seconds. Before he made his decision, the inspector, who had not been impressed with anything I had said, addressed the judge:

"Sir, can I just add…" The judge cut him off.

"No, you cannot. Be quiet, Inspector… Gents, thank you. Sergeant, please monitor the public gallery on my behalf and let me know if there is anything that I need to address. I will now continue with my trial." As we left the judge's chambers, the inspector was smarting from the judge sawing him off at the knees, turned and said:

"When this goes pear-shaped, and the punches start flying, and believe me, they will please do not think that I will be rushing to your aid. You detectives are all the bloody same, a bunch of bloody smart arses." The conduct of the families for the duration of the trial, in the circumstances, was commendable. I saw the security inspector five days into the trial he looked a bit disappointed that I hadn't been hospitalised.

At Belroy Blake's trial Melbourne Inman QC was excellent. He had a bustling manner; I could see that the jurors liked him. The prosecution case was assisted when Blake chose to address the court before he gave evidence.

"Ladies and gentlemen of the jury, something really bad happened in my house last year, but can we all please move on and put it behind us?" Mr Inman pulled Blake's defence of diminished responsibility apart. Blake claimed he had low personal esteem, a reduced sex drive, and that he had lost his appetite. Mr Inman pointed out that his assessment had taken place while Mr Blake was remanded in custody charged with murdering his son. Following the jury finding Blake guilty of murder, the judge addressed Blake before sentencing:

"Mr Blake, may I remind you of the statement that you made to the court at the beginning of your evidence, and say you were partly right? We will all move on, but you will serve a minimum of fifteen years in prison. This will give you plenty of time to reflect on your actions, then you can also move on."

The Birmingham Evening Mail Reported on April 26, 2002.

A father of three who killed his two-year-old son by punching him in the stomach has been jailed for life at Birmingham Crown Court. Belroy Blake (34), of Magdala Street, Winson Green. Was found guilty of murdering two-year-old Tyrese Gayle, his son after a jury deliberated for almost four hours. Melbourne Inman Q.C., prosecuting, said Blake delivered the fatal blow to Tyrese, who was living with his mother in Hockley while he was looking after him one evening in September last year.

He then put the toddler to bed and did not call for help until the following morning. Mr Inman said the boy suffered serious internal injuries including lacerations to his liver and bowel parts and extensive bruising.

He also had two broken ribs, which he said could have been the result of further blows from Blake. The court heard Blake, a Jamaican national, originally lied to the police about the toddler's death by claiming he fell down the stairs, which caused his injuries. Blake, who had pleaded guilty to a charge of manslaughter before the start of the trial, admitted punching Tyrese, who he said had been jostling another child over some crisps in' the front room but denied intending to kill him or cause really serious harm. Nigel Rumfitt Q.C., defending, said there was no evidence Blake had ill-treated the child in the past and that witnesses had given evidence about his qualities as a father. Detective Inspector Vince Smith, of Winson Green CID, said. 'It is a tragic incident, and my thoughts and prayers are with the family. It would have been nice to know what actually happened. Blake never told us, so Tyrese's last moments will never be known.'

I was never a detective inspector, but the Birmingham Mail *reporter liked me and said I should have been.*

CHAPTER 19
MURDER, HE WROTE

The day I started work on the Gladstone Johnson murder was also the day I left the Rose Road CID. I started an attachment to the Major Investigation Unit (MIU), and that move became permanent. As a detective sergeant at Rose Road, I learned a lot from John Davies. I attended court at every opportunity, bail applications and trials whether or not I had been warned as a witness. That allowed me to conquer my inner demons. I left behind some exceptional detectives. The Rose Road CID had an 'all hands to the pump' approach, which worked because we made it work. My new role on the MIU took me up to the end of my West Midlands police service. It meant the investigations that I worked on were a lot more structured.

Templates and guidelines dictate how a major investigation must be conducted. The cases that you are about to read about were all major crime investigations: let me just give you a brief explanation. Just a bit about the structure, mechanics, personnel, and a little bit of history. Not enough for you to investigate serial murders from your lounge, granted, but sufficient to understand the roles of some of the people in a major investigation. A senior investigating officer (SIO), usually a detective chief inspector (DCI), is appointed and heads the enquiry. The SIO will have a nationally accredited qualification. The defined areas of investigation will have identified strategies, which are recorded in the SIO's Policy Book. Topics include witnesses, informants, forensics, telephones, CCTV tapes, interviews and the media. The MIU used HOLMES for all enquiries: it is a massive data warehouse that contains everything related to a case. It's a brilliant system for storing, searching and cross-referencing information. Everything that is input stays in the system and is retrievable for future investigations. HOLMES was created in 1985. Something had to be done about the lack of cooperation between police forces. Whenever there were cross-border enquiries, each force treated the other police forces as rivals instead of allies.

In the 80s, my inspector told me: "Wolfie, in 1975, I was a young detective working on the Black Panther enquiry. The West Midlands police were in direct competition with the Staffordshire Police and West Mercia Police, as to which was going to take the credit for identifying and arresting the offender. The neighbouring forces knew the Panther was responsible for three murders and a string of armed robberies. His crimes included the kidnap and brutal murder of 17-year-old Leslie Whittle. However, there was a minimal amount of trust between the forces. Having reached an investigative impasse, senior investigating officers from the West Midlands police and Staffordshire agreed to an exchange of all the details of their investigations.

Two experienced detective sergeants left their forces with instructions to meet at a motorway service station. They were to exchange sealed boxes of documents and return to their headquarters so that their respective detective chief superintendents could open the packages. The West Midlands sergeant returned to his incident room. The box was opened: it was full of crime papers. The incident room staff broke out into spontaneous cheering. They were delighted. They knew there would be no cheering when their counterparts opened their package to discover that it contained old copies of the *Birmingham Evening Mail*."

Donald Neilson, the Black Panther, was arrested in 1975 for three murders and a series of armed robberies. He made an eighteen-page statement of admission to Detective Chief Superintendent Harold Wright of the Staffordshire CID. Maybe the newspapers the West Midlands had sent were of some use after all. Neilson was sentenced to life imprisonment, and he died in prison in 2011.

During the initial stages of an investigation, operational briefings are conducted twice daily. They are critical to all murder investigations. Everyone in the incident room can, and should contribute: typists and indexers are crucial, as they read, type and input every document onto the system. Through briefings, an investigation gathers momentum, and that encourages positivity. Without briefings, an investigation is solely reliant on the SIO for direction and progress. The first takes place in the morning to bring everyone up to speed, and issue actions, which are written tasks allocated to the outside crew detectives. Their level of priority is clearly indicated. The second briefing is conducted late in the day, to ensure that all priority actions have been carried out, and if not, then why not?

Detectives were always able to look busy, but their allocated actions ensured that they actually were. The briefing was also a platform to shine, experienced detectives knew exactly when to interject and impress the SIO, and when to say nothing. Officers who had taken statements had a forum to expand and explain, and also to give their assessment about the statement maker. The more important the statement, the more the incident room staff probed the statement taker to ensure that no detail of any importance had been missed. The SIO reviewed the investigation overnight, and decided on priority tasks for the following morning, and the cycle repeated.

Incident rooms have an inbuilt system of checks, and the theory is that nothing is ever missed. All documents pass through at least six individuals whose role is to scrutinise submitted work. Was it done thoroughly? Yes, there is nothing that raises your profile more than finding mistakes made by other people and highlighting them to the boss. MIU sergeants had supervisory duties as well as investigative responsibilities. A sergeant was nominated as the officer in charge of the case (OIC). That officer would be responsible for the preparation of the Crown Court file. Most tried to avoid this role, as drafting the case summary involved a lot of hard work and required a detailed knowledge of the case.

As a fledgling detective, I was at a conference and was unable to answer some of the barrister's questions. He was disappointed with my performance, and he chided me, suggesting that I should have been better prepared. Well, I inferred this from what he actually said, which was, "DC Smith, you had better up your fucking game, and start sparking. Otherwise, you can fuck off and take your case with you."

Murder investigations in the West Midlands followed a well-practised route. If no one was charged within 28 days, DCI Glen Moss and his review team turned up at the incident room. Glen Moss cast his experienced eye over all aspects of the enquiry. He accepted no excuses: police officers, staff and often SIOs were casualties of his reviews. The importance of the timing of this review was that it was not too late to retrieve evidence or launch fresh lines of enquiry. I liked Glen Moss, he was an experienced SIO who also had responsibility for cold case investigations. Mr Moss's only obligation was to ensure that all investigations were expedited and effective.

When a suspect was charged, the OIC submitted the case summary and liaised with CPS. John Davies would always try to get the right barrister for each case. Unfortunately, due to many circumstances, his original selection was not always available for the trial, and a replacement was nominated. At the start of a trial, the prosecution case is outlined to the jury. This should be powerful enough to capture the jury's full attention. The importance of the barrister selection is captured by the following timeless quote from an Anglo-French historian:

A jury is a group of people, who are randomly drawn together, to decide who has the best barrister. - Hilaire Belloc.

Following a charge, the police and the CPS would build and develop the case. Once charged and remanded, a suspect would be put before Birmingham Magistrates' Court. Suspects made repeated and determined bail applications, initially to the magistrates, and later at the Crown Court. The police would oppose these applications, and they usually did a much better job than I was able to with Mr Donovan in 1980. The case would then be sent to the Crown Court for trial. Very rarely does a suspect ever plead guilty to murder.

A Crown Court judge would set a non-negotiable timetable for submissions by the prosecution and the defence. Witnesses were traced, and their statements obtained. CCTV tapes recovered, viewed and evidenced. Seized exhibits would be forensically examined and become evidence. Telephones, both mobile and landline, would be scrutinised, and all the available data collected from the phone companies. All of this information was meticulously fed into HOLMES by the indexers. Suspects were traced, interviewed and either eliminated or charged. Dedicated officers were responsible for exhibits, disclosure and family liaison. Using specially trained officers reduced the number of issues at trial. Under the microscopic examination of a trial, the police investigation will be scrutinised by, in my experience, up to fourteen defence barristers, two prosecution barristers, CPS, the judge and jury.

Add the media to the equation, and you can see that not much was going to be missed.

I dealt with Yohanne Martin, on many occasions before he was murdered on the streets of West Bromwich in December 2002. I first met Yohanne in 1996. Uniformed officers Chris Rigby and Liz Devaney arrested Yohanne, and his brother Nathan, following a routine vehicle check. The car was okay, but the officers were less than happy about the bag of drugs they found stuffed up Nathan's jumper. A scuffle ensued, and the brothers were arrested. Ray Lomas was a local solicitor who always represented Yohanne and Nathan whenever they were arrested. As the Martins were connected to an organised criminal gang, I was tasked to deal with them. Mr Lomas warned me about Yohanne:

"I do hope you have a good case, Sergeant Smith," he said in his soft, Welsh lilt, "because if you don't, Yohanne will tear you to pieces in the interview. Yohanne doesn't need me, he has the mind of a top criminal barrister."

An hour or so later, following consultations with his clients, Mr Lomas seemed a little agitated. I made him a cup of cell-block coffee and asked him what the problem was. He explained that Nathan wanted to say, in his interview, that the police had planted the drugs on him. Though charged with defending Nathan, this did not sit well with Mr Lomas. He said that if Nathan maintained that stance, then he would have to instruct another solicitor. I liked Mr Lomas. Yohanne, in his interview, pointed out several issues with the prosecution case.

He was released without charge. Nathan made a full admission to possessing drugs with intent to supply; he was charged and later received a custodial sentence.

In August 1998, while he was at his home, Yohanne Martin was shot in the leg. His injuries were serious but not life-threatening. Within 24 hours, two men, who were suspected of that shooting, were also shot, wounded and hospitalised. I visited Yohanne, in hospital. Nathan declined to make a statement or name his assailants. Eloquently, he offered a hypothetical scenario for me to consider.

"Officer," he said, sitting up in his hospital bed, "if I made a statement naming who tried to murder me, and they just happened to be the two people who were shot the following day, then they might also make statements to the police, naming who had shot them." He stared at me to make sure I was getting this. "There would be two trials. If my attackers were acquitted, but the person who shot them was convicted, then that person might get a 25-year prison sentence. Now if that person just happened to be related to me, then I might wish that I had not spoken to the police at all." Well, that was food for thought, and he certainly had a point. With no leads and no complaint from the victim, that enquiry was going nowhere. I know that we could never be considered to be on the same side, but I enjoyed Yohanne's candour.

Four years after Yohanne's criminal investigation lecture, a midnight phone call instructed me to report to the incident room at Bloxwich police station at 7 am for a briefing.

Yohanne Martin had been shot and killed while he was sitting in a Mercedes SLK. This was a first for me. I had never been involved in a murder enquiry where I had met the victim while they were still alive. The investigation into Yohanne's murder was complicated. It involved three armed criminal gangs: The Raiders - a West Bromwich-based gang, were believed to be involved. They were affiliated to The Johnson Crew - another violent gang, from Birmingham. The ongoing turf war between these two gangs and The Burger Bar Boys, also Birmingham-based, and to which the Martin brothers were connected, was intense. This period was probably as busy as the West Midlands police had ever been. We could do almost nothing, proactively: we only just had enough officers to respond and investigate the murders and shootings.

After Yohanne's murder the BBC reported:

A man died in a hail of bullets in a "ruthlessly executed" gangland shooting. 24-year-old Yohanne Martin died instantly when he was shot six times as he sat in his Mercedes car on High Street, West Bromwich. The motive for the killing was based on the territorial rivalry between gangs operating in the Birmingham area.

If you can recall my ridiculous pre-joining comment about "Policing the area of my birth", well, the Burger Bar Boys were defined by their B21 postcode, the Johnson Crew by a B6 postcode. The postcode, in Birmingham, that separated those two areas is B19, the postcode for 38 Alma Street, my first home. Talk about being careful what you wish for. Following

Yohanne's murder, most of the Raiders decamped to Sheffield to lie low. Our enquiry gathered pace, suspects were charged, and John Davies was able to secure the excellent Timothy Raggatt QC as lead prosecution counsel.

A month after Yohanne's murder, in January 2003, Charlene Ellis aged eighteen and Letisha Shakespeare aged seventeen both died in a hail of bullets. They were the victims of a drive-by shooting outside the Uniseven hairdressing salon in Aston, Birmingham. The girls were killed with a MAC-10 machine gun, which empties a 32-round magazine in less than two seconds. It is almost impossible to control, and gun experts assess its reliability and accuracy as *spray and pray*. As that investigation continued Nathan, Yohanne's brother became a person of interest. Yohanne's murder and the Charlene and Letisha murders were linked. However, they were run as separate murder investigations.

In March 2003, during a case conference, Mr Raggatt had a query. The Mercedes that Yohanne Martin was sitting in when he was murdered had blacked-out windows. Yohanne had only borrowed the car that day, and the owner of the vehicle had confirmed that it did not have blacked-out windows when he lent it to Yohanne. It was not a major issue, but as always, if Mr Raggatt had a question that he needed the police to answer, then we had best just get on with it. Nathan Martin was the only person who could answer Mr Raggatt's query. Nathan refused to meet me at a police station. He was a member of an armed criminal gang and a person of interest in an ongoing double murder investigation. Worryingly, the firearms for that offence were still outstanding. I had a difficult decision to make. Either face Nathan or face Mr Raggatt.

I went to Nathan's home. I was armed with some statement paper and a pen. I would have preferred a ballistic vest and a firearms team. I was relieved to see Nathan's mother was home. She made me a cup of tea and told Nathan to be polite, and for that, I was incredibly grateful. While I sat on the sofa drinking his mum's tea, Nathan signed a witness statement. That confirmed that he had seen Yohanne blacking out the windows of the Mercedes with a kit he had bought from Halfords, on the day he borrowed the car. Yohanne, apparently, had thought it made him look like a music promoter. On that fateful night, the only thing that Yohanne was armed with were flyers promoting Dynamite Entertainment, a company that he had set up with his brother. Following a trial the *Birmingham Mail* reported:

Three people who murdered a rival gang member in a 'merciless and clinical shooting execution' in a Midland street were jailed for life. The three - a 22-year-old man Gavin Simms; Kieron Richards a 17-year-old youth; and 18-year-old Chantella Falconer - were convicted of the murder of Yohanne Martin, aged 24, who was shot dead as he sat in his parked Mercedes in West Bromwich in December 2003.

I am not sure if it is sad, ironic or prophetic, but many people knew Yohanne as Carlito, from the film *Carlito's Way*. The story of a gangster who decided to go straight, who was betrayed, ambushed and murdered. Yohanne's mother is one of the kindest people I have ever met. I do not know how she has ever been able to come to terms with the hand that life has dealt her. Having buried Yohanne, she has also had to come to terms with the murder conviction of Nathan. *The Guardian* newspaper reported:

Four gang members convicted of killing the teenagers Charlene Ellis and Letisha Shakespeare at a New Year party in Birmingham were jailed today for life by a judge at Leicester Crown Court.

Mr Justice Goldring recommended that Charlene's half-brother Marcus Ellis, Michael Gregory and Nathan Martin serve a minimum of 35 years and that Rodrigo Simms serve at least 27 years in jail.

Charlene, 18, and Letisha, 17, both college students, were killed two years ago when a semi-automatic sub-machine gun was fired from a slow-moving car outside the Uniseven hair salon in Aston, Birmingham.

In 2003 Kirk Robinson's trial for the murder of Wayne Johnson began. The defence barrister was Pat Thomas QC. He had a significant advantage over the prosecution as he had been working on the case for months. Mr Philip Parker QC was a very late replacement for John Davies's first choice, Timothy Raggatt QC. Because of this, Mr Thomas was able to outmanoeuvre the prosecution at every turn. He embraced all of the evidence and was polite and engaging to all the prosecution witnesses. When I was giving evidence, his cross-examination consisted of questions more to do with my welfare and professional ability than a test of my evidence.

"Gosh, you worked very long hours on this enquiry, Officer," and "My word, the people of Birmingham are incredibly fortunate to have such a dedicated police officer as you involved in an investigation of this magnitude." This was disconcerting stuff.

Mr Thomas accepted that his client's legal status in the UK was questionable; and that Robinson had repeatedly lied to the police throughout every interview. He agreed that Robinson had met the murderer and that his client was within a few feet of the gun when the fatal bullets were fired. He even accepted that his client had a firearm hidden in his house and that it belonged to him. Ballistics had confirmed that it was not the murder weapon: throughout the trial, Mr Thomas referred to that firearm as *the innocent gun*. He pointed out that his client was a criminal and a liar, but all of that did not make him a murderer.

The gunshot residue expert we produced as a witness was Robin Keeley. It was his evidence, almost alone, that had convicted Barry George of the murder of Jill Dando. Having secured that conviction in 2001, he was recommended to SIOs nationally as a gunshot residue specialist. In the Jill Dando case, Barry George had one particle of gunshot residue. We could prove that Kirk Robinson was practically wearing a gunshot residue suit. However, Mr Keeley did not perform at all well in the witness box. A sword of *Damocles* was hanging over him. If you followed the Jill Dando murder investigation, then you might be aware that following a further appeal, Barry George was acquitted. With weak testimony from Mr Keeley, our case began to sink. A superb performance from Mr Thomas ensured that the jury acquitted Robinson of the murder of Wayne Johnson.

Shortly after, the press reported:

A man accused of taking part in a plot involving the gunning down of a reveller at a Birmingham nightclub has walked free from court. Kirk Robinson was found not guilty of murdering Wayne Johnson by a jury at the city's Crown Court on the directions of Mr Justice Astill, following legal submissions. He also directed the jury to acquit Mr Robinson, aged 31, of Brixham Road, Winson Green, of charges of assisting an offender by receiving and concealing a firearm and possessing a firearm.

To prove he was a 'joint participant' in the killing, the prosecution needed to show he took possession of the murder weapon afterwards, which they had failed to do, he said. The judge said they had relied on there being a similar kind of gun discharge residue on the accused's jeans, but the evidence indicated that guns were fired on a frequent basis there, with bullets found in the roof. A spokeswoman for West Midlands police said enquiries into the shooting were continuing. She said: we note the decision of the judge. We are still keen to hear from anyone who may have information about this incident.

In the early hours of Saturday 20 November 2004 Ishfaq Ahmed, a nightclub doorman was shot and murdered outside the Premonition Night Club, Birmingham. The entire MIU were recalled to duty. It was gang-related, and the initial information indicated that the Johnson Crew were involved. Punchy Waldron was working on the intelligence side of the enquiry. The incident room was set up at Canterbury Road. Rather than going directly to the police station, I drove straight to the scene. I could never visualise roads and locations from maps, they looked like *Rorschach inkblots* as far as I was concerned. I always had to attend the location and examine the scene. I took in as much information as I could, and then I went to Canterbury Road. Once there I fielded some phone calls from officers who had also been recalled to duty. Some officers explained that they could only work on this job for the weekend because they had other commitments. I told them to come in but put a pencil line through their names. If they could only stay for 48 hours, then they were unlikely to locate and charge all the offenders involved by Monday. Other detectives turned up with a more positive attitude: Steff Hooton, Jason Kolar, Barry Bevan and Kevin Coley, to name a few, all worked tirelessly.

Sometimes a police investigation of this scale with numerous unknown suspects becomes a massive intelligence-gathering operation before any arrests are made.

As a result of Punchy Waldron's actions, the arrest phase started on day one. Punchy put a firearms team in an area where he believed one of the suspects lived, and at 8 pm, a vehicle of interest was stopped, and the first suspect arrested. Steff Hooton, Kevin Coley and I were tasked to interview Dean Smith. Forensic issues and other enquiries to trace witnesses and suspects were continuing. Four days of interviews resulted in Smith being charged and remanded. Punchy kept pushing the investigation. The day after the first suspect was charged, William Carter was arrested; Steff Hooton, Kevin Coley and I dealt with him. Following four days of interviews, Carter was charged. The incident room was gathering pace. With suspects now charged, all enquiries had to be done straight away. This did not suit everybody, but Punchy and I relished the speed of the enquiry. The operation continued. John Davies, our CPS guru, was liaised with as often as possible: he managed to obtain the services of the excellent Anthony Barker QC as lead prosecuting counsel.

On 14 December 2004, at 5 am, a further suspect was arrested. I was again in charge of Steff Hooton and Kevin Coley, the interview team. Identification procedures were arranged, and for the most part, the day went smoothly. I was scheduled to attend the funeral of Dave Harbon's mother that afternoon. She was a beautiful lady who had been able to battle cancer long enough to see her son get married to Sarah, who was stunning, albeit ginger. I only ever met Dave's mum at that wedding. Dave asked me if I would attend the funeral. I said I would. Adrian Atherley, the SIO, knew where I was going. Just after midday I put on my black tie and was just about to leave the station. The Handsworth CID was a proactive group of individuals and included DC Mick 'Bam Bam' Hobson.

Just before midday, Mick saw Carl Spencer, one of our suspects, walking into the notorious Black Cat café in Lozells, Birmingham. The café was almost a no-go area for the police. To enter those premises, it usually required serials of OSU in full riot gear. Mick chased Spencer into the café and arrested him. Bam Bam's actions were nothing short of heroic. Officers, backing up the arrest, searched the premises and found, a firearm, cash and drugs. The denizens of the café took umbrage, matters escalated, and a pretty serious public order situation developed.

Chief Superintendent Steve Jordan, my posh old sergeant from Kings Heath, was called out. Mr Jordan, though impressed by Mick Hobson, was angrily disappointed with Adrian Atherley's attitude. Our SIO insisted that we already had one prisoner and could not deal with another. I could hear Mr Jordan screaming at Atherley, telling him that his officer had risked his life to arrest a man for murder. I couldn't have agreed more.

I sat down. I thought long and hard, and then I made the wrong decision. In hindsight, I should have just gone to the funeral. The West Midlands police is big enough to deal with Spencer without me. I put my work tie back on and drove to Handsworth police station to deal with Spencer. At the station, I was greeted by a group of detectives who were very annoyed, and I couldn't blame them. I found an empty cupboard and started work; this was going to be difficult. A tannoy message instructed me to attend the superintendent's office.

I saw Superintendent Tom Coughlan: he shook my hand and pointed at his computer. He showed me an email sent to him by Steve Jordan. I skimmed past the first two paragraphs, which just slated Adrian Atherley, and then I read: 'The MIU is sending Detective Sergeant Wolfie Smith. If anyone can sort out this total debacle, then he can. He is a good man, so please look after him.' I can't tell you how much I appreciated his support. Following two days of hard work, Spencer was remanded in custody and eventually charged with murder. Even though he was sentenced to 30 years' imprisonment, I am haunted by the decision I made that day. I am genuinely sorry to Dave Harbon for letting him down.

Looking back, it seemed that those years were just a constant stream of murders, shootings and gang-related reprisals. I enjoyed the work and found it rewarding, but eventually, it started to take its toll. With extended hours and no rest days, I collapsed with exhaustion: my doctor diagnosed pharyngitis. She signed me off work and sent me home. I slept for a week. That investigation resulted in seven suspects being charged with Ishfaq Ahmed's murder, and they were to stand trial later that year.

The assistance and advice that John Davies gave, at the start of the enquiry, ensured that the case stayed on track. Case conferences were held as regularly as possible. There were problems with witnesses, facial recognition and case progression, but Mr Barker and John Davies ensured that the prosecution negotiated every hurdle. Mr Barker's patient and thoughtful approach instilled confidence in those who attended his conferences.

There were issues throughout the trial, and it was the first in Birmingham that had armed officers assigned to guard just one Crown Court. Four officers armed with machine guns stood outside the entrance, just out of view of the jury. Not long after the trial started, for legal reasons, a retrial was ordered. Justice Mitting was determined that the second trial would proceed and conclude. While the trial was in full flow, I found Adrian Atherley hiding in the police duty room at Birmingham Crown Court. He was terrified that he might have to give evidence. I knew the feeling, but surely this could not have been his first time in court.

Ishfaq's father, Afsar Khan, went to court every day; it must have been harrowing for him. The grainy CCTV footage of Ishfaq's murder was referred to and shown on numerous occasions. Before the video was played, Mr Khan was allowed to leave the court, ensuring that he did not have to repeatedly see the last moments of his son's life. As a mark of respect, the judge also paused the trial on 20 November 2005, the first anniversary of Ishfaq's murder. Following the trial, the BBC reported:

Six men who killed a doorman and wounded three others when they tried to force their way into a nightclub have each been jailed for life. Ishfaq Ahmed, 24, was shot in the back as he attempted to stop the group entering Premonitions nightclub in Birmingham in November last year. Four of the men are linked to a street gang called the Johnson Crew, Birmingham Crown Court heard.

Mr Justice Mitting said the defendants must serve at least 30 years in prison. Dean Smith, 20, William Carter, 29, Carl Spencer, 37, and Michael Christie, 33 - allegedly all part of the Johnson Crew - along with Leonard Wilkins, 35, and Jamal Parchment, 22, were found guilty of murder. They were also convicted of attempting to murder three of Mr Ahmed's colleagues, who were also shot and wounded. During the trial, an armed convoy brought the defendants to and from court every day. The gang had used 9mm handguns to shoot dead the father of two, after being refused entry to three nightclubs, the court was told during the two-month trial. Mr Justice Mitting told the men he was satisfied they were members of an armed gang and that the jury's verdict meant it had accepted that the shots were fired with the intention of committing four murders. He said, 'One such gun was fired and killed a blameless man for no other reason than that he was doing his duty as a doorman at a nightclub, and so caused you loss of face or annoyance, or both. It's merely a matter of chance that only one man died.' Detectives said the convictions were a significant breakthrough in the war against gun crime in the West Midlands. The Johnson Crew has been one of the most violent gangs in Birmingham over the past decade. Ishfaq's partner, Penny Morris, said that Ishfaq was a 'hero' for standing up to them."

When the guilty verdicts were returned, a brave, post-trial Adrian Atherley stood on the steps of Birmingham Crown Court talking to the press.

The BBC reported on 3 December 2005:

DCI Adrian Atherley said: 'This just goes to show what can be achieved with the help of the community and the hard work and commitment of the officers and staff who worked on this murder enquiry. Our thoughts today are with Ishfaq's family and we hope the verdict brings them some kind of peace and allows them to get on with their lives. This murder was committed by a group of men who cared nothing for the lives of others and showed no remorse for what they had done. The victim was an innocent man who was simply doing his job. This case was brought to trial because of witnesses being prepared to come forward and by police working with the courts and CPS to provide special measures in court so they could be allowed to give their evidence. The message is clear. If you carry guns or accompany those people carrying guns on the street, you are likely to go to prison for a very long time. I would also like to thank my team, I will not single anyone out.'

CHAPTER 20
31 DAYS

On Saturday 3 December 2005, the same day that six members of the Johnson Crew started their 30-year sentence, Jack Macleod was at home getting ready for his first proper night out in Leamington Spa. Jack was a good-looking, blond-haired lad. Five feet nine tall, but his slim build made him seem a little younger than his actual seventeen and a half years. Jack was aware of how young he looked and knew that getting served in a pub in Leamington Spa was going to be difficult. Getting ready to go out, Jack gelled his hair, wore shoes, a grey Bench jacket, jeans and a Saint Patrick's Irish Club T-shirt which indicated that he worked at the local Irish social club. Jack checked himself in the mirror and thought this might just work. Once dressed, he joined his mum downstairs.

"What have you got on, then?" asked his mum, Sheena. She meant the Diesel aftershave that Jack was wearing. She added, "You look gorgeous, and smell lovely." She fixed his collar, in that way that mums do. Jack was her only child, her little boy: he looked so grown up. Where had the years gone? She ruffled his hair, as much as his hair gel would allow. She told Jack to make sure that he kept enough money for a kebab and a taxi home. Her last ever words to her son were: "I love you, babes."

Sheena never saw Jack again. An uncle drove Jack the short distance to Leamington and dropped him off. Jack joined his best friend, Sean Rellis, for a night out. Between 8.15 pm and 10.45 pm, the clothes and the big shoes worked just fine, as the Ocean Bar was almost empty, and Jack drank unchallenged. However, once the bar filled up, the staff became a little bit more age selective. Something happened just before 11 pm, something so innocuous it shouldn't have mattered. Mark Hoolichan, a lad that Jack went to school with, came into the bar with four of his friends. Jack and Mark didn't hang out much at school. Jack was seldom in trouble, but the same could not be said about Mark. None of Mark's friends bothered to get him a drink, even though they were all over eighteen. Jack spotted Mark, realising that he didn't have a drink, and trying to impress, he ordered two Liquid Cocaine's (Schnapps and Jagermeister). The staff chose this moment to query both his and Mark's age, and without any ID, real or fake, Jack and Mark were escorted from the bar. None of Mark's friends went outside to check on him and probably were only with him to split the cost of the taxi home. Sean Rellis had gone for a game of pool. Sean didn't know Jack had been kicked out of the pub. Jack phoned Sean, who had just finished his game and had started to walk in the direction of his home. Sean turned back and joined Jack and Mark. It was 11 pm on a Saturday night, and Mark had not even had a drink yet. They now needed to find somewhere that they could get served.

"What about St. Pat's?" Jack suggested.

"Where's that?" asked Mark.

"It's not that far, but it closes at 11.30 pm. Sean will show you where it is," Jack said. In the absence of any other suggestions, Jack jogged to St Patrick's, an Irish club. It was next to the Adelaide Road Bridge which spans the River Leam. Sean and Jack were part-time glass collectors and had actually worked at the club the night before. Jack spoke to the manager of the club, Phil Tormey, and asked if the three of them could have a drink. Not a problem, was the reply. Sean and Mark joined Jack a few minutes later.

The St Patrick's social club was definitely not where Mark wanted to be. He was dressed for clubbing, and he wanted to be with his mates, but they had abandoned him. He was now stuck with these two clowns from school, in a crappy Irish social club. Mark had been working at Burger King until 8 pm, looking forward to his night out, which seemed to be going down the toilet.

"What a place," Mark mumbled as he walked into the main function room. Little seeds of jealousy and anger started to sprout in his gut. *Match of the Day* was on the TV. Liverpool, Mark's team, had won, but then so had Manchester United, the team that Jack supported. Some regular asked Mark if he wanted a game of pool. Why not ask Jack Macleod who plays pool for the county? Anyone could probably play for the county if their mum and dad had built a poolroom at the back of their house for them, thought Mark. "Yeah sure, I'll give you a game," said Mark.

The football on the television was okay, the game of pool was okay, but Mark really wanted to be with his mates. Jack was talking about Old Trafford, trying to explain that he had been there on a school trip, and remembered the pitch from ground level looking slightly curved, but as he'd been drinking, it didn't come out exactly the way he wanted.

"Jack, don't talk like a muppet: football pitches are not curved, everyone knows they are flat," rebuked Mark. Jack just smiled, but then Jack smiled at almost everything.

When last orders were called, Mark ordered six Jack Daniel's and Coke; Jack told him that he had no money left. Jack did have money, he had more than enough for a kebab and a taxi, but he did not want to spend any more on drink. To his annoyance, Mark had to pay for the drinks. Everybody was fussing over Jack and Sean. A barmaid came over to give Sean and Jack a cuddle. Shortly before the club closed, some family friends offered Jack a lift home. Jack declined. He didn't need a lift, he was out with his best mate, and his house was only a mile and a half away. Last orders were called at the club. It was a waste of a night for Mark, but at least he'd had some drink. Jack and Mark shared the Jack Daniel's, as Sean did not want any. Sean, Mark and Jack were the last three customers to leave the St Patrick's club when it closed just after 1.30 am. Phil Tormey said to a barman that he was giving a lift:

"Them fellows will be a long-time getting home." He pointed at the three young men slowly walking up the dark gravel path towards the well-lit and inviting Adelaide Road Bridge. In Jack's case, Phil Tormey was right: Jack never actually made it home.

Jack was reported missing the following morning. Sheena knew that Jack was dead. She has no idea why, but she was absolutely sure. She was right. Jack's body was recovered from the River Leam 31 days later. Sheena's brother Liam, a police sergeant in Warwickshire, formally identified Jack's body at the mortuary.

CHAPTER 21
ALL HE DID WAS

My finishing line with the West Midlands police was now in sight. I was an experienced detective sergeant, and I actually relished appearing in court. I would put on my three-quarter length grey Crombie coat, suit, neatly ironed shirt, unblemished silk tie and polished shoes, and attend to object to bail or give evidence. I made a point of checking the soap dispenser nozzles in police buildings before I used them. I could never be too careful, as there were some unsavoury uniform officers about who would tamper with that sort of thing just to ruin a detective's tie.

Giving evidence at court, knowing that defence barristers would try to tear police officers into little pieces, is so daunting that some colleagues avoided Crown Court at all costs. I can certainly understand why. Others accepted the responsibility as part of their job. I thought that Theodore Roosevelt could have been talking about those officers when he said:

It is not the critic who counts, nor the man who points out how the strong man stumbled, or where the doer of deeds could have done them better. The credit belongs to the man who is in the arena; whose face is marred by dust and sweat and blood;

who strives valiantly, who knows the great enthusiasms, the great devotions, and spends himself in a worthy cause. Who, at best, knows the triumph of high achievement; and who, at the worst, if he fails, at least he fails while daring greatly, so that his place shall never be with those cold and timid souls who know neither victory nor defeat.

Though I was approaching the end of my career with the West Midlands police, I was still involved in some fairly complex investigations. It seemed there was no chance of my just being able to wind down before I left. Luckily, I had done very little in the first ten years of my service, I guess I must have been pacing myself. One of my cases was a manslaughter investigation into the death of a drug addict. The victim had been breaking into a car belonging to a woman who had died of cancer aged just 52. The area where her vehicle was attacked was usually secure, but on that night, the gates had been left open to allow the family to visit and pay their respects. The press reported:

5 January 2006, *Birmingham Post*:

A thief who broke into a car died after being given a severe beating by two brothers, Birmingham Crown Court was told. Osman Jabber (23) and Saqib Jabber (20) have both denied the manslaughter of 34-year-old Tariq Rashid. Anthony Barker, QC, prosecuting, said the victim, a married father of two from Small Heath, was a drug addict who stole from cars. Mr Barker said the defendants, who were effectively all members of the same family, lived at an address in Alum Rock Road, Alum Rock, and in August 2004 spotted Mr Rashid on

CCTV breaking into one of their cars. The Jabber brothers and possibly others, he said, went to where the vehicle was parked. Mr Barker said they pulled Mr Rashid out of the car and gave him a severe beating. Mr Rashid died later the same day. A post-mortem examination revealed he had suffered a fracture of the skull, which had caused internal bleeding. Both were convicted of manslaughter.

In another case, a corrupt prison officer, Gulab Zaman, was supplying class A, B and C drugs, mobile phones and SIM cards to a criminal gang from Coventry, while the they were remanded in custody for murder. There had been two unsuccessful police operations that had targeted Zaman. Punchy and I went through everything. I noticed that it was not until Zaman was arrested that the authority to search his home was applied for. That is standard police procedure, but it took over an hour to obtain written authority and start the search, which explained why no drugs were found. Punchy applied for a search warrant in advance of Zaman's arrest, and as soon as Zaman was nicked, the search warrant was executed. Thousands of pounds' worth of drugs were found at his house. They were clingfilmed and moulded for plugging into the recipient's anus. Punchy and I interviewed Zaman. After we had both retired, Zaman was sentenced to seven years' imprisonment. Unsurprisingly, Punchy and I were not mentioned in dispatches:

Drug pusher guard jailed - by Mark Cowan, *Birmingham Mail*

A Court security guard was today behind bars himself after being caught plotting to smuggle drugs to prisoners attending trials in Birmingham. Gulab Zaman was arrested following a police swoop on the cells at Birmingham Crown Court, where he worked, and his home. Officers found capsules of drugs wrapped together in cling film in such a way they could be easily hidden away to avoid detection. Police are convinced the drugs, including diamorphine and cannabis, were intended for inmates being held in the court cells. Zaman, 25, from Bordesley Green, was jailed for seven years on Monday after pleading guilty to four counts of possession with intent to supply drugs. The cells beneath Birmingham's Crown Court house people who have been transferred from prison, where they are on remand, each day to stand trial. Detectives from the Major Investigation Unit were called in, in October 2006, after police received a tip-off that drugs may have been getting into prisons via people attending Crown Court. Zaman was working for Reliance Court Security at the time. He was arrested and later charged with drugs offences. An operation was conducted in conjunction with Reliance Security, the Courts and Prison Service at Birmingham Crown Court. At Zaman's home address we found drugs packaged up in what looked like large suppositories wrapped in cling film.' DCI Scriven said it was believed Zaman was passing the drugs to prisoners.

I enjoyed working with Punchy. He could do all the parts of an investigation that I couldn't: telephone call enquiries, intelligence, surveillance, and he could drive. He was great behind the wheel of a car and could navigate, eat a Big Mac meal and still get us to any place on time. I could handle the Big Mac but struggled with the rest. I would put case files together and liaise with CPS and prosecution counsel. We both conducted interviews, arrests and searches, which just about covers all bases on most criminal investigations. We had chequered but technically unblemished careers and dovetailed into an efficient team. We worked for whatever senior officer happened to be the SIO, and we usually had a good relationship with them. They wanted the job cleared so they could claim the credit and as much publicity as possible. Punchy and I just wanted to do our job. In my last year in the police, I worked from the new MIU building in Nechells. It was a large, open-plan office, loads of cliques, petty jealousies, and lots of history between warring factions of staff and officers.

I popped into the office at the end of a tour of duty just to book off. I sensed that the atmosphere was even more toxic than usual. I saw an unusually vexed Punchy Waldron who said that he needed to have a word with me. Something, or more likely someone, had upset him. We found an empty office. Punchy explained his problem. The phone on Punchy's desk had been ringing and Andy, an officer Punchy knew but had never really liked, had theatrically answered it.

"You want who? Punchy Waldron? No, mate, he's not here, in fact, he's hardly ever here. Call back if you want, but it'll probably just be me again. Bye." Given the unpleasant atmosphere that we worked in, no one wanted any bad press. The gaffers picked up on tittle-tattle and loaded their annual career review machine guns with gossip. Andy had probably just meant to impress those who overheard him. However, one of the ladies in the office was a big fan of Punchy's, and she told him. I asked what he wanted me to do about it.

"Right, Sarge," he started. He rarely called me Sarge and never in private. "Usually, I would have just put him up the wall and marked his card." That was pretty much the least that I thought that he would already have done. "Well, like you, I've only got a few months left in this job."

"Okay, Punchy, what do you want from me?" Punchy took a deep breath and seemed to wrestle internally before he blew out and answered, "Sarge," he said hesitantly, "it's about time I started acting like a grown-up, and not like a bully in the school playground. You're my sergeant, I'd like you to speak to Andy tomorrow morning before I come to work. Let him know that I've been told what he said. Tell him if it happens again, I'll put him in hospital." Wow, Punchy Waldron was no longer a Neanderthal. I was impressed but a little disappointed: Punchy's occasional flare-ups had always been entertaining.

The following morning, I arrived at work at 8 am. As I took my seat at my desk, I could see a distraught Andy head in hands and in a right state. I wasn't sure what had happened at first, and then I spotted an animated Punchy Waldron, bouncing around the office. He was wearing a combat jacket, a fucking combat jacket. That could mean only one thing. Punchy quietly said to me:

"That thing I spoke to you about last night, let's just say, it's been sorted." Normal service had been resumed.

There was a council leisure centre quite close to our office. To get a break from office politics, Punchy and I took up badminton. It only took 45 minutes to play, shower and change. It was just our refreshment break, remember - 45 minutes per man, per day, perhaps. It shouldn't have caused a problem, but it did. Some staff delighted in a bit of shit-stirring; they didn't say anything to us, but they made sure our boss was aware of our activities. In the circumstances, Detective Inspector Kevin Mulligan had no choice but to have a word with us. The evidence was pretty damning; our badminton rackets were sticking out of our work kitbags; I would sweat profusely for at least two hours after playing; Punchy and I would openly talk about our great shots, rallies and matches. We were doomed. Mr Mulligan called us into his office for a chat. He said that he had received a complaint from a person who wished to remain anonymous that we played badminton every day. He told us it was to cease forthwith. Mulligan dismissed us. Within seconds, Punchy identified four individuals who were going straight onto his probably-going-to-have-to-be-killed list. From that day on, Punchy and I played badminton every day that we were at work, including the day I retired. We even played once when I had a sprained ankle, just out of principle. I am sure Mister Mulligan was a good enough detective to know what we did. We ended up liking him, and he had his own issues with the West Midlands police.

In April 2006, I was on my pre-retirement course at Tally Ho. I was given advice about my police pension and how to apply for jobs. The course was okay, but what happened at lunchtime was an eye-opener. I was sitting on my own at a table in the canteen. The surrounding seats were taken up by a brand new batch of recruits: they were attending one of the many courses they had to attend. They all looked smart in their white shirts. They looked so young. I suppose I must have been that young once, but it seemed like an awfully long time ago. The recruits were chattering amongst themselves. I wasn't listening, at least I wasn't trying to, but the conversation kept looping back to the same thing and was hard to ignore. It was about another recruit by the name of Dave, who had done something and been sacked. They kept coming back to refrains of:

"I can't believe he got sacked just for that... it was very heavy-handed, the way they dealt with him." I was finishing my coffee but just a little intrigued. I introduced myself and asked what Dave had done to get sacked. One of the policewomen explained:

"Dave joined at the same time as us and was posted to the airport." The rest of the group were nodding. She continued. "Anyway, he fancied one of the women that worked in the perfume section of a duty-free shop." So far, so good: they can't have sacked him for that. "Dave showed her some funny YouTube videos." This Dave bloke seemed like an all right lad. I could feel myself starting a campaign to get him his job back.

"Well, all he did was - *it was incredible just how many times, in my service, that expression preceded an absolute atrocity -* show the woman a video of him masturbating."

"That was all he did?" The group nodded. I wouldn't have

sacked him. I would have had him publicly flogged to within an inch of his life.

"Incredible," I muttered. The group mistakenly thought that I sympathised with Dave's plight.

"The world has changed, mate," said one of the youngsters. "The gaffers have no idea. One of the policewomen on our shift has had her clitoris pierced: she's taken a picture of it, and most people at the nick have it as a screensaver on their mobile phone." I left before he could show me the photograph. He was right - the world had changed. I had joined 30 years too late.

CHAPTER 22
ALL LIES AND JEST

In May 2006, the MIU team I was on started work on a complex and sensitive case. The kidnap, unlawful imprisonment and wounding of Tommy Scragg. There was a whole series of issues throughout the investigation and the trial. The offence took place in Coventry. A police officer from Coventry was one of the main suspects. Other suspects had relatives who were police officers working in Coventry. The investigation was swiftly moved to Ladywood, Birmingham. DCI Philip Ball was appointed as the SIO. I have a lot of respect for Phil. As an SIO, he had a phenomenal success rate. Every one of his cases had been successfully investigated and prosecuted. His results gave him a relaxed, almost blasé approach to Crown Court trials.

At the start of the investigation, three of the main suspects, including the serving policeman Colin Hester, were identified, arrested, interviewed and remanded in custody. A fourth suspect, David French, was circulated as wanted. A few weeks later French was arrested at Heathrow Airport. Metropolitan police officers saw French driving his Jaguar and arrested him. In the boot of his car, he had a loaded handgun. Punchy and I drove to Heathrow police station to deal with him.

The custody sergeant told me that French had stripped off his shirt and was threatening anyone within earshot. The custody sergeant was concerned. French was huge, a 56-year-old bodybuilder the size of a small building. To search his house, I needed to know about the keys he had with him when he was arrested. Also, whether or not he had an alarm or a dog. I was asked to sign the custody record and acknowledge that, if French attacked us while we were in his cell, we had to accept full responsibility. Fair enough. I unlocked the cell door, and we walked in. French stood up and towered over us: he was enormous. French puffed out his chest, clenched his fists and growled.

"Do you two fuckwits have the remotest idea of just exactly who you are dealing with?" I think we were supposed to shit ourselves.

"Vince," Punchy said, "this cunt appears to have amnesia. He doesn't know who he is." French was not in the mood.

"Get out of my fucking cell," he snarled and took a pace towards us, fists clenching and unclenching. I explained that as the cell was actually in a police station, then it was ours and not his. French calmed down a fraction and said:

"Okay then, Tweedledum and Tweedle-even-fucking-dumber... say what you have to and then fuck off."

"David," Punchy said calmly, pointing to the bench in the cell and indicating that French should sit down. "We need your help. We need to know which of your keys fit the locks in your house and whether you have an alarm. I also need to let you know something else, if you have a dog and don't tell us, then we may have to destroy it to gain access to your house. So is there anything that we need to know?" French visibly deflated, then he slumped onto the bench and hung his head.

"The only Yale key on my key fob fits my front door. I don't have an alarm, but please don't kill my dog," he pleaded, "please, not my dog."

"There's a good lad," I said, patting the giant on the back. "Now, put your shirt back on and act your age. You are making yourself look like a right cunt." The custody sergeant was quite surprised to see us return unscathed.

French was interviewed, and he made no comment to all the questions put to him. He was charged and remanded in custody. While on remand, he wrote a letter to the CPS and explained that he had only made no comment throughout his interviews because his solicitor had wrongly advised him to. As he was now facing a trial, he wished to be seen and give his account.

I was working at Ladywood police station. Mr Ball had been promoted to Superintendent and was working from the police headquarters Lloyd House; most of us referred to Lloyd House as the 'Dream Factory'. Mr Ball retained SIO responsibility for this investigation. I phoned him, we caught up on a few matters, and he let me know that he had someone with him. Whenever Phil Ball spoke to me, he roughed himself up a little bit. He would become slightly more aggressive and swear: I never understood why. I could tell that the call was on his speakerphone and he was about to show off to whoever was with him. Well, that was his prerogative: after all, he was a superintendent. I explained:

"Boss, the CPS has received a letter from David French, who's currently in Leicester Prison. Apparently, he would like to speak to us and tell his side of the story."

"Vince, write back to him and just tell him to fuck off."

"Sir, we cannot do that," I said. "If we don't see French, then when he gets to court, he can make up any old rubbish and say that he would have told us earlier, but we refused to see him." There was a delay. I think Phil was just a bit disappointed that 'fuck off' didn't resolve all of the issues.

"Okay, then, Vince. What do you suggest should happen?"

"Sir, I think that French should be seen by two experienced officers, possibly Punchy and myself," I began. "This cannot be an interview, as he's already been charged, so we cannot ask him any questions. We should audiotape the conversation and just listen to what he has to say. Then get the conversation transcribed and have it on your desk within 24 hours." There was a pause. Phil Ball was now contemplating how best to impress whoever was with him. He cleared his throat and with authority addressed his speakerphone.

"Right, Vince, I want you to write this down." He paused. I did not get a pen. "I want French seen in prison as a matter of urgency, I want you and Waldron to see him, and that is an order. I want the conversation tape-recorded." I rolled my eyes. "Do not question him, he has been charged, so you cannot ask him any questions. I will then need the full transcript on my desk within 24 hours. All of this is non-negotiable." He took a breath. I waited. What he said next was the reason I liked him so much. "Now, Vince, is there anything about all of this that I don't understand?"

Stephen Linehan QC prosecuted the case, and I was the officer in charge. Remember, I said that the role of OIC required in-depth knowledge of the investigation, which would be tested - well, it was time for my examination to start. Mr Linehan stared at me from across a large table in a room at No. 5 Legal Chambers in Birmingham. It was an unusually crowded conference due to the presence of the Anti-Corruption Unit. Mr Linehan was in a bad mood due to a severe lack of nicotine. The unlit cigarette he clenched between his teeth only served as a painful reminder of his chronic habit. The fire regulations and a highly sophisticated sprinkler system prevented even Mr Linehan from lighting up. Early in the conference, I found myself directly in his cross hairs:

"Detective Sergeant Smith, what colour were the cable ties that the offenders used to bind and secure the victim?"

"They were black, sir." My cross-examination continued. "Black? Not blue, Smith?" His raised left eyebrow supported his verbal challenge. I could not falter: Mr Linehan was able to move countries across continents with that eyebrow.

"Sir, the offenders needed cable ties to bind the wrists of the victim. They couldn't find any, so dispatched two of their number to buy some from the local Halfords." Under the watchful beady eye of Mr Linehan, I continued. "While the errand-runners were away, a pack of black cable ties were found and used to secure the victim. The other men returned from Halfords with blue cable ties." I knew that Mr Linehan had based his challenge on the evidence that the police had recovered. I went for bonus points. "The blue cable ties and their receipt were found during the search of the scene." Mr Linehan's eyes twinkled. I had passed this test. I also knew that there would be other tests, lots of them. Mr Linehan was incredibly forceful in court, but in conference, he was absolutely brutal, as Phil Ball would find out later.

At murder trials, issues and problems were relatively common. If the defence can't score points on behalf of their client through cross-examination, they will try to muddy the waters by attacking police practices or behaviour. They used some well-practised tricks to weaken the prosecution team. When I was in the public gallery, the defence would often ask the judge to exclude me from the courtroom and only allow me into court to actually give evidence. If the judge queried this, the defence barrister would insist that the reason for my exclusion would become apparent during the trial; it never did. I suppose this was a compliment of sorts, at the start of my service, the defence could not wait to rip me to shreds on the witness stand. I had become an officer that they routinely applied to exclude from the courtroom as my presence and knowledge might assist the prosecuting counsel.

Police criticism at a trial is standard but how Punchy responded to that criticism was not. I always accepted that defence barristers would use every trick they could to defend their client: it was their job. Punchy felt that any challenge was a personal attack on him. During this trial, I was in the Birmingham Crown Court reception area just before the 1 pm lunch break. Punchy exited Court 1, he resembled *Aragorn* crashing through the gates at *Helm's Deep*. I could see he was annoyed and could guess why. Punchy had been cross-examined by Mr Germaine QC, the barrister defending the corrupt policeman Colin Hester. Punchy stomped towards me then spun on his heels. He was now staring at the door he had just almost taken off its hinges and was seething. There are twelve operational courts in that building; dozens of people were milling about. After about 30 seconds, the door to Court 1 opened and one of the first people to exit was Mr Germaine. Punchy cupped his hands around his mouth and shouted.

"What a waste of fucking space!" Mr Germaine saw Punchy, said nothing, clutched his briefcase to his chest, turned on his heels and went straight back into court to speak to the judge. A short discussion between Mr Germaine, Mr Linehan and His Honour Philip Gregory took place. Mr Germaine wanted DC Waldron reprimanded. The judge adjudicated that the incident had taken place outside his courtroom. If Mr Germaine wished to make a formal complaint about DC Waldron, then he should find a uniformed police inspector and do so. Mr Germaine said he reserved the right to deal with the matter in open court. Mr Linehan told us that the judge could not have looked less interested. The trial continued.

One week later, Punchy was called back into court over some spurious matter. Punchy took the stand. I sat in the public gallery: I wasn't going to miss this. Mr Linehan sat quietly, but I detected a mischievous twinkle in his eyes.

Mr Germaine now had Punchy exactly where he wanted him, in the witness box and under oath. After briefly discussing the trivial matter, which was clearly a ruse to get Punchy on the stand, he cut to the chase.

"Can you tell the court where you were last Wednesday, Officer?"

"We both know I was here," Punchy replied curtly, looking straight back at him. Germaine smiled. "And where were you at 1 pm, Officer?" Punchy looked at the large courtroom doors. "I think I was outside this court." Mr Germaine nodded. "Yes, Officer, that is also correct. Do you remember screaming something at me?" He paused to consult his notes. "Here it is: 'What a waste of fucking space': did you shout those words at me, Officer?"

"I did shout those words, but not at you." He stared at Mr Germaine. "I had just left the courtroom and was talking to Detective Sergeant Smith." He actually pointed me out to the jury. I resisted the urge to wave. He continued. "Sergeant Smith and I are both Aston Villa fans. We were talking about football, then for some reason, Sergeant Smith mentioned Lee Hendrie." Punchy spat out the name, turning to explain to the jury. "He is a player that I have never rated. I just kind of exploded with the words 'What a waste of fucking space!' I couldn't help myself!" He turned back to Mr Germaine and put his finger to his lips thoughtfully. "You know, thinking about it, that must have been the exact moment you were leaving this court." Punchy smiled sweetly. Mr Germaine was annoyed. "I don't think that you're telling the truth, Officer." No one did, but this was quality entertainment.

"Mr Germaine, I am on oath, so what I say is evidence. You are not under oath, so what you say is of absolutely no importance. Do you actually have any questions for me about the case?" Germaine pretended to read some papers, then said he didn't. Punchy left the witness box, when he was not in the line of sight of the judge and jury, Punchy winked at me.

Occasionally we fought amongst ourselves. Phil Ball in a conference during this trial overstepped the mark with Mr Linehan. Mr Ball suggested that Mr Linehan should use the letter that French had sent to the CPS from prison. Mr Linehan was even grumpier than usual. Still, no nicotine and the trial was beginning to wear on him. Mr Linehan, in short, rude sentences ridiculed Mr Ball's suggestion. It is very rare for prosecuting counsel to confront an SIO in the presence of junior officers. Mr Ball was visibly shaken; he retreated to the sanctuary of his office in the Dream Factory.

Mr Linehan had a bit of sport when he cross-examined David French. Mr French was trying to portray himself as an international businessman. He stated that he had spent a lot of time in Ghana. Mr Linehan began with a simple question.

"Mr French, just how well do you know Ghana?"

"Very well, indeed, I spent months there, working with their government."

"Ah, Ghana, now is that East or West Africa, Mr French?" The witness pondered for a moment.

"Er, it's East Africa. Yes, East Africa." Mr Linehan raised his left eyebrow.

"Really?" He stared at French, who was beginning to look uncomfortable.

French responded. "No, no, sorry, it's actually West Africa, definitely. West Africa, I think."

Mr Linehan delivered the coup de grâce.

"So, Mr French, all it took for me to move Ghana from one side of Africa to the other was for me to raise my left eyebrow and say the word really". I told you he could move countries across continents with that eyebrow.

During the trial, Mr Andrew Lockhart QC, who was defending Paul Farr, fired a shot across the prosecution's bows. Punchy Waldron and I had interviewed the principal witness for over twelve hours; each interview was tape-recorded. Mr Lockhart was clutching at straws.

"Ladies and gentlemen of the jury, we know the key witness was interviewed, and the interviews were tape-recorded. But we do not know what the officers said to the witness while the tapes were turned off. I do not wish to recall the detectives who interviewed him at this time. I am just making the observation that they may have coached that witness."

Mr Linehan practically marched Punchy and me into a conference room. Punchy was incensed if Mr Lockhart had recalled him to take the stand he may have taken a swing at him. Mr Linehan fixed me with his special stare, then said, "Well, you pair of clowns, can I rebut this, or have you just cost me my trial?"

I said, much more calmly than I felt: "Sir, we interviewed the witness for over twelve hours..." Mr Linehan went to interrupt, so I just kept talking. "Sir, please let me finish. The witness referred to the corrupt police officer as 'Chris' throughout every interview. Surely if Punchy or I had coached the witness, then we would have pointed out that Hester's first name was actually bloody 'Colin'. Don't you think, sir?" Linehan nodded, almost smiled and told us to clear off.

Yet another problem presented itself during the trial. One of the defence barristers stated in court that our victim, had given evidence in a case that year, as a prosecution witness. He added that Scragg had not been believed and was, therefore, a liar. This needed to be rebutted as soon as possible. Mr Linehan rounded on me during the break.

"Do you know anything about this, Smith?"

"Yes, sir," I confirmed.

"Well, is it correct?"

"No, sir, it is not," I replied firmly. Mr Linehan was now a human polygraph, looking for the tiniest indication that I was not telling the truth.

"Tell me more, Smith." I explained that I had been at the trial when Mr Scragg gave evidence. The defendant was convicted of all charges. Scragg's testimony was totally accepted by the court. Mr Linehan scoffed.

"Well, you would say that, wouldn't you, Smith?" He needed more. "Who was the prosecuting barrister, Smith?" Eyebrow semi-raised.

"It was Mr Paul Farrah, sir."

"Speak to him, Smith. Get him to confirm what you have just told me. Get back to me by 2 pm tomorrow."

"Don't you believ..." I began. He had already gone.

The following morning, right next to the police duty room, I saw Paul Farrah. He was dressed in his court robes and wig. This was ideal, and Mr Farrah is eloquent, polite and concise. Mr Linehan could learn a lot from his bedside manner. True to form, Mr Farrah courteously greeted me:

"Hello, Sergeant Smith, how the devil are you?" I confirmed that I was well. I explained what had been alleged about Tommy Scragg. Mr Farrah looked thoughtful. "Sergeant Smith, have you ever heard of Paul Simon?"

"Yes, sir, he is one of my favourite singers," I answered truthfully.

"Have you ever heard his song, *The Boxer*?"

"Sir, I really love that song."

Mr Farrah smiled. "Well, there's a verse in the song, that applies to all barristers, solicitors, judges and police officers. Do you know what the verse is?" It was evident to Mr Farrah from my expression that I did not. He cleared his throat and gently sang:

> ♫ *All lies and jest,*
> *Still, a man hears,*
> *What he wants to hear,*
> *And disregards the rest.*
> *Tra La La La La La* ♫

I understood and could not wait to pass this on. I went to the small room we used for storage and conferences during the trial. I could see that Mr Linehan was thrashing the life out of Punchy over something to do with the telephone evidence. I was relieved that it had nothing to do with me. I waited patiently. I knew better than to interrupt.

Superintendent Ball popped his head around the door, perhaps hoping for an apology from Mr Linehan; I suspect he is still waiting. Mr Ball nodded at me, and then with his eyes indicated that I should join him: we found another room. He asked me about the state of the trial, adding that he was struggling to make the daily conference with counsel. He asked if I could update him whenever necessary. Neither of us mentioned Mr Linehan's verbal attack at the previous conference.

"Oh, did you catch up with Paul Farrah?" Mr Ball asked.

"Sir, have you heard of Paul Simon?" I was met with a blank look.

"No, why? Is he giving evidence in our trial?"

"No, sir, he's a singer."

"Oh, the singer, yes, I've got all of his songs."

"Sir, have you ever heard his song, *The Boxer*?"

Phil Ball smiled and said, "Vince, that song is my absolute favourite."

Phil is 6' 4", he leant back in his chair, stretched out his arms, closed his eyes and started to click his fingers, then he began singing:

♩ *... Here's to you Joe DiMaggio,*
Jesus loves you more,
Than you will know,
Ho Ho Ho,
I said Ho Ho Ho ♩

Tears of laughter were streaming down my face; I was close to collapsing.

"Sir, that song you are singing is not called *The Boxer*."

"Oh, I think you will find it is, Vince."

Through the tears, I said, "Sir, the song you are singing is called *Mrs Robinson*, and just for your information, she isn't giving evidence in our trial either."

Following the 5-week trial the press reported:

Gang Tried to Cut Hostage's Hands Off with Machete!

August 2006, By Amardeep Bassey

Hooded thugs tried to hack off a businessman's hands with a machete before demanding £150,000 during a six-hour torture session in a Midland pub.

Thomas Scragg was left pleading for his life after the gang held him hostage and forced him to call his business partner for the ransom money which they claimed they were 'owed'.

More than half the money was eventually handed over to another gang member, serving West Midlands police Officer PC Colin Hester, who collected the £72,000 cash outside Little Park Street police station in Coventry where he worked.

Last week Hester, 36, of Stoke Row, Stoke, Coventry, an officer of four years who has now resigned from the force, was found guilty of blackmail following a six-week trial at Birmingham Crown Court. He will be sentenced next month. Three other members of the gang, David Houston, 31, his twin brother Anthony Houston of Bantock Road, Coventry, and Paul Farr, 36, of no fixed address, were sentenced to life in prison after being convicted of wounding, false imprisonment and blackmail.

They helped bundle Mr Scragg into a windowless upstairs room at the Prince William Henry pub in Foleshill, Coventry, after the victim arrived there with a friend, Mohammed Riaz.

He was gagged and bound before up to 12 men wearing hoods and masks began taking turns to beat and torture him with weapons, including a machete and hot iron.

Birmingham Crown Court heard how the thugs used metal cables and a machete to hack at their victim's face, slashing it down to the cheekbone.

They also threatened to drill Mr Scragg's kneecaps when he struggled to break free.

As well as the money, the gang demanded the logbook to Mr Scragg's £81,000 Mercedes and his £185,000 Lamborghini.

Giving evidence Mr Scragg, who received a two-year suspended sentence in June 2005 after pleading guilty to conspiracy to commit fraud, broke down in tears when he told the jury: 'They said they wanted the money or I would not get out of the room alive.'

He said he begged for his life and told his kidnappers he would raise as much cash as he could, eventually making contact with his business partner Paul Phillips, who began to gather together the money.

Following the sentencing of Colin Hester, the police issued a press release.

Police Constable in Blackmail and Torture plot.

A Coventry police officer has been jailed for five years for his part in the torture and blackmail of a man at a city pub. Colin Hester, who was based in Tile Hill, Coventry, collected ransom money from the victim's business partner in the city centre. He was yesterday jailed for five years after being found guilty of blackmail and pleading guilty to two counts of misconduct in a public office - at Birmingham Crown Court. Speaking after he was sentenced, Chief Supt Debbie Harrod, of the West Midlands police, said: 'The judge described this man's behaviour as utterly disgraceful and I would reiterate that.' The trial in June heard Hester - a police constable - collected the £72,000 ransom outside Little Park Street police station and took it to the now-closed Prince William Henry pub in Foleshill Road in May last year. His kidnappers demanded £150,000 and he contacted a business partner who collected the cash that was handed to 36-year-old Hester. David French, aged 57, of Windsor, was jailed for four years after being found guilty of blackmail.

The Coventry detectives always referred to this investigation as the 'Hester Ransom'.

In November 2006, I was working on an investigation into the murder of a black male. Intelligence indicated that this youth was killed in retaliation for a series of violent robberies on Asians. A suspect was arrested for the murder and detained. I was in charge of the interview team and working with Punchy who was, once again, the link to the intelligence cell. Interviews with murder suspects usually ran for days. Murder investigations would often require applications for further detention, these were made initially to a senior police officer, and subsequently at the magistrates' court.

Our prisoner was being held at Thornhill Road police station, which was another large converted house. There was nothing pretty about the building, and, although many licks of paint had been applied, it never looked any better. Once inside the recently redecorated public entrance, the station became a maze of narrow corridors, steep stairs and small offices. Mr Ahmed legally represented the suspect. I had not met him before: he was impressive, polite, well-spoken and smartly turned out. He wore Armani glasses, an expensive suit, and a shirt and tie: his entire ensemble was colour coordinated. Through the cut and thrust of the interviews, Mr Ahmed remained calm, professional and debonair. We exchanged mobile telephone numbers so that I could update him as to when his client's interviews would take place.

A warrant of further detention was applied for on Friday 17 November 2006. The hearing was held at the Birmingham Magistrates' Court. The detention extension was authorised at 9.10 pm. The police were granted a further 27 hours to continue their enquiries and conduct additional interviews. Mr Ahmed approached me immediately after the hearing and said that his client should be put on a lie-down and have no further interviews that night. I informed Mr Ahmed that he should be at Thornhill Road at 10 pm, as that was when his client's next interview would start. Persons in custody have to be allowed time to sleep, but if we didn't use the time we had been given to conduct further interviews, then that time could be halved by an early night's sleep. Mr Ahmed, of course, knew this. Our exchange had verged on almost heated. Punchy and I drove to Aqua House to collect some photographs, for the interview, at 9.45 pm my mobile phone rang, I could see from the caller ID that it was Mr Ahmed.

"Hello, Mr Ahmed, what can I do for..."

"You bastard, you fucking bastard! You, you've set me up, you fucking fucker!" Mr Ahmed was screaming. I tried to calm him down. He was shouting so loud that Punchy could hear him. I ascertained that Mr Ahmed was at Thornhill Road. I told him we would sort this out on my arrival and ended the call. Punchy was angry.

"Right, Sarge, as soon as we get to the nick and you see this cunt, punch him. If you don't, I will. No one speaks to us like that." I explained to the Punchmeister that any punches that I threw would be because I wanted to throw them, and not an instruction from someone who thought that a fist to the face should be the start of most conversations. There had to be some sort of explanation.

Punchy and I arrived at Thornhill Road and walked through the public entrance. At the back of the office, a uniformed sergeant waved at me and put his finger to his lips, indicating that I should be quiet. I complied. He led us to an empty office. Once inside, he closed the door. He then burst out laughing but tried to stifle the sound as much as he could. He established who I was and confirmed that Mr Ahmed was making a formal complaint about me to the duty inspector:

"Vince, did you tell Mr Ahmed to be here just before 10 pm tonight?"

I nodded. "Well, he arrived at 9.40 pm. He was waiting in the public area. It gets a bit lively, which is why they have metal screens dropped down to protect the staff." I had no idea where this was going or what it had to do with me. The sergeant continued. "The local drunk wandered in, he's a massive bloke, a real handful. I don't even know why he came in. Maybe it was a full moon or something. He took one look at the immaculately turned out Mr Ahmed and decided that if he was going to stand any chance of surviving in the Borough of Handsworth, then he was in immediate need of a makeover." "A makeover?" I asked perplexed.

"Yes," the sergeant carried on, starting to giggle again. "He grabbed the solicitor by his tie and swung him around like a rag doll. His glasses have smashed, his clothes are ruined, and he is pretty badly shaken up."

"And he thinks that I arranged for this to happen?" The sergeant grinned. "He knows you arranged for this to happen. Why else would you have been so specific about the time he was to get here?" The three of us were giggling as quietly as we could. I went to see Mr Ahmed he was a mess, broken spectacles skewed on his head, a knot in his silk tie that he was never going to undo, jacket ripped, one shoe missing and in a state of shock; he was sitting with the duty inspector. He had been placated, at least to some extent. A further interview was conducted; Mr Ahmed, still in a daze, left the station without saying goodbye.

Four months later, I was at Queens Road police station when, by chance, I saw Mr Ahmed. His sartorial elegance had been restored and his spectacles replaced. I opened with:

"Hello, Mr Ahmed, you are looking a lot better than the last time I saw you." I offered my hand, which he lightly shook. I then asked, "Would you like to apologise to me for your outrageous allegation that I arranged for you to be attacked at Thornhill Road police station?"

"Sergeant Smith," Mr Ahmed sighed, "I am still conducting enquiries into that matter, and at this stage, I have not been able to totally eliminate you as a suspect." He smiled, shook my hand properly and left.

Before I retired, I decided to do something about my eyesight. I had reached the ridiculous stage of my life where, even though I wore contact lenses, to read, I had to wear spectacles as well. I thought that laser surgery might resolve my optical issues. Eye surgery held no fears for me if my eyesight continued to deteriorate, then it would not be long before I was wearing sunglasses and carrying a white stick.

Following an examination at a clinic in Edgbaston, I was told that, although surgery would drastically improve my vision, I was still going to have to wear reading glasses. As I was paying privately, my procedure was scheduled to take place a month later. The clinic's instruction for post-operative care was that all patients had to be collected, as they would not be able to travel unassisted.

On the day, just before I went to the operating theatre, I spoke to my consultant who asked if I wanted to try something that might work. She explained that they could correct my left eye, but not as much as my more dominant right, and that would allow my left eye to read. The procedure had a 90% success rate, but if it did not work, I could pop back in and have my left eye strengthened. I agreed to give it a go. The operation was straightforward: 25 seconds' laser treatment on each eye. Following the procedure, my eyes were teary and blurred; a nurse led me into the reception area. An extremely busy receptionist asked who was collecting me. I said, my wife. I sat down and picked up a magazine that I pretended to read. I gave it ten minutes then pointed to the CCTV monitor next to the receptionist and said:

"That's her, just driving into your car park, thanks." I stood up and went to walk out.

"Not so fast, Mister Smith, what car does your wife drive?"

"A red Fiat Bravo."

"Sit down, Mister Smith, that was a blue BMW that just drove in." Chastened but undeterred, I sat down. I waited a further five minutes until the receptionist was even busier. I stood up and said, as I was walking towards the exit:

"That's her now, thanks for everything, see you." The receptionist turned away from the people that she was speaking to. She firmly said, "Mister Smith, the car that just came in was a white Mercedes. Your wife is not coming to collect you, is she?"

"No, she isn't. I am really sorry." I was more than a little embarrassed. Almost in a panic, the receptionist asked:

"Please, at least tell me you are not bloody driving home. For God's sake, you have just had eye surgery." I apologised for lying and showed her my train ticket. She reluctantly let me go and told me to return in two weeks for a check-up.

A fortnight later, I went back for my post-operative examination. My consultant was really keen to know whether the procedure had worked. I slumped down in a chair. Her enthusiasm slightly dampened.

"Can you read without glasses?"

"It's not good news, I'm afraid." My consultant looked disappointed. I added, "My eyes have started talking to each other, and it's rather worrying."

"Talking to each other? What on earth are they saying?"

"My right eye is saying, 'I can see really far.' And my left eye is saying, 'Yeah, but I can read', Doctor." My smile wasn't reciprocated. My eyes were fine. I have never had any reason to go back.

In our last eighteen months in the West Midlands police, Punchy and I dealt with seventeen defendants who were convicted of 42 nasty offences; the offenders were sentenced to over 250 years in prison. You might think the police would have wanted us to stay on. Not a bit of it. The organisation practically put up bunting and gave out party hats when we were leaving. No effort was made to retain our services. Still, I was a grown-up, and it didn't really bother me that much. As Punchy so succinctly put it:

"Vince, it's their fucking loss."

CHAPTER 23

A PASSAGE TO LEAMINGTON

A journey from Kings Heath to Leamington Spa takes 38 minutes in a car, and it takes seven hours to walk. From the time my police journey started, it took me 28 years to get there. In February 2007, as part of my exit strategy from the West Midlands police, I applied for a job with Warwickshire police, as a civilian investigator. DCI Adrian McGee interviewed me. I was successful and accepted their offer of a post with the serious and organised crime team, at Leek Wootton, Warwickshire. I gave the required 28 days' notice and had the pleasure of an exit meeting with the Chief Constable of the West Midlands police, Mr Paul Scott-Lee. We had a coffee and an enjoyable chat. I waited until he was ushering me out of his leather-suited office.

"Sir, I leave the organisation in three days. Can I ask a favour?"

"Of course."

"Sir, can you find out who will be the best-looking employee after I leave?" He laughed, thought about it for a second or two, then said, "You know, I think that it is actually me." I could hear him chuckling as I walked along the corridor towards the lifts. I left Lloyd House for the last time.

On my final day at work, after my game of badminton with Punchy, I went back to the office and sneaked out via the fire escape. I jumped in my car and drove home. I left behind friends and colleagues who were gathered to give me a proper send-off. Some sent me abusive text messages, but Punchy really went to town. If the swear words were taken out of his messages, they would have been blank. Flowers, cards and whisky were unceremoniously delivered to my wife while she was at work. It's probably a bit late to apologise to my well-wishers, but with hindsight, I now regret leaving the way I did.

The Warwickshire police crest is a bear and ragged staff. It is a heraldic sign that dates back to the 15th century. Warwickshire police adopted the crest in 1857 when the force was founded, it shows a bear chained to a tree and depicts the barbaric pastime of bear-baiting. For three centuries this was entertainment for all the family and Kenilworth, in Warwickshire, was a popular venue. The lack of rules made the event easy enough to follow. A bear was chained to a tree, and over several hours, it was repeatedly attacked by waves of vicious mastiffs. When the bear tired, it was torn to shreds and eaten by the dogs.

A possible conversation taking place at Kenilworth Castle, Warwickshire, on a Saturday afternoon, circa 1575. Henry Tallis, a local man, talking to a fellow spectator, waiting for the bear-baiting to commence:

I hope this is as good as last week, me and the kids were right at the front. The bear was so big they had to chain it by the neck, he must have killed about fifteen dogs before he was eventually ripped to pieces. Henry then completed his match report. We got splattered with blood, it was brilliant.

If people feel that the graphics on computer games are horrific and too realistic today, just how unpleasant was the family entertainment back then? Well, times change, and in 1999, without any fuss, the Warwickshire police crest was fine-tuned. If you look at it today, the chain is no longer there. A police officer may also airbrush the truth when asked to explain the force's crest to a group of schoolchildren:

"Well, kids here you can see a big bear. Let's call him Django. He's standing next to his favourite tree, waiting excitedly for UPS to deliver his unicycle. Django can then start training to fulfil his dream of joining a circus. All together now, children... Aaahhhhh."

In case you are wondering what happened to Django? Well, one of his descendants is in a new role, assisting Warwickshire police in their ongoing fight against crime.

The week before I started work with Warwickshire, the following article was reported in the press.

The Coventry Telegraph 26 April 2007:

A police blunder has halted the inquest into the death of tragic Warwickshire teenager Jack Macleod. The dramatic ruling was made by the coroner when it emerged that police had failed to disclose significant witness statements.

Michael Coker ordered that the enquiry into the 17-year-old's death could not continue until he had read the new documents. The blunder shocked Jack's father who said he was "gobsmacked", and the family said their confidence in the police was severely damaged.

Barney Branston, for Warwickshire police, told the hearing at Leamington town hall yesterday that nine witness statements and a 23-page police interview transcript had "fallen through the cracks" and not been submitted to the coroner.

He said the force had tried to supply all relevant statements to the court, but had been the victim of "human error". Jack's body was recovered from the River Leam in Leamington in January 2006, a month after he went missing while on a night out with friends.

The youngster, also known as Jack Fisher, was last seen alive by friends at the Adelaide Road Bridge. Earlier, the inquest heard that Jack had been drinking for a number of hours before his disappearance. The coroner said: "I am extremely disappointed that we have reached this situation, particularly for Jack's family, who had hoped to achieve closure on these tragic events." He said he needed the time to consider them and decide whether the witnesses ought to be cross-examined.

Jack's father, Kevin Fisher, said he was "gobsmacked" by the day's events.

An angry Mr Fisher said: "As a family we have been on tenterhooks for the last year. We had hoped for some closure this week. "This is a tremendous disappointment, but we must be sure the inquest is done right. If anything, this is a lesson in how it should not be done." Jack's mother and stepfather, Sheena and Ewan Macleod, of Tachbrook Road, Leamington, were too distraught to speak as they left the hearing. Earlier, their barrister Jane Sarginson told the coroner the couple were appalled by the sudden emergence of the new documents. She said: "Their confidence in the police has been seriously undermined."

A spokeswoman for Warwickshire police said the force would offer an immediate apology to Jack's family. She said: "We will also investigate how this mistake came about, and we will be explaining what went wrong."

The Independent Police Complaints Commission is supervising investigations into complaints about the police enquiry made by Mr and Mrs Macleod.

I joined a team of ten police officers and support staff on the serious and organised crime team. Some of our squad spent the day using the gym facilities; others went jogging around the grounds. Wednesday afternoon was football, and we played on a pitch in the middle of the police headquarters. An awful lot of thought and effort went into the refreshment arrangements.

I found this fascinating. I had left an organisation where the time book, and any sort of time off, was scrutinised by the management with an industrial microscope. In Warwickshire, they didn't even use a time book. I'll admit after the hustle and bustle of the West Mids it was relaxing. However, after a week, I was bored.

When I left the West Midlands police, I used part of my pension to buy a Citroën Picasso. I was insistent that the car I wanted was diesel, the garage offered me great deals on their petrol cars, but this only made me more determined to hold out for a diesel one. Eventually, I was offered a diesel car at the right price.

On Wednesday, 16 May 2007, I was driving my nearly new chariot to work. It was a beautiful sunny day. I was travelling through Middle England to Leek Wootton. I looked at my fuel gauge, and it was getting low. I pulled in at a garage and paid £50 to fill my car up. I continued my journey to work but had only travelled about ten miles when I saw, in my rear-view mirror, a smoke cloud of Batmobile proportions. I knew exactly what I had done, I had filled my Picasso up with unleaded petrol. My car coughed and spluttered, but I somehow managed to limp it to a remote plant and shrubbery garden centre, called Barnes Close Nursery.

I pulled over and made some phone calls. I rang my office and explained what I had done. I was told not to worry and that they would just have to get someone else to play centre half that afternoon. I called the RAC. They sounded helpful but said that I was not a priority. I was promised a recovery vehicle within the hour. It was 9.30 am. I took out my flask of coffee and sandwiches and then settled down with the *Daily Mail*. Two hours later, with my newspaper read, and the crossword completed, the RAC called me. They asked me to confirm the postcode of my location. I reminded the RAC they had promised to assist me within an hour. 90 minutes later, the recovery driver called. He explained that he was struggling to find me, but that he had some knowledge of the general area.

"Is Barnes Close Nursery the place that always has an enormous Christmas tree outside it in December?"

"December? December mate?" I was annoyed. "The RAC promised me someone within the hour, and it's still only fucking May." The recovery driver snorted, and then the line went dead. Five minutes later, the truck turned up. The driver was pissing himself, laughing and hardly able to speak to me. He hooked my disabled car to his truck and drove off. I could see his face in his rear-view mirror, he laughed all the way to the garage. When he separated our vehicles, he still couldn't talk, he just gave me a hug and drove off.

I worked from an old accommodation block at the police headquarters. In the next room was a retired copper, Graham Lord. He was the spitting image of the actor Gareth Hunt who played Mike Gambit in the TV series The *New Avengers*. Graham had worked for Warwickshire police for 35 years. He was one of the cops who escorted Gordon Wardell to court after he was charged with the 'Nuneaton Murder' all those years ago. Graham gave me a guided tour of Leek Wootton. It was a mishmash of buildings that ranged from a huge country mansion to an ugly 1960s brick box. Graham introduced me to some notable people within the organisation. I remember thinking that nobody seemed to be doing anything too quickly. It was not easy to recognise the existence of a rank structure; everyone was on first-name terms. Graham introduced me to Bill, Ken, Adrian and Andy - an assistant chief constable, two superintendents and a chief inspector. Where I had come from officers of that rank had first names, but I was never brave enough to use them. During the tour, Graham pointed to a building that housed the Warwickshire MIU. He gave me some advice.

"Stay away from that place, mate," he said earnestly, "the Jack Macleod job has gone a bit pear-shaped. There's talk of coppers getting sacked." It was clear that he meant this as a warning. "If you go in there," he continued, "you'll probably end up dealing with the enquiry."

Graham turned out to be surprisingly prophetic.

In June 2007, I was in a briefing room in the accommodation block. Chief Constable Keith Bristow, my superintendent from Rose Road, popped down to speak to our team. After a few minutes, most of my colleagues had made their excuses and left. Eventually, Mr Bristow and I were alone. The room overlooked the football field in the middle of Leek Wootton, and a police helicopter was landing on the football pitch. Keith Bristow pointed to it and grinned.

"Vince there you go, there's the helicopter you asked me for ten years ago."

Keith Bristow dragged Warwickshire police kicking and

screaming into the 21st century, which was no mean feat. Some of their efforts at police work left me buckled with laughter. One day our team had an impromptu drink at Warwick Racecourse, and DC Wayne Plester was hammered. He let himself down quite badly in the curry house by falling asleep and plummeting face-first into his chicken korma. He scored nil points for the approach, the flight and the entry.

The following morning our team executed a drugs warrant. Feeling just a little embarrassed, Wayne tried to recover some standing with the team, by putting the front door in. Wayne was wearing the full kit: riot helmet, body armour and big leather gloves. Wayne hefted back the weighted metal door *bosher* (possibly named after DC John Pestridge, my shoe-toting colleague) and let rip. It was an impressive strike made with all his strength. Sadly he missed the wooden door frame by inches and connected with the door's paper-thin plate-glass window. This offered somewhat less resistance than Wayne had been expecting and he followed his bosher, head first, through the broken window. As he disappeared through the door frame, there was a ripping noise as the shards of glass cut through his protective gear and gave his beer belly a foot-long caesarean scar. I'm sure it hurt a great deal, but the team were laughing so much it was hard to offer assistance. I caught my breath long enough to ask Wayne if he was trying to smash down the front door and the back door at the same time. Wayne grimaced and took himself off to the Accident and Emergency department for sutures.

CHAPTER 24
TRAGEDY STRIKES ON THE M40 MOTORWAY

On the afternoon of Sunday 12 August 2007, Gerry Tobin was riding his motorcycle on the M40 in Warwickshire, when he was shot and killed. Gerry was a leading member of the Hell's Angels and had just left the 'Bull Dog Bash'. Approximately 40,000 bikers had congregated, from all over the world, to attend the annual event at Marston Green in Warwickshire. As it was a weekend, every available member of police staff was drafted onto the murder enquiry. From the outset, this was going to be difficult. With the vast number of people that needed to be traced, it would have been easy for the investigation to be a long-drawn-out intelligence-gathering exercise. One man made sure that did not happen. No, not me, it was the Chief Constable of Warwickshire police, Keith Bristow.

Twice-daily briefings were held in a lecture theatre, which was fitted with banks of seats, and a large screen for presentations. During the briefing's officers gave updates, and a problem loomed: quite a few griped that the Hell's Angels' creed dictated that they were not allowed to speak to the police. This was going to massively hinder the enquiry. Mr Bristow sensed that unless he stepped in and addressed this issue, a wave of negativity could sweep through the incident room, and officers would use this excuse to shy away from doing their job. Mr Bristow stood up to address the troops. At 6' 4" and the only officer in the room in uniform, Mr Bristow struck an impressive figure. He laid out the ground rules.

"Ladies and gents, we are here to investigate the cold-blooded murder of a man, who was doing nothing more than riding his motorcycle on the M40 motorway." He let this sink in and continued. "Because of who he was, and where he had come from, this is going to require the incident room to have contact with hundreds of Hell's Angels and bikers. Your job is to talk to and question everyone that you've been tasked to see. If any biker makes a formal complaint that you have breached their code, then it will come to me. I personally guarantee that no disciplinary action will be taken against anyone who is just doing their job." The briefing room was quiet. Keith's eyes scanned his audience: he was looking for any sign of dissent. He saw none.

"If anyone is not clear about this, then please see me immediately after this briefing."

The investigation gathered momentum, arrests were made, and evidence secured. The suspects were identified as being another motorcycle gang 'The Outlaws'. Some members were arrested on suspicion of the murder. Keith Bristow was at most of the briefings, ensuring that the pace and positivity never dropped. After only three weeks the CPS authorised murder charges against the arrested 'Outlaws'. With the CPS decision to press charges in his hand, Mr Bristow addressed a packed briefing room; he was only about four seats away from me when he stood up to speak.

"I have worked in several police forces, and on many serious crime investigations. I can honestly say that this operation is easily the best that I have ever been involved with."

He seemed genuinely proud and almost emotional. The room was quiet: he was right, it had been an incredibly quick turnaround given the circumstances. I broke the silence and said, just loud enough for Keith to hear:

"It may be his best job, but it hasn't made my top ten." A few people giggled. As we filed out of the room, the tall and smartly uniformed Keith Bristow brushed past me. As he did, and without moving his lips, he hissed a single word into my ear, "Twat". Which I thought was fair enough. A very good source told me that he once said about me, "Vince Smith is a force of nature, and a very hard man to ignore when he is in your company. Although it is definitely worth the effort." I always liked Keith. I believe that if he had not wasted his time passing exams, then breezing through a series of promotion boards, Keith Bristow would have made a bloody good detective sergeant.

With the offenders now charged, a detective sergeant in the incident room asked me which barrister I would want as lead prosecution counsel. It was a pretty easy choice: Timothy

Raggatt QC, any day of the week, and twice on Sunday. Any Crown Prosecution Service school report for Mr Raggatt would likely include the line, 'Young Timothy is rather effective at prosecuting armed criminal gangs'.

Through the CPS, Warwickshire police secured the services of Mr Raggatt and on the 28 November 2008 *The Guardian* newspaper published the following report:

Seven members of the Outlaws motorcycle gang were sentenced to life in prison at Birmingham Crown Court today for the murder of Hell's Angel Gerry Tobin.

The men were convicted of killing Tobin on the M40 in August 2007. The last two members of the South Warwickshire chapter of the club on trial were found guilty of murder yesterday after jurors deliberated for eight days.

The seven include Sean Creighton, 44, from Coventry, who pleaded guilty to murder and firearms charges before the start of the trial last month.

The others were Simon Turner, 41, from Nuneaton, Dane Garside, 42, Dean Taylor, 47, Malcolm Bull, 53, Karl Garside, 45, and Ian Cameron, 46, all from Coventry.

In October 2010 there was a lot of jockeying for position within the police nationally: it was a period of considerable uncertainty and change. Though there will always have to be modifications, one area that cannot change is the operational front-line police officer. It is the sharp end of policing: these officers work nights, and regularly deal with angry and violent people. I was reading the *Police Review*, a monthly police magazine. I nearly snorted my coffee out through my nose when I read a superintendent's comment:

"Let's not forget about senior police officers. We are the invisible front line."

What a load of shite. Later that night, I was looking through Debbie Menzel's Facebook page. Debbie is an ex-colleague from the West Midlands and has devoted her retirement to the collection and circulation of police photographs and stories. She has well over 50,000 photos on her Facebook page. It is brilliant for prompting memories of places and people I had forgotten. Her page contains, almost exclusively, West Midlands police officers. I stumbled across a picture that showed Sir Geoffrey Dear, my previous chief constable, leading the charge in a public order situation. He was a leader, and there was nothing invisible about the front line that he was a part of. I wondered if Mr Dear had a copy of the photo. I tracked down his email address. He is now a member of the House of Lords, I emailed the photograph to him with a short message. I included my service details and a contact mobile phone number. A few weeks later, while I was walking my dogs, my mobile phone rang. I answered and immediately recognised the polished tones of Lord Geoffrey Dear. In my email, I said that we had met and had a brief conversation at Lloyd House.

"Vincent, can you tell me where and when we met? I must warn you, if I do not remember it, I will not continue with this conversation."

"Sir, it was in 1986. I had been off work for three weeks

with a head injury and had to report to the force surgeon at Lloyd House. You and your wife joined me in the lift. I looked a complete mess as my head was covered in cuts and bruises. Breaking the ice, you asked me if I had ever met your wife. I asked, what exactly am I being accused of. You both burst out laughing." Mr Dear was chortling on the other end of the phone. He told me that whenever he and his wife had words she jokingly threatened him with, "I can always go and live with that bloody man we met in the lift at Lloyd House, Geoffrey."

The actual circumstances of my head injury, all those years ago, was that I fell off my pedal cycle at 2 am while cycling home from work. Moseley to Solihull was a ten-mile journey and contained a few treacherous hills. I had made the trip considerably more challenging by being pissed, and that had pretty much sealed my fate. On one long downhill stretch, I fell asleep on my bike and hit a pothole. I woke up in an ambulance. With a bleeding head wound, a lack of motor skills, and slurred speech, the ambulance crew were convinced that I was horrifically brain-damaged. I eventually managed to persuade them that I was just drunk.

Regarding the photograph, Mr Dear confirmed that he did not have it, but asked, "Are you sure it's me?" I told him I was. I intended to send Mr Dear two copies of the photograph, requesting that he signed and returned one for my son, as a keepsake. A week later I emailed Mr Dear:

Sir,

Hopefully, you had a good week away. When I spoke to you last Sunday, I could tell from your voice there was some doubt it was actually you in the photograph: this caused me to make some further enquiries. The picture was taken in June 1984, in South Yorkshire during the miners' dispute. It ended up on a West Midlands police officer's Facebook site. The reason for it being on her page is that there were hundreds of West Mids officers present. I believe the West Mids OSU were at the forefront.

The senior officer, leading the charge, was actually a chief superintendent John Nesbit, South Yorkshire Police. If my enquiries are correct, on this day he not only led the charge, he also arrested Arthur Scargill.

I feel he bears a remarkable resemblance to you. My apologies for misleading you. On the plus side, it was really nice to hear your voice. I also know that if you had been there, then you would have led from the front because you always did.

Vincent Smith (sheepish)

Five days later, Mr Dear responded:

Dear Vince

C'EST LA VIE! I always wanted to lead a charge like that, and now I know that I did not! It was a pleasure to chat with you and to know that you are enjoying retirement.

I hope things continue to go well for you.

With my very best wishes.

Geoffrey Dear

It was great to hear from Mr Dear, even though it was for all the wrong reasons. Mr Dear was the man who smartened up a police force. The force of a thousand raincoats was issued with tailored barathea tunics and NATO-standard sweaters. He gave the West Midlands police a much-needed makeover.

In November 2010 the government finally decided to do something about the national police budgets. They realised that unless they made working conditions a little less cosy, no one was ever going to leave. In Warwickshire, a new shift pattern was implemented. It was not unknown, but it was a big step away from the cosy four days on, and four days off, that had been worked for years. The moaning and whining started, and everyone walked around in a complete huff. Who was going to pay for the petrol for the extra journeys to and from work? What about childcare costs?

One man in Warwickshire wasn't having any of it. He took one look at the new shifts and decided that the organisation could shove them up their arse. Everyone that he spoke to was in total agreement that it was time to leave. There were plenty of opportunities in the outside world. Screw the police. Buoyed by his support, he picked up the flag and led the mass exodus. Unfortunately, when he burst through the exit door, he turned to see that no one else had actually followed him. He started his brand new job as an assistant bailiff in Worcester and was promised untold wealth, albeit on commission. How hard could it be? Seizing legally recoverable assets from members of the public. Well, he found out exactly how hard it was on his first day while trying to recover a TV, Xbox and DVD player from a two-bedroomed flat. He said the terraced squat contained a menagerie of obnoxious children, assorted exotic pets, and a shaven-headed, fat, tattooed parent who had a pit bull tied to his wrist. He received more threats in twenty minutes than in his eight years in the police. Realising that he'd been a little bit hasty, he rushed back to Stratford-upon-Avon police station to see if there was any possibility of a return to the comfort and safety of police work. He was told that he had no chance.

I worked at Stratford-upon-Avon, and one of the blokes on our team was a total spanner when it came to computers. His machine never seemed to work, it couldn't do this, or wouldn't do that, and he was forever onto the IT department to fix the damn thing. His computer skills were poor, but his huge sausage fingers pummelling the keyboard probably did not help. The technical chap would turn out and sit at the broken computer for a few minutes. After which he would report back to his boss:

"It's all right, the computer's fixed. It was a picnic, yeah, a total picnic." He'd smile and leave. I witnessed this about four times in a fortnight, and he always said the same thing on the phone. The next time he came to our office I made him a cup of tea before I asked: "What do you mean by a picnic? You keep saying it, so picnic has to mean something." He looked around to check we were alone. "It's a code we use, but don't tell anyone. Picnic means, *problem in chair not in computer.*"

In February 2011, with the organisation under threat of drastic budget cuts, I was waiting to find out if I still had a job with

Warwickshire. When redundancies were needed, they didn't make decisions and avoided confrontation at all costs. They operated on rumour, innuendo and implied threats. The longer-serving members of staff felt that they were safe, and they knew where the bodies were buried, and, more significantly, who had buried them. I was given four days to apply for enhanced voluntary redundancy. Warwickshire police was desperate for civilians to retire so that serving cops could take their jobs. I wanted to take voluntary redundancy provided I could leave on 3 December 2011. That should have been an option as this type of redundancy can be deferred. However, once I opted to leave, it was the organisation's decision as to the date I could go. So the question was: could I trust them? I felt confident that I could not. Not through paranoia, you understand. In the four years that I had worked for these jokers, my three internal job applications went as follows:

In 2008, I applied for a post and the essential application criteria, just to apply, was changed two weeks before the application deadline. This was done to ensure that the successful candidate could make her application.

In 2009, I came second in a two-horse race to a person who had already been promised the job. The inspector, who interviewed me, told me that after the interview.

In 2010, I applied for a major investigation manager's job. I didn't even get an interview for that one: the two successful applicants were assessed and selected by the senior civilian they'd worked under for the previous twenty years. The process was reviewed, and the Head of Human Resources, Bob Davies, wrote to me. He apologised and accepted that the entire procedure was 'fundamentally flawed'. The advertised posts were withdrawn.

In May 2011, I started work as an investigator at Leamington Spa police station. It was a farce. 60 staff, not enough desks, phones, cars or radios. The whole place was a flurry of inactivity. I had never seen so many people trying to hide in plain sight. In late July 2011, a wounding investigation was nudged in my direction, but I was about to go off duty and start annual leave. I suggested someone else was tasked but was met with a sea of blank faces. Eventually, DC Mark Hewston was cornered and reluctantly accepted the job. Before I left, I read the papers and spoke to the victim who confirmed that, because of the attack, he was now blind in his left eye.

"Christ on a fucking bike!" Mark Hewston announced, starting to read the report. "The so-called victim actually started the fight! He got exactly what he deserved."

"Mark," I sighed, "the victim threw the dregs of a pint of lager over the offender, who glassed him in the face. He's lost an eye, Mark. An eye."

"Well," said Mark, "he should have thought about that before he started." DC Hewston had taken a well-known Biblical proverb and turned it into, *An eye for a lager-dampened T-shirt.*

September 2011: I was posted to a potential murder enquiry. A 42-year-old man had been violently attacked in his flat. He was in the hospital on a life support machine and not expected to live. Including me, there were five officers on the team. On a tea break, four of us were discussing the rugby World Cup. The fifth member, of our team, Vicky Stephens, walked in ashen-faced and clutching a cup of tea. She cleared her throat and declared:

"Well. That was the worst weekend of my life." None of us really knew Vicky, and this was clearly an opportunity to learn more about her.

"What on earth happened?" I asked, mustering up all the sincerity I could. "Well," she preened, glad to have an audience, "it all started in Argos on Saturday morning." Bollocks. What half-decent story ever started like that? Vicky was standing in the doorway: there was no escape, we were boxed in.

"I selected an item from the catalogue, wrote the item's number on the slip and handed it to the cashier," she droned on. "I recognised the girl behind the till because a couple of months ago, I crashed into some cars, including hers. It was all my fault, you understand." We did. "I admitted everything. Well, I had no choice really what with all the witnesses and the CCTV." I made a mental note to seek out the footage of Vicky's demolition derby on Leamington Spa's High Street.

"I realised she recognised me. I was trapped." We knew the feeling. "I'd paid for my stuff and was waiting for my order number to come up. I saw the cashier talking to a man at the back of the shop. I started to hyperventilate. I went to collect my order and dash out. But then the man behind the counter started to ask me really personal questions. Like, 'Are you off duty today?' and 'Were you involved in the riots?' I just grabbed my item and ran out of the shop!' I was losing the will to live. Do you know what I did then?" Vicky enticed, hinting at a grand finale. Part of me hoped that she had fired up her car, and driven it straight through Argos's window, but I doubted it.

"I went straight into Greggs the bakers and bought ten doughnuts. I went home and ate nine of them straight away. I was almost sick." I confess I never understood her logic and still dread to imagine the crisis that would have justified a full ten-doughnuter. I'd just lost five minutes of my life listening to this inane drivel, but I was keen to show some sort of support, and more importantly, bring her tale to a conclusion. I said, "That'll teach the fuckers, Vicky."

A few weeks later, I was working with DC Bruce Irving. We interviewed two men who had been arrested on suspicion of murder. We worked hard and were able to assist the SIO in obtaining plausible accounts from both suspects. Their interviews explained everything. Bruce and I took a well-earned break and popped to Costa Coffee in Stratford-upon-Avon. It was lunchtime and busy. Bruce sipped his black coffee and told me about a job of his, specifically about the abdominal injuries that a child had received. Bruce thought that the violent brute in the house, and not his wife, must have been responsible. I remembered the words of wisdom that John Davies had imparted all those years ago. Keen to impress, I pushed my cappuccino aside and shared my knowledge.

"Bruce, a small person can actually cause massive injuries to a young child," I said, knowingly.

"How do you work that out?"

"Like this." I slid my chair back. I raised my right foot and slammed the heel of my leather brogue into the floor, exactly how John Davies had demonstrated. Disappointingly, we were sitting at a table on a raised wooden floor, and the hollow area underneath produced incredible acoustics. When my heel hit the deck, it sounded like a gun had gone off: every item of cutlery for ten tables around us jumped. A sea of terrified patrons shrieked: most spilt their drinks in shock, and one person dived under a table for cover. The chatter in the busy café stopped. I finished my coffee and decided it was time to leave. Bruce followed. Near the exit sat a smartly dressed elderly lady. Her impeccable outfit was spoilt only by the gingerbread latte that she was now wearing. As I was passing, she tapped me on the arm and leant forward, and with an ice-cold stare, she said in a frail voice:

"You, sir..." She racked her brain to deliver the most hurtful insult that she could. I braced myself, and finally, she said, "... are not from Stratford-upon-Avon."

That was well over the top if you ask me.

In June 2012, I was wiped out by a severe attack of shingles. My illness required complete bedrest for over a month. I felt vulnerable and had no energy; I thought that I was never going to recover. By September I was still unwell but jumped into my blue Ford Fiesta to take my son Tommy to Coventry for training. It was a 60-mile round trip in light traffic.

At 9 pm, we set off to go home. With hindsight, I should

probably have visited the toilet before leaving. Sadly, I had not.

My return route meant taking the A46, the M40 and then the M42. My nine-year-old son was in the front passenger seat playing on his iPhone and listening to music. As I turned onto the M40, I felt an uncomfortable rumbling in my tummy. There are no exits on that stretch of motorway, and it is ten miles before it joins the M42. It was a foul night and the rain and spray from the lorries made driving particularly hazardous. The rumbling in my stomach was now causing me to have serious concerns, I felt like I was going to explode. I needed a toilet and soon. I started to sweat. Every mile seemed to take an age, and it was becoming increasingly difficult to hold things in. I took deep breaths. My sweat trickle became a torrent; I leant forward in my seat and prayed for help. After five long, slow, torturous miles, I had run out of options. I checked my clothes. I was wearing tracksuit bottoms that had a drawstring around the waist and were elasticated at the ankles.

I checked on my son: he was oblivious to my predicament. I took another deep breath, turned the music up, and in spite of the weather, I opened my window a tad. Then I released an absolute avalanche of shit. The immediate relief was overpowering, and my vision blurred. For a couple of minutes, I emptied the contents of my bowels into my tracksuit bottoms. I thought it was never going to stop. Tommy continued to play on his iPhone. I wiped the tears from my eyes and concentrated on my driving. This was more difficult than usual, as I was sitting in my own personal shit swamp.

I made it to the driveway of my house with Tommy none the

wiser. I could see into my lounge. I saw that my bloody teenage stepsons had their friends round, and they were all standing chatting to my wife. I sent Tommy in first as a distraction. I knew his mum would ask him about his training. Once he was through the front door, Tommy walked into the lounge, and his mum took the bait. I waddled up the stairs as fast as I dared. I headed into my bathroom and locked the door. For over an hour, I dealt with the horrendous aftermath. I saved most of my clothes, but my Marks & Spencer's underpants were beyond redemption. An inspection of my car the following day revealed a stain on the driver's seat that proved impossible to remove. Lucky for me, 'We Buy Any Car' really do buy any car. So, if you purchased a 08-registration plated blue Fiesta Zetec in Birmingham in 2012 and are wondering what caused the stain on the driver's seat, well now you know. Sorry.

On 18 September 2012 two unarmed policewomen from Greater Manchester were lured to a burglary, ambushed and murdered in a horrific gun and grenade attack. The severity of the violence shocked the world. The news reports were harrowing. It was a nightmare, unimaginable, a worst-case scenario that should never happen. Like the rest of the decent members of society, I felt angry and helpless. I read a poem that was written in tribute to a policeman who had died in service, years ago. The author is unknown. I tweaked the poem and have made it my personal tribute to Fiona Bone and Nicola Hughes.

THE FINAL INSPECTION

The policewomen stood and faced their God,
Which must always come to pass.
They hoped their shoes were shining.
Just as brightly as his brass.
Step forward now, policewomen.
How shall I deal with you?
Have you always turned the other cheek?
To my church have you been true?'
The policewomen squared their shoulders and said,
'No, Lord, we guess we ain't,
Because those of us who carry badges
Can't always be a saint.
We've had to work most Sundays,
And at times our talk was rough,
And sometimes we've been violent,
Because the streets are awfully tough.
But we never took a penny,
That wasn't ours to keep
Though we worked a lot of overtime
When the bills got just too steep.
And we never passed a cry for help,
Though at times we shook with fear.
And sometimes, God forgive us,
We've both wept many tears.
We know we don't deserve a place
Among the people here.
They never wanted us around

Except to calm their fear.
If you've got a place for us, Lord,
It needn't be so grand.
We never expected or had too much,
But if you don't, we'll understand.
There was silence all around the throne
Where the saints had often trod.
As the policewomen stood waiting,
For the judgment of their God.
'Step forward now, the both of you,
You've borne your burdens well.
Come walk a beat on Heaven's streets,
You've served your time in Hell.

Rest in Peace, Fiona and Nicola. God bless you both.

CHAPTER 25
FINALLY BOOKING
OFF DUTY

By the end of September 2012, though I was back at work, I was still a long way from being fully fit. Whenever possible, I partnered up with Camilla Goddard, a tall, extremely attractive lady who was heavily pregnant with her second child. She was a good laugh and kept me sane. Unfortunately, Camilla had joined 30 years too late to have her arse date-stamped. Never mind. Even though she was heavily pregnant, Camilla never allowed me to drive our police car. My driving had not improved - if anything, I was getting worse.

Camilla drove to the bottom of a cul-de-sac on a council estate on the outskirts of Leamington. I jumped out of the car and knocked on the door of a ground-floor flat. Camilla waited in the car. Eventually, a female troll opened the door: she was fat, sweating profusely and wearing a tight T-shirt with no bra. Her huge nipples were pointing south. It was impossible to guess her age, and I don't mean that as a compliment. It was her eighteen-year-old son whom I wanted to speak to, as

Camilla required him to attend Leamington police station for an interview. The troll grunted in the direction of her lounge. A younger male elf shuffled to the door. He was a mess, too, and his last seven meals were easily identifiable from the stains on his T-shirt. I asked the lad when he could get himself to Leamington. His eyes glazed over, and he began mumbling. Camilla, perhaps fearing that I was distracted by the woman's nipples, jumped out of the car to join me. The lad seemed to perk up at the sight of Camilla. I thought she might have more luck with him, but then I realised he wasn't looking at her, but past her. He finally stopped mumbling and now using actual words:

"Your car," he said slowly, "is rolling down the fucking hill." Out of the corner of my eye, I could see he was right. Camilla sprinted into action, correctly assessing that I was worse at running than I was at driving. She caught up with the car, jumped into the driving seat, and applied the handbrake. The car stopped just inches from a garage wall. The nipples, the lad's T-shirt and the pregnant detective chasing a runaway police car were too much for me. I just couldn't stop laughing.

In October 2012 I popped into Stratford-upon-Avon police station. A woman had just started work there, and as I walked in, she greeted me.

"Hi, Vinnie, long time no see." The regular office staff looked surprised, and someone asked her how she knew me.

"How on earth could I ever forget him? He drilled me every single day for ten weeks." It was Maggie O'Hare. She did explain that it wasn't what they were thinking and that I had been her class drill prefect at Ryton.

I never fully recovered from my bout of shingles. I had a second attack, and that was even worse. I think my body was telling me to leave work while it was still my choice. In August 2014, after a further period of illness, I retired from Warwickshire police.

After leaving the West Midlands police in 2007, I didn't immediately sever all ties. I stayed in touch with Ishfaq Ahmed's father. On the 20 November each year, the anniversary of Ishfaq's murder, I phoned Afsar Khan to offer my condolences. In February 2008 a concerned Mr Khan rang me. He was worried that I might not attend the High Court appeal of the men convicted of murdering his son. John Davies and Mr Barker had already spoken to me about the appeal; I assured him that I would be there.

After some years I wasn't sure if I was making my annual call to Mr Khan for his benefit or mine. In 2014 I decided not to make the call. I felt that it might be time to move on. On 21 November, Mr Khan rang me: he wanted to make sure that I was all right. He also let me know that he looked forward to hearing from me every year. He said it pleased him to know that someone from the police still remembered his son. What he then said means more to me than all the medals, awards and commendations that I received during my service:

"Mr Smith, you will always have a special place in my heart". A man who had lost his son in a hail of bullets phoned me to make sure that I was okay. I was truly humbled. I am now committed to calling Afsar Khan on 20 November every year until one of us is not there to make or to take that call.

So far, you have joined me on a whistle-stop tour of my memories and shared the journey of a fifteen-year-old boy who joined the Army and then worked for the police for over 35 years. The experiences I have had were not unique, but some of the people I met along the way were. I wanted to share these tales before I have forgotten them. This book is my legacy. I have written about only some of the investigations that I was involved with. Most of the cases that I worked on were upsetting and have left emotional scars that will stay with me forever. The offences I investigated included child murders, gang murders, cot deaths, rapes and assaults. My coping mechanism was to focus on my job and deal with the tasks I had to. That stopped my reflecting on the real horror of what had happened. I put everything into boxes, statements, interviews, telephone data and exhibits. I then submitted the files to the CPS. My job was to find the answers for families and not just to convict the suspects. Because I worked with some incredibly brave witnesses, extremely talented detectives and the gifted John Davies, almost all of my cases were put before the courts.

I would like to say that no bowling greens or ferrets were harmed by my book's production. Unfortunately, they were. Sadly, many people that I have written about are no longer alive.

Thank you to the Band of Brothers and Sisters, who shared my journey, especially those who helped, supported and made me laugh along the way. To anyone who enjoyed my jokes and stories, well, you are at least partly to blame for this book. I am grateful that so many have allowed me to use their real names. For those that I didn't ask, well, I doubt that you would have said yes.

A special thank you to all of my family. To Sarah, *my raison d'être*, and my editor-in-chief Peter and his able assistant Tommy, my stepsons Marcus and Josef, and thanks to my sister Frances and brother Anthony. Sadly my other sister Kathleen died of anorexia in 1982: she was only 23 years old.

In July 2018 Hughie McGowan phoned me: he was in a pub and was with someone who had heard that I had been writing my memoirs and was not impressed. Hughie passed his phone over.

"Wolfie, what have you written about me, you wanker?" I recognised the voice, it was Johnny Mac: it was great to hear him. I asked if we could meet up and suggested the following Thursday at midday in Moseley. John burst out laughing.

"You will not believe why I can't make Thursday because I am at Birmingham Crown Court, I am doing jury service."

"Bloody hell, John, that's the hat-trick for you, then. You have been to Crown Court as a copper, a criminal and now a juror. Well done."

On 14 January 2019, at the age of 73, Pete The Feet McKenzie died in his sleep. Pete stopped wearing shoes in the mid-1960s. He was one of a kind, and his legend lives on. I bid you a fond farewell, Pete, and may, 'Your Soles Rest in Peace'.

Whenever a case file is forwarded to the CPS, it contains all of the available evidence, statements and a case summary. That file also includes a schedule of sensitive and unused material which is not to be disclosed to the defence. I have neither the skill or will to write about my marriages, so I have deemed that area of my life as sensitive and unused material.

I always wanted to read a book about policing that covered the area and the era in which I served. I never found that book, so have written it. I hope you have enjoyed it. As someone once said, "Everyone should sit down and write a book, it is an excellent form of therapy and a lot less expensive."

I would like to book off-duty with Derek Whitehouse's favourite poem, Vitai Lampada. Derek introduced me to it, I learned it and recited it to him. I can now pass on this *Torch of Life* to those that have chosen to patrol the same streets that I did.

VITAI LAMPADA

There's a breathless hush in the Close tonight
Ten to make and the match to win.
A bumping pitch and a blinding light,
An hour to play and the last man in.
And it's not for the sake of a ribboned coat,
Or the selfish hope of a season's fame,
But his Captain's hand on his shoulder smote
'Play up! Play up! And Play the game!'

The sand of the desert is sodden red,
Red with the wreck of a square that broke.
The Gatling's jammed and the Colonel dead,
The Regiment blind with dust and smoke.
The river of death has brimmed his banks,
And England's far, and Honour a name,
But the voice of a schoolboy rallies the ranks:
'Play up! Play up! And Play the game!'

This is the word that year by year,
While in her place, the school is set,
Every one of her sons must hear,
And none that hear it dare forget.
This they all with a joyful mind
Bear through life like a torch in flame,
And falling fling to the host behind
'Play up! Play up! And Play the game!'

- Sir Henry Newbolt

CHAPTER 26
FOR THE LOVE OF JACK

One particular investigation still haunts me, and in the interest of full disclosure, I feel it warrants a place in my book. I confess this chapter was the hardest to write. I would not have written anything about the Jack Macleod case without the consent of Jack's mum, Sheena Macleod. She has read my book and been kind enough to add her thoughts. In a previous chapter, you read about the murder of Gerry Tobin and how well organised Warwickshire police were. How officers were briefed, debriefed and supported throughout. That was very different from how the Jack Macleod case was conducted, and yet the same detectives were involved in both investigations.

In July 2007 DCI Adrian McGee contacted me. He was in charge of the MIU, and his remit included the investigation into Jack Macleod's death. The caustic media reports regarding the second adjourned inquest and the pressure from Jack's family to find answers meant that he was in a dark place. Mr McGee asked me to have a look and see if anything had been missed. I asked him for the operational name for the investigation: he told me it was Operation Enact. I half-expected him to say, 'The Leamington Murder'.

By accessing HOLMES, I worked my way through the statements, interviews and documents. Though there was no one else working on the case, I was extremely grateful for the assistance of Detective Julie Sidaway. In a force where the attitude was, 'Hasn't this investigation gone away yet?' Julie Sidaway kept an open mind, listened and helped me whenever I asked.

Detective Inspector Bob Bradbury was the SIO initially in charge of this enquiry. Adrian McGee was appointed SIO in February 2006, and Bob Bradbury retired from the police shortly after. By the time I had joined Warwickshire police in 2007 Graeme Pallister - the SIO for the Gladstone Johnson murder in 2002 - had transferred to Warwickshire as a superintendent. He was a joint SIO with Adrian McGee. I had never heard of joint SIOs. If one officer outranks the other, then they are the senior investigating officer, it's that simple. The reason for the dual appointment was that Sheena refused to speak to Adrian following the collapse of the case at the second coroner's inquest. Senior and junior officers were terrified of Sheena Macleod, as she had made dozens of formal complaints about them.

I went through everything systematically and found a thread to pull on. Rachel Wood, a policewoman just out of her probation, was tasked to collect and interview Mark Hoolichan on 4 December 2005. Mark was the last person to see Jack Macleod alive. She obtained an account via a voluntary interview. Hoolichan spoke freely, but as she had not been briefed, WPC Wood was in no position to challenge anything he said.

Mark Hoolichan's summarised account:

I bumped into Jack in the Ocean Bar. I knew him from school as we had been in the same year. We were both age-checked and told to leave. Sean Rellis joined us outside. We went to St Patrick's Social Club, where Jack and Sean worked. We got served and drank Jack Daniel's and Coke. We left the club when it closed. I was drunk, we all walked to the Adelaide Road Bridge. Jack was very drunk and kept falling over. Just after Sean Rellis went home, Jack passed out on the Adelaide Road Bridge. Initially, I carried Jack in a fireman's lift, but I kept dropping and picking him up. I left Jack by a riverside bench. I went to get my friends and returned to where I had left Jack; he was no longer there. I then went home in a taxi with my mates.

Following the interview, Rachel Wood seized the clothes, including a black, long-sleeved T-shirt that Mark Hoolichan had been wearing the previous night.

Mark Hoolichan was arrested for the murder of Jack Macleod on 7 December 2005. Several Warwickshire officers and staff have always contested that this investigation was only ever a missing person enquiry. Sorry, but if a suspect is arrested for murder, then it becomes a murder investigation and must follow the Major Incident Room Standardised Administrative Procedures (MIRSAP), a manual that contains a step-by-step guide on how to conduct a homicide investigation. All of the SIOs connected with this case had been MIRSAP-trained.

Jack Macleod was recovered from the River Leam 31 days after he went missing. Jack had drifted 300 yards before becoming snagged near the riverbank. He didn't have any injuries consistent with a serious assault, his clothes were intact, and he still had his mobile phone. In his pockets, he had sufficient money for a kebab and a taxi home, just as his mum had told him to. These facts eliminated assault and robbery. Jack's full bladder supported the cause of death as *dry drowning* - a sudden and unexpected immersion in cold water.

As an investigator, there was plenty of work to do. Far too much time had been spent reviewing the investigation. After I started working on the case Punchy, having retired from the West Midlands police, took up the offer of a job in Warwickshire working in their intelligence cell. He was happy enough but was a lot more concerned with the process of taking his family, lock, stock and barrel, to live in Canada. Punchy's immediate supervisor was DS Steve Beardsmore.

"Hey, Steve", said Punchy, "I've just seen Vinnie Smith. Apparently, he's working on that Jack Macleod job." Steve didn't even look up from his computer.

"What a waste of time," he scoffed. "That case is going nowhere, and it's certainly never going to see the inside of a courtroom."

"I think you're wrong," said Punchy, defending me. "Vinnie always gets his cases to court." Steve was a lot more interested in finishing his report than talking about the Macleod case.

"Look, mate," he sighed, "that case has been to CPS, and it's been reviewed twice. I tell you, it's going absolutely nowhere."

"Steve," Punchy said, getting annoyed that he was being ignored, "I've just read the original file that was sent to CPS. I'm not surprised it never made it to court: the case summary read like it had been put together by the force gardener while he was still pissed." Steve stopped typing and looked directly at Punchy. There was a short pause before he spoke.

"I did that file, mate." Punchy left his office and jogged down to tell me.

Regarding the Jack Macleod enquiry, there is a poem which pretty much sums up both my position and the stance of Warwickshire police and CPS. Only you can replace the word 'Somebody' with 'Everybody'.

IT COULDN'T BE DONE

Somebody said that it couldn't be done,
But he with a chuckle replied
That "maybe it couldn't," but he would be one
Who wouldn't say so till he'd tried.
So he buckled right in with the trace of a grin
On his face. If he worried he hid it.
He started to sing as he tackled the thing
That couldn't be done, and he did it.

Somebody scoffed: "Oh, you'll never do that,
At least no one has done it,"
But he took off his coat and he took off his hat,
And the first thing we knew he'd begun it.
With a lift of his chin and a bit of a grin,
Without any doubting or quiddit,
He started to sing as he tackled the thing
That couldn't be done, and he did it.

There are thousands to tell you it cannot be done,
There are thousands to prophesy failure,
There are thousands to point out to you one by one,
The dangers that wait to assail you.
But just buckle in with a trace of a grin,
Just take off your coat and go to it,
Just start to sing as you tackle the thing
That "cannot be done," and you'll do it.

Edgar Albert Guest.

As a priority, I needed to obtain and clarify statements. Even the suspect's original interview transcript was incomplete. The CPS did not know what the defendant had said in his interview. Based on the shoddy case summary that was submitted to them, the Warwickshire CPS decided that there was insufficient evidence to charge anyone. From what I saw, I couldn't blame them. Except that the CPS never asked for any further work to be done: I could definitely blame them for that. My initial thought about the investigation was that there was no structure, strategy or plan. Operation Enact was not a complicated enquiry. Warwickshire police encouraged Mark Hoolichan to take part in the *Crimewatch* appeal, possibly believing that the media pressure may cause him to panic, as it had done with Gordon Wardell in 1994.

The incident room's only tactic was to pepper Mark Hoolichan with questions, put to him by a string of interviewers. Apart from the initial interview by Rachel Wood, the other interviews with Mark Hoolichan never achieved anything. Whenever Mark was challenged about the differing accounts, he had given to people that he had spoken to on 4 December. His response was 'No comment', or 'that because he had been drunk, so he couldn't remember'.

There had only ever been one suspect, Mark Hoolichan. I did everything I could to eliminate him. I spent three weeks working through the evidence held on HOLMES and was unable to. I was then left with a circumstantial case against him. To put any case before a court, there has to be evidence, I took stock of what was available. If something was retrievable, I recovered it. There was no point complaining about anything, and there wasn't anyone to whom I could complain. Apart from Julie Sidaway, I didn't get much help from anyone else. I think I understood why; most believed I was preparing a list of those who should be sacked for incompetence. There was a degree of paranoia that surrounded this investigation.

It was time to meet Sheena Macleod, so we had a coffee in Leamington. I was a long way from being invited into her home. I let Sheena know I would do my best. It was clear that she had no confidence in Warwickshire police. She had hoped that the inquest would give her some of the answers that she was desperate to hear. But because of a 'police blunder' (*The Coventry Telegraph*) that hearing had been adjourned. From what I had seen and read, Sheena had every reason to be angry. She was quite rightly suspicious of me. I might just be another Warwickshire tosser who wanted to make this enquiry just go away. Sheena was lovely. She has an incredible family, and they have always been there to support her.

With the fresh evidence that I had gathered, it was time to re-interview Mark Hoolichan. He was rearrested on suspicion of the manslaughter of Jack Macleod. For two days in March 2008, Punchy and I interviewed him. He replied, 'No comment,' to all the questions that we asked. I expected that: why should he say anything? He had an absolute legal right to say nothing, so he maintained his original story, declining to explain which of the many accounts that he had made was correct.

Over months, a series of case conferences were held with the Warwickshire CPS. I would update them with developments in the case. CPS had a master and pet relationship with Warwickshire police. The CPS had already made their decision not to prosecute, and they were not going to be changing it anytime soon. They were so confident that no barrister would disagree with their view that they asked me to suggest one who could advise on this case. I thought about it, and briefly considered Stephen Linehan, but decided that Anthony Barker would be the best choice. They were both brilliant, but Mr Barker's conferences were less violent.

I had worked for Mr Barker on previous cases and knew exactly how he expected the police summary to be presented. My case summary was 38 pages. I then paginated the appended statements - over 160 pages - and I cross-referenced the relevant page number next to the witness I was referring to in the summary. Mr Barker always asked for this, as it made his job a lot easier.

At the first conference, unusually for him, he seemed a little vexed. He asked me why the case summary was incorrectly cross-referenced with irrelevant page numbers. The CPS sat smugly watching me squirm. I asked Mr Barker if I could see his copy of the file. CPS had randomly inserted twenty other statements and repaginated the pages in a way that made a nonsense of my case summary. A heated exchange followed: at least Mr Barker realised that it was the CPS who had caused the problem. The conferences followed a pattern. Mr Barker and I would suggest ideas and lines of enquiry while the CPS played *Devil's Advocate* and pulled our suggestions apart.

CPS requested numerous tasks to be undertaken by the police - namely me - including Army cadets performing firemen's lifts. Also at 1.44 am on a Saturday night in December 2008 I shouted, "Jack" from the Adelaide Road Bridge. Which Punchy recorded as being audible from a distance of 1,000 yards. Punchy and I visited an eminent professor who was an expert on alcohol consumption and how it affects a person's memory. I flew to Jersey to see a key witness and take a statement that should have been routinely obtained two years before. I jumped through a series of hoops and impressed the CPS, not one jot.

CPS submitted my advice file to Mr Barker for his consideration. In spite of their promise, they would agree with his instruction; when he recommended a charge, the CPS prevaricated for a month. Cruelly this was another 31 days for Sheena and Ewan to endure. On 6 June 2008 arrangements were made to charge Mark Hoolichan with the manslaughter of Jack Macleod. Warwickshire police had Sheena and Ewan brought to their headquarters at Leek Wootton to be given the news, mostly so that Adrian and Graeme could repair their relationship with the Macleod family. I was asked to stay away. Sheena was pleased that the case was going to court. Finally, she might get some answers.

Shortly after Hoolichan was charged Paul Waldron immigrated to Canada. Punchy would have been a useful ally at the trial provided he behaved himself. Best of luck, mate, and thanks for everything. Don't worry about me getting around these days, I have bought a sat nav.

Before the trial, I visited the 52 potential witnesses, and I read their statements to them. I was conscious of how much time had elapsed between the incident and the trial. I did not speak to any of the expert witnesses, police officers, medical staff or the Spartan Rescue team who had recovered Jack Macleod from the River Leam.

At the trial, at the defence's request, I was excluded from the public gallery. Mark Hoolichan's barrister said that the reason for my exclusion would become apparent during the trial; needless to say, it didn't. Incredibly, Sheena and Ewan Macleod, for reasons that I still do not understand, were also excluded. Sheena had to rely on her sister Siobhan, who was not a witness, for updates. Sheena and Ewan had expected to receive some compassion and understanding from the court as they had lost their son, but that never happened. In court, the defence barrister confused them and challenged their integrity; they both left the Crown Court feeling angry and let down.

Mr Barker did the best he could. I just hope that the Macleod family appreciated his efforts. I had done the best I could, but I just wish that John Davies CPS had been available to assist with the case preparation.

When the trial reached half-time, the defence submitted that there was no case to answer. The judge deliberated and agreed.

8 May 2009 the Warwickshire police website reported:

Following the successful submission of the defence counsel that there is no case to answer, Senior Investigating Officer Detective Chief Inspector Adrian McGee said: 'My first thoughts are with Jack's family who, despite a determined police investigation still do not have the answers that they want about Jack's death. Over the past three years, we have carried out a thorough investigation. Our determination to discover what happened to Jack did not waver. We never stopped searching for the truth. In considering the submissions, Judge Inman said that "the prosecution had left no stone unturned". Following the decision to end court proceedings, we will be considering what action, if any, should be taken.'

Following the trial, Graeme and Adrian invited Sheena and Ewan to The Saxon Mill pub just outside Warwick. Adrian had thought that the Macleod family would like to join them for a drink so they could lick their post-trial wounds together. Boy, was he wrong? Sheena charged at Adrian, and if Ewan had not intervened, Adrian could have been seriously hurt. Sheena had not forgotten or forgiven Warwickshire police for how badly they had conducted the investigation, and how poorly they had treated her family.

In April 2013 the then Chief Constable of Warwickshire, Bill Holland, publicly apologised to Jack Macleod's family for the "botched investigation". Detective Inspector Bob Bradbury, the original SIO, also apologised and agreed that the force had "messed up" the early stages of the enquiry while he was in charge. Sheena and Ewan fought hard to get those apologies. What is the point of apologising unless you explain exactly what you are apologising for? I would like to clarify precisely how this investigation was botched and messed up by Warwickshire police.

In February 2006 a senior Warwickshire police officer produced a review of the investigation. In that document, he confirms that he also reviewed this investigation on 5 and 19 December 2005. That review strongly criticised Detective Inspector Bradbury and stated that there were no strategies in place for any area of the investigation. Several courses that Bradbury should attend, as a priority, were recommended. Bob Bradbury opted to retire from the police instead. The review's summary of events was flawed and inaccurate. The time that Jack Macleod was last seen appears to be a guess. The statement 'that all three young men were drunk, as they had been drinking all day' is totally wrong. Mark Hoolichan's first alcoholic drink was not until 11.30 pm.

The case summary was sent to the CPS on 26 April 2006

for a decision. I thought surely, with the family and media pressure, everything that should have been done had been. It most definitely had not. It did not fill me with confidence that Jack's surname was misspelt throughout that document. No reference was made to the telephone evidence except to say that Mark, Sean and Jack had all used their mobile phones that night. There was no mention of forensic evidence. Also, the statements made by the Burger King staff about disclosures Hoolichan made on 4 December were not mentioned. If I had sent that case summary to John Davies, he would have had to visit a WH Smith's to buy a big box of green pens.

A retired superintendent from the West Midlands police conducted two further reviews. Bob Bradbury had retired, so it was quite easy to slide most of the blame in his direction. Bob Bradbury publicly admitted that he made mistakes. The initial stages of any enquiry are crucial, but Bob Bradbury was only in charge for twenty days. There is nothing that he missed that could not have been put right by those who followed. 22 recommendations were made by the reviewing officer, almost all of which were designed to assist future investigations. The Gerard Tobin murder enquiry definitely benefited from those suggestions, but that is no consolation to the family of Jack Macleod.

The media pressure and Sheena Macleod's persistence forced Warwickshire police to embarrassingly deem this investigation a Critical Incident - *'where the effectiveness of the police response is likely to have a significant impact on the confidence of the victim's family or the community'.*

The MIU investigation team, three reviews and the Warwickshire CPS missed the crucial lines of enquiry that I am now going to highlight. These were not difficult or complicated. In MIU terms, they were routine and would have provided both answers and probably evidence. For reasons I will explain, some of the opportunities that Warwickshire police missed were not retrievable.

While I was building the case, and searching for evidence, I knew that Jack, Mark and Sean had all used their mobile phones on the night that Jack went missing. There was a box in the incident room that contained the telephone data. It had never been examined as potential evidence and was not included in the submissions to CPS. I checked the details of the calls and messages that the three had made that night. I was frustrated that the only data requested was for that weekend. A month's data would have allowed pre-incident and post-incident comparison. The next area I needed to examine was the cell site data. Cell site pinpoints a mobile telephone's precise location. It is a technique that had been used in police investigations since 2000. Incredulously, Warwickshire police never requested that data and it is only available for the six months following an incident. That data may have included the critical shutdown time of Jack Macleod's mobile phone. This was both negligent and inexcusable as the financial cost is minuscule.

Hoolichan was arrested on suspicion of murder, as he had given differing accounts about his movements following the last independent sighting of Jack and Mark on the Adelaide Road

Bridge. The original investigation team never obtained an account from Mark that they accepted, or that could be corroborated. The time between 1.44 am and 2.30 am was lost to the investigation. The only activity that was ascertained, for that critical period, was that Mark Hoolichan had spent a lot of time on his mobile phone. Without the cell site data to pinpoint the suspect's location and the exact timing of his movements, the case could, and maybe should, have hinged on the forensic evidence.

When Mark Hoolichan was arrested for murder on 7 December 2005, his jacket was seized, and then sent to the laboratory where it was examined. The laboratory searched for traces of Jack's clothing and hair, Adelaide Road Bridge paint, tarmac and anything else they could think of. Eventually, the jacket was destroyed through repeated testing. Mark Hoolichan had not worn a jacket on that fateful night. The exhibits officer and the SIO should have browsed HOLMES before the jacket's submission. Eleven independent statements confirmed what Mark Hoolichan had worn on the night of 3 December 2005.

Jack Macleod's jacket and jeans shed fibres but would not have retained them; the River Leam made sure of that. The laboratory found just one fibre matching Jack's jacket on Mark Hoolichan's long-sleeved, black T-shirt. In their original statement, the laboratory stated that a single fibre indicated minimal contact between those two garments. But as the police had told the laboratory that Mark's T-shirt was an inner garment, the find was not thought to be significant. I informed Graeme Pallister and Adrian McGee that Mark Hoolichan had not been wearing a jacket on the night that Jack went missing. Finally, a breakthrough.

387

Hazel Johnson, the head of the forensic laboratory, was not impressed. She believed that her department had been totally misled by the police's incompetence. I tried to explain that it was just a genuine mistake. Hazel Johnson was someone whom I had dealt with many times before and she is excellent at her job. She agreed to re-examine Mark's T-shirt. The lab found cellulite and hairs on the T-shirt, but nothing that could be attributed to Jack Macleod. This was crucial.

I wanted the laboratory to give their expert opinion on a single point. Was Mark Hoolichan's account, that he had repeatedly carried and dropped Jack Macleod over a distance of 100 yards using a fireman's lift, forensically compatible with finding a single fibre on his black T-shirt? The technician produced a further statement that her forensic findings were, in her expert opinion, inconclusive. And that would be her stance if called to court. She didn't expect to be called by either the defence or the prosecution, as her position was neutral. Mr McGee accepted their findings. I was crushed.

The team leader of Spartan Rescue was called to give evidence at the Crown Court. His statement included the details of the original, unsuccessful search, and the subsequent recovery of Jack Macleod on 3 January 2006. I hadn't met him before, but he seemed to know his job. Adrian McGee took him into a consulting room at court to go through his statement. I could see that there was a lively discussion taking place. The Spartan team leader was explaining to Adrian that, as an expert, he could tell the court exactly where Jack Macleod had entered the River Leam. He said that the flow of the river, the debris on the river floor, added to the recovery location meant that he could identify Jack's point of entry into the River Leam. He said that in his expert opinion, Jack had entered the river from the Adelaide Road Bridge. It was the exact location that an independent witness had last seen Jack and Mark.

This evidence supported the prosecution case. A further statement was taken and presented to Mr Barker. The trial judge considered the statement but decided that it was too late in the day to be allowed as it would not be fair to the defence. I felt disappointed. The Spartan Rescue team leader gave his evidence regarding the search and recovery only. As he was leaving the court, he looked pretty annoyed. I asked why he had not told the police where Jack had entered the river:

"Because nobody ever bloody asked me, that's why."

Leadership, direction, an independent review or CPS support would have ensured that all of these evidential opportunities were taken. A lack of briefings was highlighted by one of the reviewers. Three simple questions at any briefing would have resolved some serious issues:

'Have we applied for the cell site data for Mark, Jack and Sean's phones, sir?'

'Why are we sending Mark's jacket to the lab? He wasn't wearing a one.'

'Do Spartan Rescue have any idea about where Jack could have entered the River?'

If none of the critical areas of the investigation - witnesses, interviews, forensics or telephone enquiries - has a strategy, then there is little point in having briefings. What would you even talk about?

The forensic findings, cell site evidence, and the expert testimony of the Spartan Rescue team leader could have challenged Mark Hoolichan's version of events, possibly rendering his account unsustainable at the trial. There may indeed have been a case for him to answer.

The decision to make an appeal on *Crimewatch* was criticised by both reviewing officers. Mark Hoolichan was part of the television appeal while he was on police bail for the murder of Jack Macleod. The programme included a reconstruction of the night's events and the actor playing the role of Mark Hoolichan wore a jacket. Mark Hoolichan said on the programme:

"The most disappointing thing, for me, was that I cannot remember the most important bit, you know when it was just Jack and me."

A Warwickshire officer handled the police contact telephone number which was given out on *Crimewatch*. A caller said that Jack had been thrown over the bridge following an altercation with his friend. That absolutely critical call was not recorded, and no telephone number trace facility had been put in place. If the National Crimestoppers number had been used, their calls are recorded and traceable. The caller has never been traced.

The full picture of the investigation includes lost exhibits, witness statements that were not taken for weeks, months and in one case years. A complete lack of operational briefings, telephone data that was never requested, and the slipshod submissions to the forensic laboratory. I concur with Warwickshire police's own assessment that this enquiry was indeed "a messed-up, botched investigation".

Sometimes incidents are tragic accidents, and the truth may never be known; I do not think this investigation ever fell into that category. I would describe the Warwickshire investigation as - An absolute masterclass in how to avoid the collection of routine evidence.

The Macleod family only ever wanted the police to do their job and provide answers. In my opinion, most of those answers were available. Sheena Macleod has every right to still feel angry and entirely let down. Sheena's raft of formal complaints about officers' actions, or lack of them, did not result in a single officer being disciplined.

I never met Jack, but because of Sheena and Ewan, I feel that I actually know him. I am proud to call Sheena and Ewan my friends and I enjoy spending time with them. I just wish it could have been under different circumstances. Sheena and her family are still waiting. They will never give up and they shouldn't. They know that there are people who have the answers that they so desperately need. They hope that, as allegiances change, and consciences are pricked, one day someone with those answers will come forward.

Sheena has kindly written the following and asked for its inclusion:

When you lose a child, whether in an accident or a deliberate act, your natural desire is for the truth about how and why it happened. When Ewan and I last saw our beautiful son, Jack, at 7.45 pm on Saturday 3 December 2005, he was a happy, contented young man, excited about his present and his future.

When we woke up on the morning of Sunday 4th to find he was not in his bed, our world began to crash around us. Our ordinary lives became a horror show, shared by family, friends and people we didn't know from the media and the police.

We knew on that morning that we would never see Jack again. Endless desperate days were spent waiting; Christmas came and went, as did the New Year. We put our total trust in the police to find Jack and give us the answers we so desperately needed. While we lived in a terrifying limbo, the police took their Christmas leave, which ensured there was no possibility for a swift recovery of Jack's body. 31 days later, on 3rd January 2006, Jack was finally found where we all knew he was: in the River Leam. He had lain undiscovered for a whole month.

We soon realised that answers were not going to be provided by the police. Over the next few months and years, what should have been a straightforward enquiry into our son's death became clouded by police incompetence on a monumental scale. Only after the collapse of the Coroners' inquest in 2007 did we really start to understand just how many mistakes had been made.

It was at this time that Vince Smith came into our lives:

a no-nonsense man, whose very involvement in completing an unfinished investigation has convinced us that we know who killed our son and why and how he did. We also realised the reason why he was not convicted. Thank you, Vinnie, for allowing me the chance, as Jack's mum, to add a few words at the end of this chapter. We will never give up hope that one day those who conspired to lie, to protect themselves, rather than give us some peace of mind, will be crushed by their guilt and finally confirm what everyone already knows and should have been proved beyond a reasonable doubt over a decade ago!

Sheena Macleod